The Design and Management of Effective Distance Learning Programs

Richard Discenza
University of Colorado, Colorado Springs, USA

Caroline Howard
Emory University, USA

Karen Schenk
K. D. Schenk and Associates Consulting, USA

IRM Press
Publisher of innovative scholarly and professional
information technology titles in the cyberage

Hershey • London • Melbourne • Singapore • Beijing

Acquisitions Editor:	Mehdi Khosrow-Pour
Senior Managing Editor:	Jan Travers
Managing Editor:	Amanda Appicello
Development Editor:	Michele Rossi
Copy Editor:	Jane Conley
Typesetter:	LeAnn Whitcomb
Cover Design:	Deb Andre
Printed at:	Integrated Book Technology

Published in the United States of America by
IRM Press (an imprint of Idea Group Inc.)
701 E. Chocolate Avenue, Suite 200
Hershey PA 17033-1240
Tel: 717-533-8845
Fax: 717-533-8661
E-mail: cust@idea-group.com
Web site: http://www.idea-group.com

and in the United Kingdom by
IRM Press (an imprint of Idea Group Inc.)
3 Henrietta Street
Covent Garden
London WC2E 8LU
Tel: 44 20 7240 0856
Fax: 44 20 7379 3313
Web site: http://www.eurospan.co.uk

Library of Congress Cataloging-in-Publication Data

Design and management of effective distance learning programs / [edited by] Richard
  Discenza, Caroline Howard, Karen Schenk.
       p. cm.
   Originally published: Hershey, PA : Idea Group Pub., c2002.
   Includes bibliographical references and index.
     ISBN 1-931777-80-2 (paper)
      1. Distance education. 2. Instructional systems--Design. I. Discenza, Richard. II.
Howard, Caroline, 1953- III. Schenk, Karen, 1955-

   LC5800.D47 2003
   371.3'5--dc21
                                                                        2003040630

Previously published in a hard cover version by Idea Group Publishing.

eISBN 1-59140-001-5

British Cataloguing in Publication Data
A Cataloguing in Publication record for this book is available from the British Library.

New Releases from IRM Press

The Design and Management of Effective Distance Learning Programs

Table of Contents

Section I THE ROLE AND EVOLUTION OF DISTANCE LEARNING INTO HIGHER EDUCATION

Chapter 1 1

Distance Education: What is it? Utilization of Distance Education in Higher Education in the United States
   Diane A. Matthews, Carlow College

Chapter 2 21

Distance Education in the Online World: Implications for Higher Education
   Stewart Marshall, Central Queensland University
   Shirley Gregor, Australian National University

Chapter 3 37

The Potential Attraction of Online Distance Education: Lessons from the Telecommuting Literature
   Geoffrey N. Dick, University of New South Wales

Chapter 4 55

The Future of Distance Learning in the Traditional University
   Gary Saunders, Marshall University

Section II FACULTY, STUDENT AND PROGRAM CHALLENGES

Chapter 5 ....**75**
Faculty Perceptions and Participation in Distance Education:
Pick Fruit From the Low-Hanging Branches
 Kim E. Dooley and Jane Magill, Texas A&M University

Chapter 6 ....**93**

The Challenge of Teaching Effectively from a Distance
 Valerie E. Polichar and Christine Bagwell, University of California,
 San Diego

Chapter 7 .... **108**

A Preliminary Exploration of Social Needs in Distance Education
 William B. Martz. Jr. and Morgan M. Shepherd, University of
 Colorado, Colorado Springs

Chapter 8 .... **125**

Online Courses: Strategies for Success
 Linda Cooper, Macon State College

Chapter 9 .... **141**

Institutional and Library Services for Distance Education Courses and
Programs
 Elizabeth Buchanan, University of Wisconsin-Milwaukee

Chapter 10 .... **155**
Quality Assurance of Online Courses
 Richard Ryan, University of Oklahoma

Section III IMPLEMENTING DISTANCE EDUCATION: PROGRAMS, DESIGNS AND EXPERIENCES

Chapter 11 .... **171**

Distance Education Quality: Success Factors for Resources, Practices
and Results
 Cathy Cavanaugh, University of North Florida

Chapter 12 .... **190**

Establishing Successful Online Distance Learning Environments:
Distinguishing Factors that Contribute to Online Courses and Programs
Lynne Schrum and Angela Benson, University of Georgia

Chapter 13 .... **205**

Case Study in Managing a Distance Education Consortium
Vicky A. Seehusen, Colorado Electronic Community College

Chapter 14 .... **218**

Using Tutored Video Instruction Methodology to
Deliver Management Education at a Distance in China
L.William Murray and Alev M. Efendioglu, University of San
Francisco

Chapter 15 .... **233**

Leveraging Distance Education Through the Internet:
A Paradigm Shift in Higher Education
Zeynep Onay, Middle East Technical University

Chapter 16 .... **262**

Teaching Enterprise Systems in a Distance Education Mode
Michael Rosemann, Queensland University of Technology

About the Authors **288**

Index **296**

Preface

"Anytime, anyplace, any subject" is an emerging theme for distance learning in higher education throughout the world. Portable wireless devices and other emerging interactive media are giving traditional classroom and distance education professors a growing array of tools to provide instruction wherever it is needed or desired. Educators now have an expanding repertoire of interactive media enabling both traditional pedagogical options and "just-in-time" situational learning in a wide variety of environments. Currently about 16 million Americans attend colleges and universities of all kinds. With the growth in distance education, this figure could rise significantly. People who could not attend a class now have the opportunity. Many predict that by this time next year handheld devices and virtual classrooms will be ubiquitous, enabling students to log on to the Internet for assignments and to participate in chat room discussions with students across the globe.

While the new technology is complex and expensive, it is a growing necessity for higher education. Christopher Dede of Harvard's Graduate School of Education says, "Within a couple of decades refusal to use interactive media in teaching will be considered professional malpractice."

Although online education is still in the early stages, it is now starting to show its impact as it extends through adult and lifelong learning. It is growing fastest in the area of higher education. Universities are the most wired community on the Web with more than 90% of college students accessing the Internet. In 1999, Market Data Retrieval reported the results of a survey that 72% of two-year and four-year institutions offered online courses, up 48% from a year earlier. By next year (2002), 2.2 million students are expected to enroll in distance learning courses, up from 710,000 in 1998, according to Merrill Lynch researchers. They expect the online higher education market to grow from $1.2 billion in 1999 to $7 billion in 2003.

Not all students, faculty and university administrators agree that the Web is the answer to the problems of the world of education. In fact, some say that the Internet may create some new challenges and problems. There is a growing backlash among professors and administrators who question the merit of computers in the classroom or in place of the classroom. They believe students are distracted by technology and understaffed institutions are unable to maintain the costly infrastructure and the computer clutter associated with high-tech classrooms. Many top-tier universities are taking a cautious approach as professors battle with administrators over intellectual property rights concerning who has ownership of courses and materials. Instructors see technology changing their ranks to that of a "knowledge disseminator" who spreads information for a profit. These challenges are described in Section II of this book. Detractors of distance education point to the high-profile venture at Western Governor's University that has not been a great success.

Software and e-learning programs have made a world of difference for those involved in distance education. For a distance student, all one has to do is look online to find what must be done. Students are more in control of their time and are less occupied with logistics. Parking for classes is no longer a problem. This has made life easier for them, but it has forced instructors to provide more structure for their classes. Since web-based classes are often required to be online weeks in advance, a professor can no longer prepare for classes at the last moment. Increased quality control is seen through the use of course directors or administrators.

While a growing number of students and instructors have enthusiastically embraced distance learning, some point out that they may be losing human contact with their counterparts. There are concerns about finding a balance between information technology on the one hand and traditional, humanistic learning on the other. Martz and Sheppard's chapter (Section II) presents a study and discussion on some of the human aspects of distance education.

The purpose of this book is to increase understanding of the major issues, challenges and solutions related to distance education. With such large numbers of individuals learning at a distance from traditional central locations, it is critical that we understand the impacts of these arrangements, the major issues and challenges, and how to best manage and develop distance education programs. This knowledge will enable organizations to implement and improve programs. It will also further our understanding of the impact of technology, particularly when it is used to replace face-to-face communications among both individuals and groups.

ORGANIZATION OF THE BOOK

The book is organized into three sections. The first part identifies the role and evolution of distance education into higher education. This part reports on the development of educational experiences as they have changed in the distance environment. Besides the availability of new technology, much of the motivation for distance programs stems from the perceived need to accommodate nontraditional students when university budgets are squeezed to the point that localized convenient educational experiences are out of the question. There is a clear demand for new course delivery, content, and curriculum. This section shows how organizations have changed, grown, and progressed to meet this demand.

Section II brings a multidimensional discussion of the faculty, student, and program challenges of distance education programs. The evolution of computers and online capacity into the world of higher education has evoked in many a sense of foreboding and fear, while others have welcomed this new approach as a valuable cost-effective tool for delivering educational needs in today's world. Course delivery methods have been modified due to the physical distance between the instructor and the student. The dimensions described in this section point out the significant impact on course delivery, student-to-professor interactions, student-to-student interactions, and assessment vehicles.

Section III gets down to the business of implementing programs and examining the designs and experiences of those who have had their organizations commit resources to distance programs. These are the early adapters or pioneers of this technology who have already made significant progress in the use of computers and the World Wide Web for teaching courses completely online or for adding course sections taught at a main or distant location. Today, these are examples of only a very small portion of the educational work force in the world. Opportunities are awaiting those who are willing to step up and move into the arena of the ever-evolving educational challenges of education at a distance. This part tells the story of experiences and includes technical, pedagogical, and organizational issues. A brief description of each chapter follows:

Chapter 1 describes and identifies distance education as a serious alternative to the standard classroom environment, presenting enormous opportunities for both the organizations and players involved with this version of education. Matthews examines the technology and the types of students involved. She comments also on the advantages and disadvantages for instructors, virtual universities, state governing bodies, and consortia members.

Chapter 2 begins by identifying forces leading to change in organizations involved in the online world. These include rising global competitors, powerful consumers of education, and rapid changes in technology. Also included are the formation of alliances, outsourcing, and the re-engineering of systems and work practices of distance education providers. A model is presented that outlines "glocal", a networked education paradigm that separates out global and local resource development. The result is that university academics are finding themselves responsible for the learning of hundreds of students with whom they may never find themselves face-to-face.

Chapter 3 reviews the telecommuting literature and proposes a model that provides a basis for consideration of the appropriateness of the attributes associated with various distance education tasks and the suitability of those tasks. This model could be useful for managing issues presently encountered in distance education programs.

Chapter 4 presents the impact that Internet courses have on the traditional university and also examines whether these courses represent a new and significant improvement over traditional pedagogy for educating students or just a lessening of the rigor in academic programs. The chapter shows the results of a departmental survey on the reactions to distance programs by accounting chairpersons and college of business deans.

Chapter 5 addresses the motivation of faculty members to teach at a distance. The concepts and challenges of distance programs involve adapting traditional classroom approaches, attitudes and barriers to the technologies associated with distance education methods. Dooley and Magill present an extensive survey of faculty opinions about teaching at a distance, as well as several case studies describing incentives and training made available for distance education.

Chapter 6 describes the potential of distance learning to be as successful in instruction as conventional classroom learning. The approach is to take advantage of the known principles of perception and learning gleaned from cognitive behavioral, educational and perceptual psychological research. The principles are presented and applied in conventional learning packages that include web page development, course-in-a-box software, chat rooms, MUD/MOO environments, bulletin boards, and real-time online lectures.

Chapter 7 explores the concern for social needs in distance education. Several themes that integrate learning and technology are identified and analyzed. In addition, the results of an exploratory study are presented on the "need for affiliation" among students who work in groups in distance courses versus those who work in groups for campus classes.

Chapter 8 reviews the experiences of offering an online Business Computer Applications course that provides instruction in basic computer concepts and terminology as well as instruction in using software programs. Various strategies that were successful in the course are reported for those who are interested in offering online courses. Topics of importance include the initial class meeting, providing diverse instructional material, the value of student evaluations, and the determination of student assessment procedures.

Chapter 9 examines the use of institutional resources and structures for embracing distance education. The areas scrutinized include registration, advising, library, and technical support. Institutions must have clear, well-planned strategies in place in order to maximize a student's experience and overall satisfaction. These strategies prevent attrition and maximize retention for institutions considering distance education.

Chapter 10 explores the issues surrounding quality assurance with online courses. As demand for distance education grows, the Internet delivery method raises questions about the quality assurance of these offerings. Ryan addresses the question that administrators and participants must ask themselves: "Should there be a trade-off of class quality with the convenience of the delivery method?" If not, then how do we keep course quality from being compromised using this new medium?

Chapter 11 describes success factors used by institutions, course developers, professors and students that lead to high-quality educational experiences. These have been found through practice by institutions, course developers, instructors, and students. Guidelines are presented on the three stages of the distance education development cycle: resources, practices, and results. In addition, two distance education programs are described as case illustrations that exemplify the successful application of success factors.

Chapter 12 looks at factors that promote development and implementation of successful online distance learning environments from the perspectives of educators and learners. Schrum and Benson provide an overview of current tensions between the requirements of the faculty, the needs of the students, and the forces driving the development of online programs. This work is based on the authors' current research and past experiences in the design and development of online distance learning environments.

Chapter 13 describes the unique distance education consortium called CCC Online developed by the Community Colleges of Colorado System (CC of C). CC of C is comprised of fourteen Colorado community colleges and delivers courses, certificates and degrees to more than 250,000 students per year. The CCC Online consortium, managed by the Colorado Electronic Community College (CECC), provides centralized management of faculty and curriculum, and the consortium member colleges provide most of the student services to their students enrolled in the program.

Chapter 14 presents the results of a study comparing classroom performance and student attitudes of distance education students to on-campus ("live") students enrolled in classes leading to a Master of Business Administration (MBA) degree. The faculty from the School of Business and Management at the University of San Francisco developed the program. Contracts to deliver these courses were negotiated with two large Chinese companies. The off-site students of this distance education attended class sessions in Hong Kong and in three other locations within the Peoples Republic of China, using a Tutored-Video Instruction (TVI) methodology.

Chapter 15 provides an overview of the different models that have emerged, and addresses the key issues that need to be resolved for integrating Internet-based learning in traditional universities. The breadth of strategic, administrative, academic and technological concerns encountered through the evolution of an Internet-based education system, from its inception to implementation, are discussed and illustrated by the e-learning initiative of Middle East Technical University in Turkey.

Chapter 16 discusses the needs and opportunities for teaching comprehensive business applications, Enterprise Systems, in the form of academic distance education courses. Specific factors of the educational market in Enterprise Systems, such as high demand, limited resources and the increased importance of Application Hosting Centers will be described. An appropriate learning model will be selected, which stresses the role of the lecturer as a moderator. The subject, Process Engineering at Queensland University of Technology, is used as an example to discuss different forms of distance and collaborative education in Enterprise Systems. The summary includes recommendations and sketches possible future directions.

ACKNOWLEDGMENTS

The editors want to acknowledge the many people who made the project possible. We appreciate the help and cooperation of the authors of the chapters included in this volume. It has been a pleasure to work with them. Many served as referees for chapters submitted by other authors. We especially want to thank those authors who took the time to provide comprehensive reviews and constructive comments. These were indispensable during the final selection and revision process. Reviewers who provided the most comprehensive, critical and constructive comments include Valerie Polichar, Christine Bagwell, Benjamin Martz, Morgan Shepherd, Cathy Cavenaugh, Lynne Schrum, Angela Benson, Richard Ryan, Elizabeth Buchanan, Zeynep Onay, Gary Saunders, Vicki Seehusan, Geoffrey Dick, Stewart Marshall, Shirley Gregor, and Kim Dooley.

The assistance of the staff at Idea Group Publishing has been invaluable. We would like to extend our greatest thanks and appreciation to all the editors and staff at Idea Group Publishing, without whom the writing of this book would not have been possible. Michele Rossi's support and quick responses to our inquiries helped facilitate the process. We benefited from Mehdi Khosrowpour's guidance in developing the initial idea. Jan Travers has both provided guidance and helped keep the project on schedule. We thank Carrie Stull for helping to develop the marketing plan.

The preparation of a book of this kind is dependent on excellent colleagues and the three of us have been fortunate in this regard. It has been a team effort, start to finish.

Last but not least, I, Carol, want to thank my husband and children for their love, support and patience during this project. From Dick to my wife, Suzanne, who taught me that virtue is possible in marriage, family and life as well as one's profession. From Karen to Robert and Katie, whose love and support has encouraged me in this fun and fulfilling collaboration.

Caroline Howard
Richard Discenza
Karen D. Schenk

Section I

The Role and Evolution of Distance Learning Into Higher Education

Chapter I

Distance Education: What Is It? Utilization of Distance Education in Higher Education in the United States

Diane A. Matthews
Carlow College, USA

Technology-based distance education is emerging as an increasingly visible feature of post-secondary education in the United States (U.S. Department of Education, 1999). Educators have the opportunity to define, design, and manage effective and robust teaching and learning systems, programs, and courses. As distance learning becomes a serious alternative to the standard classroom environment, enormous opportunities and dilemmas present themselves for the players. This chapter examines the technology used in distance education; the type of student utilizing distance education; advantages and disadvantages for the student, the instructor, and the institution in the use of distance education; and the players involved—including higher education institutions, virtual universities, states, and consortia.

INTRODUCTION

Technology-based distance education is emerging as an increasingly visible feature of post-secondary education in the United States (U.S. Department of Education, 1999). Technology is changing the way the university functions as an institution of higher learning. Publications such as *The Chronicle of Higher Education* regularly feature articles about the distance education efforts of various higher education institutions and systems, states, and consortia. Distance education specialists and academic policymakers expect technology to help higher education institutions provide a wide range of programs, including degree programs, to larger proportions of the student population (U.S. Department of Education, 1997).

In distance education, or distance learning, the students and instructors emain geographically apart. Today, the ability to take courses from a remote location utilizing the Internet is referred to as "e-learning" (Quan, 2000); e-learning is the dot-com term for distance education. Concepts of lifelong learning, individualized or personalized learning, and time-free, space-free, "just-in-time" learning arrangements have emerged, all of which allow learning away from the traditional campus (American Council on Education, 1996). Distance education is a key strategy in meeting the massive demand for higher education.

Distance education is first and foremost a movement that sought not so much to challenge or change the structure of higher learning, but to extend the traditional university in order to overcome its inherent problems of scarcity and exclusivity. Second, distance education developed as a creative political response to the increasing inability of the traditional university structure to grow bigger (Hall, J., 1995). Distance education dealt with the problem of too many students in a single physical space.

The increasing diversity in demand for education means the virtual campus is a model for the future. Developed societies are moving further from the traditional model, where people complete their education at an early age and then dedicate themselves solely to work (Warden, 1995). Simple desktop computers can now function on the Internet as powerful, multimedia, interactive communication centers. New Internet tools, such as bulletin boards, electronic tests, hyper-linked texts and sources, and enhanced computer systems with greater speed and more memory, allow viewers to see more information and tune in on discussions, meetings, theatrical performances, even operas, around the world (Gallick, 1998). Such features offer rich opportunities for distance education.

Distance learning is emerging as part of mainstream education (American Council on Education, 1996). So, "What is distance education and what is its use in the United States?" To answer this question, we examine the media used in distance education, the type of student utilizing distance education, advantages and disadvantages in the use of distance education, and the players involved.

MEDIA USED IN DISTANCE EDUCATION

Distance education employs media in many forms and to varying degrees. It uses mail, facsimile, radio, television, satellite broadcasts, video-tapes, teleconferencing, electronic mail, chatrooms, bulletin boards, CD-ROM, the Internet, and the World Wide Web.

The "first generation" of distance education technologies included print, radio and television. The "second generation" added audiocassettes, video-tapes, and fax. Both generations of technology were primarily one-way (asynchronous) communication from the faculty to the student.

In 1985 and for the next ten years, CD-ROM technology was developed and used to deliver instruction. We also witnessed two-way interactive capabilities (synchronous or simultaneous, real-time communication) utilizing computers and computer networks, including the Internet and the World Wide Web. Audioconferencing and videoconferencing came into being. High-quality interactive videoconferencing provides additional enhancements to distance teaching. In videoconferencing, a faculty member teaches a class in a traditional classroom setting while concurrently instructing a different group of students in another classroom via interactive video. Introducing an audio link from the remote site back to the lecturer allows live interaction and enables questions.

The use of the "virtual classroom" is a growing development in distance learning. It is usually based on computer groupware, but can be operated over the Internet. Both groupware—or "courseware"—and the Internet utilize synchronous and asynchronous instruction. In general, the student uses a local computer (usually from home) to access a range of services and facilities. These include online registration, dissemination of prepared course materials (such as the course syllabus, assignments, and practice tests), access to online video materials, and communication with instructors, tutors, and other students via electronic mail (email). Frequently, courses have their own Web page where instructors post their syllabi and assignments, as well as links to other informative Web sites, periodicals, and shared audio and video files. "Classes" and discussion groups are conducted in online chatrooms; assignments and exams are emailed to the instructor. Discussion topics are posted to discussion or bulletin boards ("threaded discussions"); students comment on the selected topics, and they may also post new topics.

The Web is used in teaching in two different ways. A Web-Assisted Course (WAC) has a traditional classroom setting and uses the Web to exchange email for communication between students and instructors in chatrooms and to download course materials and obtain grades. A Web-Based Course (WBC) is a stand-alone course delivered to students who do not meet in a traditional classroom; these students take the course from a remote location via the Web.

The United States Department of Education (1999) conducted a survey on distance education and found the following regarding the then current use and the planned use of technology:

> Distance education courses were delivered by asynchronous Internet instruction at 58% of post-secondary institutions, by two-way inter-active video at 54%, and by one-way prerecorded video at 47% of the institutions in the 1997-1998 academic year. Nineteen percent of the institutions offered courses using synchronous Internet instruction. Thus, more institutions used several types of video technologies and the Internet-based technologies than other modes of delivery. (p. 38)
> Institutions planned to start using, or to increase their use of asynchronous Internet instruction as a primary mode of delivery more than any other type of technology, with 82% of the institutions planning to start or increase their use of this technology. Two-way interactive video (cited by 61%) and synchronous Internet instruction (cited by 60%) were also indicated as technologies planned for an increasing role in delivering distance education in the next three years. (p. 39)

The methods by which higher education institutions provide instruction are changing rapidly. The integration of computers into teaching as we are now experiencing may be one of the most significant contributions to education ever known (Buikema & Ward, 1999). Now faculty have a growing range of distance education tools allowing them to bring information resources, simulation capabilities, and other enhancements to instruction.

TYPE OF STUDENT

Distance education has a long history of serving isolated and remote learners (American Council on Education, 1996). Today, in addition to serving the learner who lives far from campus, distance education is aimed at part-time students, time-strapped adult learners, and students trying to work full time while earning degrees. Virtual classrooms are not aimed at the traditional market of young college people, but rather are meant to serve disciplined adult learners (Guernsey, 1998). Students are typically older than traditional undergraduates (On Line, 1998, May 22). Interestingly, the typical distance learning student is a 43 year old woman, with a $73,000 household income, who is looking for a career change or career enhancement (Lucas, 1998, as cited in Buikema & Ward, 1999). The age profile of students, whether men or women, suggests that many will have family commitments. It is unlikely that they would be willing or able to leave home to attend a full-time, campus-based course (Miller, Smith & Tilstone, 1998). Distance learning primarily attracts women with children. Sixty-six percent of the adult distance education market is female, and 80% of them have children (Bremner, 1998). As a rule, the distance learner is serious, disciplined, conscientious, and demanding (O'Leary, 2000). According to professors who teach online courses, virtual classes require unflagging self-discipline, self-motivation, and efficient time management by the student.

In a survey conducted by the U.S. Department of Education (1997) in 1995, more higher education institutions offered distance education courses designed primarily for undergraduate students (81% of the institutions) and graduate students (34% of the institutions) than for any other type of student. Professionals seeking recertification were targeted by 39% of institutions offering distance education courses, and other workers seeking skill updating or retraining were targeted by 49%.

In the fall of 1998, another student population emerged—students already enrolled in regular classes eager to ease their schedules by taking courses online. Many colleges and universities find students enrolled in distance education courses simultaneously enrolled in on-campus courses ("The Costs of Teaching," 2000). Many of these students work part-time or full-time jobs and they need the freedom to manage their time (Guernsey, 1998).

ADVANTAGES AND DISADVANTAGES OF OFFERING DISTANCE EDUCATION

There are benefits and drawbacks to offering distance education. Advantages accrue to both the student and to the institution; however, there are numerous disadvantages that must be considered.

Benefits to the Student

Benefits to the student include: increased access to higher education (particularly for the nontraditional student), flexible scheduling of personal time, convenient location (students can attend class from any corner of the globe), individualized attention by the instructor, less travel, and increased time to think about and respond to (via email or discussion boards) questions posed by the instructor (Matthews, 1999). Shy students can anonymously speak up in chatrooms. Often students who participate in online courses say they get to know one another better than in a traditional class (Buikema & Ward, 1999); chatrooms build a sense of community. Increased access to certificate and degree programs can have the further benefit of encouraging students to undertake these programs or to complete them more quickly (Turoff, 1997, as cited in U.S. Department of Education, 1999).

Benefits to the Institution Offering Distance Education

The institution also reaps benefits from offering distance education. It increases enrollment, attracts more qualified students, increases retention and graduation rates, and increases institutional prestige (Buikema & Ward, 1999). In addition, offering distance education attracts new teaching staff (those interested in distance education), allows instructors freedom to be more creative in the classroom, reduces the need to build and maintain university campuses and buildings, offers a new level of communication with students, requires the university to keep abreast of new technology, and signals the public that the institution is forward thinking and technologically advanced (Matthews, 1999).

Disadvantages

There are numerous disadvantages to the student, the instructor, and the institution that must be considered when deliberating distance education. These disadvantages include, but are not limited to, the following:

Costs of Entry and Ongoing Support

The entry and ongoing support costs to quality distance education can be substantial. Distance education is a capital-intensive business. Investments in state-of-the-art technology, computers, virtual libraries, central servers and data networks, program development costs, ongoing technical support, equipment maintenance, hardware and software upgrades, and marketing can be expensive. Early results from a study conducted by the Western Cooperative for Educational Telecommunications on the costs of alternative forms of instructional delivery suggest that modes of delivery that rely on technology consistently cost more than face-to-face instruction ("The Costs of Teaching," 2000).

The Alfred P. Sloan Foundation commissioned studies at six universities to explore the financial costs and potential profitability of distance learning. The universities included Drexel University, Pace University, Pennsylvania State University, Rochester Institute of Technology, the University of Illinois, and the University of Maryland-College Park. The researchers who conducted the studies concluded that "universities aren't losing a lot of money on distance learning, but they aren't making much, either. How well the programs appear to be doing depends, in part, on how their costs and revenues are defined" (Carr, 2001, p. A42). The costs of expanding programs are, in some cases, greater than anticipated. "Several distance-education leaders predict that some administrators will slow or stop their expansion into online learning as they develop a better sense of the costs" (Carr, p. A41). Robert E. Myers, executive vice president of the University of Maryland's University College, states that it is a myth that online learning is cheaper to produce and cheaper to deliver than face-to-face instruction (Carr). "After proclaiming that distance learning would save money, business schools are now discovering that 'presence' teaching is less expensive" (Ramanantsoa, 2001, p. 12).

One sobering reminder of the extent of the difficulty in implementing distance education is California Virtual University (CVU). CVU served as a clearinghouse for distance education programs for 98 public colleges and universities in California. Less than one year after its creation in 1997, CVU ceased operations. Although CVU faced a number of difficult issues, the decision to cease operations came after the venture's partners—the state's three public college systems and the Association of Independent Colleges—balked at putting up $1 million a year for three years to cover proposed operating costs for advertising and marketing (Blumenstyk, 1999; Young, 2000, June 30).

Accreditation and Quality Assurance

According to Emmert (1997) in *New England's Journal of Higher Education and Economic Development*:

> One hindrance to globalization of distance education is the issue of quality control—an area in which U.S. institutions begin with a disadvantage. Today, quality in American higher education is assessed by a complex, some say arcane, system of accreditation. The American accreditation system relies heavily upon the assessment of proxies for educational quality, such as hours spent in classrooms, student-to-faculty ratios, availability of facilities, and total resources spent on each student. Many other nations,

particularly in Europe, approach quality control through competency examinations for each discipline. Such competency assessment de-emphasizes time to degree, instruction mode, and the reputation of the institution providing the instruction. These nations therefore may be better positioned to adopt quality control in distance education. (p. 21)

Furthermore, the Internet is an ideal breeding ground for diploma mills; a school could be fraudulent (Terry, 2000). Students must determine if a school is properly accredited.

Concern for Online Course Quality

The overall lack of standards in distance education is an issue (Imel, 1996). There is no standard format for conducting an online class; therefore, course quality is a concern. In January, 2001, the American Federation of Teachers, one of the nation's largest unions of educators, approved 14 quality standards for online colleges. The guidelines call for, among other principles, clear standards for content, technical support and counseling for students and faculty, and training for professors in effective online teaching methods ("Is Online Education Off Course?" 2001; Carnevale, 2001).

The quality of instructors in the online environment is an issue. Research has shown that some virtual universities require minimal qualifications when hiring instructors. "The instructors hired …need only a master's degree; they do not enjoy tenure; they are replaceable cogs in a profit machine" (Stross, 2001, p. 37). Hiring distinguished faculty is a luxury when evaluating the profitability of online education. "In fact, it is the opportunity to not hire full-time Ph.D.'s [sic] that makes the online university such an attractive financial proposition" (Stross, p.37).

In addition, business leaders, whose needs are often cited by promoters of online education, seem less certain about the quality of virtual degrees. In an October 2000 survey, 77% of human resource officers did not consider a degree from an online-only institution to be equivalent to a campus-based diploma (Press, Washburn & Broden, 2001). As participation in distance education by prestigious universities increases, and students with online degrees join the work force, business leaders will be able to reevaluate their position.

Other critics argue that online learning could "facilitate the rise of a two-tiered educational system—prestigious campus-based diplomas for the children of elites, and mass-marketed online degrees for those less fortunate" (Press, Washburn & Broden, 2001, p.35).

Labor Intensity

Distance education is more time-consuming (Guernsey, 1998); it is more labor intensive to teach an online class than it is a regular chalk-and-talk class (Bremner, 1998). It takes an average of 18 hours of personal time to create one hour of stand-alone Web-based instruction. This is a two- to fourfold increase over a traditional classroom lecture (Boettcher, 1998, as cited in Buikema & Ward). The conversion of curriculum from classroom to Internet is not easy or intuitive. "It is vastly harder than preparing a classroom course, 20 times the effort," says Eli Noam, professor of economics and finance at Columbia Business School (Svetcov, 2000). In addition, there is usually more time spent corresponding (email, chatrooms) with students enrolled in an online course than in a traditional classroom (Buikema & Ward, 1999). An American Federation of Teacher's survey revealed that 90% of those polled found a significant difference in preparation time necessary for the development of a distance learning course ("Is Online Education Off Course?" 2001). A recent University of Illinois study found that "high-quality online teaching is time- and labor-intensive" (Press, Washburn & Broden, 2001, p. 34).

Effectiveness of Distance Education

The effectiveness of distance education is a hotly debated issue. An oft-cited report compiled by Thomas Russell in 1999 entitled *The No Significant Difference Phenomenon* indicates that learning outcomes of distance education students are similar to the learning outcomes of traditional on-campus students. Russell compiles this information from 355 research reports, summaries, and papers. This body of work also suggests that the attitudes and satisfaction of distance education students are generally positive. Other reviews of this body of evidence are more critical, arguing that there is no conclusive evidence to indicate this. Still others argue that the existing evidence on the effectiveness of distance education is generally inadequate because of experimental design flaws in the research (Van Dusen, 2000). In addition, other studies report that students see distance education as a convenient but less effective and less satisfying alternative for delivering education. Among academics, the debate continues to rage about the effectiveness of distance education.

Commercial Versus Pedagogical Forces Driving Distance Learning

"While most educators support using technology to broaden educational opportunities, a growing number fear that commercial rather than pedagogical considerations are driving the distance learning trend" (Press,

Washburn & Broden, 2001, p.35). A number of universities are determining how this technology can be used to generate a profit, rather than how this new technology can enhance the quality of learning. Many universities have launched for-profit subsidiaries to market online courses, which has aroused strong opposition among professors. Virtual education threatens to shift control over the learning process from college educators to administrators and marketers.

In addition, government officials, anticipating a boost in demand for post-secondary degrees, but reluctant to commit resources to public education through increased taxation, embrace distance learning as a way to expand "cheaply"—by using technology rather than bricks and mortar (Press, Washburn & Broden, 2001).

Need For Faculty and Staff Training

Distance education requires a high level of instructor and staff training (Connell, 1998). Staff and faculty need to be trained in the use of technology (Hall, P., 1996). Faculty also need formal training in curriculum design and development, and in the development of techniques that promote learning for distant students.

Development of Educational Materials

There is a need to develop world-class educational materials (Emmert, 1997). Learning materials must be constructed that anticipate the learning problems of the isolated student and provide a wide range of activities that will support learning (Hall, P., 1996). Pedagogical adjustments are required, particularly in the areas of class participation and course-related activities.

Inaccessible Libraries

Most academic and corporate libraries provide remote access to materials, including journals, newspapers, magazines, and reference books. To serve distance learners, institutions will have to digitize local materials, such as course-related print sources. In addition, students need to have access to books and other print sources for research; a recurrent difficulty with the distance learning institutes is providing access to libraries. Consequently, there is a need to convert existing physical collections into digital form (Lynch, 2000).

Faculty Compensation Issues

There are significant and substantial challenges to faculty compensation practices and existing norms of faculty development, including issues of promotion and tenure, release time, course load, course updating, publishing, faculty mentoring, and consistency across departments (U.S. Department of Education, 1999).

Inadequate Infrastructure and Technical Support

In many institutions there is limited technological infrastructure to support distance education (U.S. Department of Education, 1997). Communication systems can be unreliable (Hall, J., 1995) and equipment failures numerous. In addition, ongoing technical support for students and faculty is lacking or insufficient at many institutions.

Technology Limitations

Vagaries of the Internet, such as dropped connections, network congestion, and software incompatibilities, are an issue. In addition, current bandwidth in most homes is limited to 56K; therefore, interactive video may be too choppy and distorted for student use. Performance limitations of the Internet inhibit the full use of rich multimedia content and communications.

Equity of Access For Students

Distance education requires that students have access to technology. The cost of equipment and access charges are issues for lower-income students.

Inadequate Reflection, Conversation and Intellectual Dialogue

Distance learning might be inadequate for deliberation and discourse among students, their instructors, and their peers. Distance education limits the extent to which students can reflectively browse in their subject matter with their peers and engage in exploratory discussion of their discipline (Curran, 1997). There is value in being at a university campus interacting socially and intellectually with fellow students and teachers (Plant, 1996).

Maintaining Sufficient Student Contact

A fundamental problem with distance education is how to maintain sufficient student contact, including timely assistance and adequate performance feedback (Hall, J., 1995). The Further Education Funding Council, in visits to 50 colleges during the year 2000, and in surveys of 1,400 distance learning students, found inadequate guidance and support, leading to "unacceptably low" achievement rates. The report stated that most colleges do not take the initiative to keep in contact with students (Tysome, 2001).

On the other hand, recent research also indicates that through email and chatrooms, faculty are establishing better contact with students than through a traditional classroom environment.

Possible Fraud in Authenticating Submissions

There is always the problem of authentication (Hall, P., 1996). How do we verify that persons sending assignments and tests are who they say they are? Distance education offers a unique venue for academic dishonesty and requires a software infrastructure to support authentication.

Legal Issues of Intellectual Property Rights

Traditionally, teachers have been considered the owners of lectures and course materials. The market potential of online education has led numerous schools to attempt to claim these rights, prompting protest from faculty organizations (Press, Washburn & Broden, 2001). In addition, syllabi or course outlines on the Web might be absorbed into the public domain and could be used and adapted by others (Gallick, 1998). Ownership of intellectual property is a source of debate.

Inadequate Financial Aid Policies

There are restrictions on financial aid availability for distance learners (Selingo, 1998). The "50% rule" prohibits the granting of federal aid to students who are not in a classroom seat at least 50% of their academic program. This class-time requirement has effectively barred online colleges from arranging federally backed financial aid for enrolled students.

Global Issues

When looking at distance education from a global perspective, translation remains an issue. In addition, because of differences in culture, the content of the educational materials, the values implicit in the materials, and the underlying assumptions about educational processes need to be reviewed and might need to be transformed (Hall, P., 1996). Underdeveloped countries might not even have access to technology. In a keynote address concerning global distance education to officials from 30 nations, Jacques Hallak, assistant director general for education of UNESCO, states, "There are political concerns about sovereignty and control, important differences in education policy and regulatory environments and in the ways education institutions are chartered and governed, as well as the realities of language, culture, and geographic perspective" (Young, 2000, September 29, p. A46).

It is a dynamic time for post-secondary education institutions facing the opportunities and challenges brought by technological innovation. There is no question that the use of technology has advantages and disadvantages for both users and providers of distance education.

THE PLAYERS IN DISTANCE EDUCATION

Distance education in the United States is offered by individual institutions as well as a range of new, some may say "unconventional" providers of education. According to the U.S. Department of Education (1999), other providers include:

> Consortia or collaboratives that represent cooperative pooling and sharing arrangements among institutions (typically, traditional colleges and universities). In these arrangements, multiple institutions join together to provide distance education on a statewide or regional basis. The authority to award degrees and credits, however, remains with each member institution and does not shift to the consortium....

> Contracted or brokered arrangements that are configurations of institutions, faculty, or other providers brought together solely for the purpose of delivering distance education. In contrast to consortia or collaboratives, the authority to award degrees and credits rests with the contracting or organizing entity, not with the originating institution....

> Virtual universities, or institutions that offer most or all of their instruction via technological means and are distinguished by their nearly exclusive use of technology as the educational delivery device. (p. 6)

A sampling of the various types of players in distance education in higher education follows.

Many states have active distance education programs. For example, the Education Network of Maine is an independent arm of the Maine university system. Colorado established the Colorado Electronic Community College as the state's 12th community college (*The Chronicle of Higher Education*, 1995, December 8, as cited in U.S. Department of Education, 1997). Among the other notable education systems are EdNet in Oregon, the Iowa Communications Network, the TeleLinking Network in Kentucky, and BadgerNet in Wisconsin (U.S. Department of Education, 1997).

California State University (CSU) is one of the leading practitioners in distance education (Primary Research Group, 1997). CSU is the largest system of state colleges in the country, with 23 campuses and 255,500 full-time students. CSU embraces the digital revolution, including the virtual classroom and online applications. To finance educational technology, CSU is proposing the California Educational Technology Initiative—a 10-year, $4 billion revenue partnership with four private corporations: Microsoft Corporation, Hughes Electronics Corporation, GTE Corporation, and Fujitsu Ltd. (Gallick, 1998). This initiative will have a major impact on distance education at CSU.

Universities, such as Columbia, Cornell, Duke, NYU, Temple, Maryland, and Nebraska, have all established "for-profit" subsidiaries to market distance education programs. Many more schools are collaborating with commercial and nontraditional providers. For instance, Columbia Business School, the University of Chicago, Stanford University, Carnegie Mellon University, and the London School of Economics and Political Science have agreed to develop content for Cardean University, a virtual school for business education (a division of UNext) launched by Oracle CEO Lawrence Ellison and former junk-bond magnate Michael Milken (Terry, 2000).

Other states and institutions have joined together in cooperatives and consortia to support and offer distance education. The Committee on Institutional Cooperation is an example of such a cooperative. It consists of 12 large institutions including Pennsylvania State University, the University of Iowa, Ohio State University, the University of Minnesota, the University of Wisconsin, and the University of Illinois (*The Chronicle of Higher Education*, 1995, December 8, as cited in U.S. Department of Education, 1997).

As more colleges consider collaborations as a way to move quickly into distance education, two notable models are Western Governors University and the Southern Regional Education Board's Electronic Campus. Both span huge geographic regions, but their approaches and records diverge (Carnevale, 2000, May 19, p. A53).

In the west, 13 members of the Western Governors Association created Western Governors University (WGU), a degree-granting virtual university (Ashworth, 1996). WGU has administrative headquarters in Salt Lake City, Utah, and academic headquarters in Colorado (Gallick, 1998). The university was founded in 1997 and began enrolling students in September, 1998. This virtual university has no campus and relies on computers and other technology, such as interactive video, to deliver instruction (U.S. Department of Education, 1997). Students can gain knowledge in courses offered by 40 colleges and universities in 22 states and Guam. WGU brings together, under a single academic banner, courses created at a variety of member institutions, and awards degrees under its own name. WGU promises to revolutionize higher education by offering degrees—based on a new, competency-based testing system—that will compete with those offered by existing colleges.

On the other hand, WGU found, as have other players, that entering into the distance education environment can be arduous. "WGU...has failed to meet any of its enrollment targets, is running a deficit, and lacks accreditation" (Carnevale, 2000, May 19, p. A53). Today, WGU enrolls 200 degree-seeking students. When first conceived, WGU anticipated 500 degree-seeking students by the year 2000 (Carnevale, 2000, May 19; Carr, 2001). Utah's auditor general released an audit of WGU, criticizing it for low enrollment and poor performance in competing with other distance education programs (Carnevale, 2000, October 6). WGU also found that gaining accreditation is a slow process. After two years, in November, 2000, WGU was awarded candidate status in the accreditation process. WGU expects to gain accreditation after further evaluation, which typically takes an additional two to five years. In WGU's favor, other virtual universities, such as Jones International University and Regents College, have already gained accreditation. In addition, Regents, like WGU, also awards degrees through competency-based assessments (Carnevale, 2000, December 15).

The Southern Regional Electronic Campus is a consortium of 16 southern states. It is made up of more than 262 colleges and universities that enroll 20,000 students in distance education courses. The Electronic Campus lists more than 3,200 courses (it began with 40 in 1998), and 102 degree programs (Carnevale, 2000, May 19). The Electronic Campus is a loose collective that started out providing members little more than a common Web site to publicize online offerings. Students earn course credits and degrees from the individual participating institutions. The Electronic Campus has a policy of not setting strict rules for its member institutions. It is essentially a free-trade zone where states can develop their own online course material and then share it with other states. Its purpose is to share resources and help market the courses that its institutions create.

In contrast to WGU, the Southern Regional Electronic Campus "hasn't attempted to reshape academe or to compete with anyone, but rather, to give students easy access to online courses offered by participating colleges" (Carnevale, 2000, May 19, p. A53). Many new collaborations are being modeled after the Southern Regional Electronic Campus rather than WGU.

Officials of WGU announced in November, 1998, that they were establishing a distance education consortium with Britain's well-known Open University. The new organization, called the Governors Open University System, serves as a front end for the two universities, and students enrolled in either institution are able to take courses through the other (McCollum, 1998). In 1999, Britain's Open University opened a new sister institution in America—the United States Open University.

In higher education, the highest-profile virtual college is the University of Phoenix, which has a complete curriculum and a sophisticated delivery system (O'Leary, 2000). Started in 1989, the University of Phoenix is the largest private school in the U.S., enrolling more than 75,000 students; 13,800 students from 25 countries take online courses. In September, 1999, the Apollo Group, parent company of the University of Phoenix, raised $70 million from investors on Wall Street in a stock offering tied directly to the distance education unit. It is the first test of a public offering of stock in a distance learning institution. Table 1 lists a few virtual universities.

Investors are pouring millions into Web education. So far the biggest player is Michael Milken, his brother Lowell, and Oracle's Larry Ellison. They own Knowledge Universe, a venture hatchery for education and training companies. The Washington Post Company is also knee-deep in edu-ventures, including the ownership of Kaplan College. Wall Street magnate Herbert Allen of Allen & Co. has earmarked $20 million to launch and sustain Global Education Network, a clearinghouse of courses from America's top colleges, including Brown, Wellesley, and Williams. (Svetcov, 2000). In 2000, billionaire Michael Saylor donated $100 million toward the creation of an online university that will offer an "Ivy League" level of education free of charge.

Technologies for an advanced Internet are now being actively studied for use in higher education by a three-way partnership that includes government, industry, and academia (Houweling, 2000). The "Internet2" project focuses on new technologies and applications and on the convergence, or the unified delivery of services such as text, voice, video, and data. Since it began in October, 1996, the Internet2 project has grown to include over 150 universities, more than 50 companies, and dozens of other organizations focused on advanced networking (Houweling, 2000).

As distance learning becomes a serious alternative to the standard classroom environment, enormous opportunities and dilemmas present themselves for the players in distance education. Software developers, telecommunications companies, hardware makers, publishers, Internet and Web service providers, and many other technology- and education-based services are developing systems for this emerging market that capitalize on the special capabilities of different technologies.

Table 1: A few virtual universities

Name	Year Founded	Courses/Degrees
Capella University	1993	500 courses, Certificates, BS, MS, MBA, PhD
Cenquest	1997	100 courses, Certificates, MS
Fathom	2000	7,000 courses through member institutions
Jones International U.	1995	80 courses, Certificates, BA, MA, MBA
Kaplan College	2000	500 courses, Certificates, AS, BS, JD
UNext	1997	100 courses through Cardean University, MBA

CONCLUSION

The ever-accelerating growth in information technology and the prolif-eration of distance education are exciting developments in higher education that could bring about some of the most profound changes to the ways we teach and learn. They provide extraordinary opportunities to transform the when, where, and how of what we teach (Matthews, 1999). Taking a class and ultimately receiving a college degree are being added to the list of stay-at-home electronic activities.

Educators have the opportunity to define, design, and manage effective and robust teaching and learning systems, programs, and courses. It is no longer a question of whether or not the new higher education will develop, but how fast it will occur (Connick, 1997). Adopting new approaches to education is not an option—it is imperative. No generation will have the opportunity that we have to put a mark on the look of education in the future. Technology has penetrated all aspects of education and will change it dramatically.

REFERENCES

American Council on Education Center for Adult Learning and Educational Credentials. (1996). *Guiding Principles for Distance Learning in a Learning Society*. Washington, D.C.: ACE Central Services.

Ashworth, K. H. (1996). Virtual universities could produce only virtual learning. *The Chronicle of Higher Education*, September 6, 43(2), A88.

Blumenstyk, G. (1999). California Virtual University will end most of its operations. *The Chronicle of Higher Education*, April 2, 45(30), A30.

Bremner, F. (1998). On-line college classes get high marks among students. Cyber courses handy but more work for teacher. *USA Today*, November 16, 16E.

Buikema, A. and Ward, B. (1999). *Plain Talk About Using the Web in Teaching*. New York: Saunders College Publishing.

Carnevale, D. (2001). Union offers standards for distance education. *The Chronicle of Higher Education*, February 2, 47(21), A33.

Carnevale, D. (2000). Two models for collaboration in distance education. *The Chronicle of Higher Education*, May 19, 46(37), A53.

Carnevale, D. (2000). Legislative audit criticizes Western Governors University. *The Chronicle of Higher Education*, October 6, 47(6), A48.

Carnevale, D. (2000). Accrediting panel grants candidate status to Western Governors U. *The Chronicle of Higher Education*, December 15, 47(16), A51.

Carr, S. (2001). Is anyone making money on distance education? *The Chronicle of Higher Education*, February 16, 47(23), A41-A43.

Connell, T. (1998). Distance holds the key to growth. *Times Higher Education Supplement*, July 17, (1341), 12.

Connick, G. (1997). Issues and trends to take us into the twenty-first century. *New Directions for Teaching and Learning*, Fall, 71, 7-11.

The Costs of Teaching With Technology. (2000). *NCHEMS News*, December, 2-4.

Curran, C. (1997). ODL and traditional universities: dichotomy or convergence? *European Journal of Education*, December, 32(4), 335-346.

Emmert, M. (1997). Distance learning tests America's higher education dominance. *New England's Journal of Higher Education and Economic Development*, Summer, 12(2), 20-22.

Gallick, S. (1998). Technology in higher education: Opportunities and threats. Faculty Association of the University of California-Los Angeles. (ERIC Document Reproduction Service No. ED 415 929)

Guernsey, L. (1998). Distance education for the not-so-distant. *The Chronicle of Higher Education*, March 27, 44(29), A29-A30.

Hall, J. (1995). The convergence of means. *Educom Review*, July-August, 30(4), 42-45.

Hall, P. (1996). Distance education and electronic networking. *Information Technology for Development*, October, 7(2), 75-89.

Houweling, D. (2000). Inventing the advanced Internet. In Luker, M. (Ed.), *Preparing Your Campus for a Networked Future*, 29-40. San Francisco: Jossey-Bass Publishers.

Imel, S. (1996). Distance education: Trends and issues alerts. Columbus, Ohio: ERIC Clearinghouse on Adult, Career, and Vocational Education, the Ohio State University. (ERIC Document Reproduction Service No. ED 414 446)

Is online education off course? New AFT report proposes standards for online colleges. (2001, January 17). U.S. Newswire.

Lynch, C. (2000). The academic library in the networked information age. In Luker, M. (Ed.), *Preparing Your Campus for a Networked Future*, 15-28. San Francisco: Jossey-Bass Publishers.

Matthews, D. (1999). The origins of distance education and its use in the United States. *T.H.E. Journal*, September, 27(2), 54-67.

McCollum, K. (1998). Western Governors University forms consortium with Britain's Open University. *The Chronicle of Higher Education*, November 27, 65(14), A23.

Miller, C., Smith, C. and Tilstone, C. (1998). Professional development by distance education: Does distance lend enhancement? *Cambridge Journal of Education*, June, 28(2), 221-230.

O'Leary, M. (2000). Distance learning and libraries. *Online*, July-August, 24(4), 94-96.

Online. (1998). While most colleges and universities are setting up chairs and clipping grass to prepare for spring commencements, some institutions that offer distance education have been readying television studios and tuning up World Wide Web servers instead. *The Chronicle of Higher Education*, May 22, 44(37), A27.

Plant, M. (1996). Technology, Open Learning and Distance Education, Studies in Distance Education. *Assessment & Evaluation in Higher Education*, March, 21(1), 103-104.

Press, E., Washburn, J. and Broden, F. (2001). Digital diplomas. *Mother Jones*, January-February, 26(1), 34-41.

Primary Research Group. (1997). *The Survey of Distance Learning Programs in Higher Education* (Report No. ISBN-1-57440-008-8). New York, NY. (ERIC Document Reproduction Service No. ED 414 874)

Quan, M. (2000). E-learning is a 24 x 7 endeavor. *Electronic Engineering Times*, July 31, (1124), 66-67.

Ramanantsoa, B. (2001). Why far-sighted schools will keep their distance. *The Times Higher Education Supplement*, January 5, (1468), 12.

Russell, T. (1999). The no significant difference phenomenon. As reported in 355 research reports, summaries and papers. Raleigh, NC: North Carolina State University.

Selingo, J. (1998). Congress moves cautiously on aid for students in distance education. *The Chronicle of Higher Education*, June 5, 44(39), A30.

Stross, R. (2001). The new mailbox U. *U.S. News & World Report*, January 15, 130(2), 37.

Svetcov, D. (2000). The virtual classroom vs. the real one. *Forbes*, September 11, 166(7), 50-52.

Terry, L. (2000). The digital diploma. *Internet Life*, November, 6(11), 132-136.

Tysome, T. (2001). Distance learning fails students. *The Times Higher Education Supplement*, January 5, (1468), 7.

U.S. Department of Education. (1997). Distance education in higher education institutions (National Center for Education Statistics Report 98-062). Washington, DC: Author.

U.S. Department of Education. (1999). Distance education at post-secondary education institutions: 1997-98 (National Center for Education Statistics Report 2000-013). Washington, DC: Author.

Van Dusen, G. (2000). *Digital dilemma. Issues of Access, Cost and Quality in Media-Enhanced and Distance Education.* San Francisco: Jossey-Bass Publishers.

Warden, R. (1995). Metaphor made real with an open mind. *Times Higher Education Supplement,* October 13, (1197), pIi.

Young, J. (2000). Logging in with... Stanley A. Chodorow. *The Chronicle of Higher Education,* June 30, 46(43), A44.

Young, J. (2000). Officials from 30 nations seek global coordination in distance education. *The Chronicle of Higher Education,* September 29, 47(5), A46.

Chapter II

Distance Education in the Online World: Implications for Higher Education

Stewart Marshall
Central Queensland University, Australia

Shirley Gregor
Australian National University, Australia

In this chapter, the authors identify forces leading to change in industries in the online world, including increasing global competition, increasingly powerful consumers and rapid changes in technology. In the higher education industry, outcomes are evolving, but include the formation of alliances, outsourcing and re-engineering of systems and work practices. The communication and information technologies that created the online world also link lecturers, tutors, and teaching resources to create the possibility of networked education. The authors outline a "glocal" networked education paradigm that separates out global and local resource development and global and local learning facilitation. By embracing this separation, it is possible to develop ways of working that allow the creation of a flexible model of education delivery that is scalable and hence globally competitive. In this model, the work of the university academic is changed considerably. The functions traditionally performed by a single university academic are differentiated and are performed by a network of learning facilitators. In this scenario, university academics may find themselves responsible for the learning of hundreds of students, but they may never find themselves face-to-face with a single student.

INTRODUCTION

As the world moves online, pressure increases on industries and organizations to change the way they do business. According to Turban, McLean and Wetherbe (1999), pressures acting on industries and organizations result from: the market, technology, and society. *Market pressures* include global competition and consumers who are becoming more demanding; *technological pressures* include the use of e-commerce to lower the costs of production and transaction costs; and s*ocietal pressures* include government regulations and economic conditions (for example, through the use of subsidies, tax policies, and import/export regulations).

The higher education industry and universities are subject to the same pressures as other industries and organizations in the online world. For example, in Australia, enrollment of foreign students was the country's eighth largest export earner during 1997/8 earning A$3.1 billion [the larger ones being: coal (A$9.5b), tourism (A$8.0b), transport (A$6.7b), gold (A$6.2b), iron (A$3.7b), wheat (A$3.6b) and aluminium (A$3.2) (AVCC, 2000)]. Because of the Internet, Australian universities must now *compete* with universities from other countries offering online programs to those students in their own countries. So universities must change the way they do business.

Those institutions that can step up to this process of change will thrive. Those that bury their heads in the sand, that rigidly defend the status quo - or even worse - some idyllic vision of a past that never existed, are at very great risk....The real question is not whether higher education will be transformed but rather how and by whom?

(Duderstadt, 1999, p.1)

To understand how universities need to be transformed, it is necessary to look at the impact of distance education in the online world on higher education organizational structures and work groups, including organizational roles, workgroup dynamics, and communication. It is also necessary to examine which structures and processes are needed to allow a university to exist and prosper in an age of globalization and rapid changes in the information technology underlying remote education and work. This chapter tackles these issues using a model based on Giddens' (1977) theory of structuration in which process (activity) and structure are reciprocally constitutive, and the application of this theory to information technology by Orlikowski and Robey (1991). Central to this model is the view that change is not solely "technology led" or solely "organizational/ agency driven." Instead, change arises from a complex interaction between technology, people and the organization.

The authors then consider, as a case study, Central Queensland University (CQU), which is a university in Australia that is responding to the challenge of remote education and operation on a national and international basis. CQU has been a distance education and on-campus education provider since 1974 and is now Australia's fastest growing university. Inherent in all CQU's operations is a model in which the organization, its members and its partners are all constituents of a "glocal" network of learning facilitators.

IMPLICATIONS OF THE ONLINE WORLD FOR STRUCTURE AND PROCESS IN INDUSTRIES AND ORGANIZATIONS

In considering the implications of the online world for industry, it is necessary to consider both *structure* and *process,* where process includes *change processes* (Gregor & Johnston, 2000; 2001; Johnston & Gregor, 2000). For example, one defining characteristic of an industry structure is the degree to which vertical integration has occurred. Vertical integration and alliances are formed by negotiation over periods of time. The result is a structure that becomes formalized to some extent. Further activities and processes are needed to maintain the alliance and modify it as needed.

In Giddens' theory of structuration, process (activity) and structure are reciprocal (Giddens, 1977, 1984, 1991). As Giddens (1977, p. 121) states, "Social structures are both constituted by human agency, and yet at the same time are the very *medium* of this constitution," or as Rose (1999, p. 643) puts it, "Agents in their actions constantly produce and reproduce and develop the social structures which both constrain and enable them."

This link between process and structure is also important at the organizational level. In order to develop technology and systems to survive in the online world, an organization must engage in certain processes, such as business process re-engineering. These processes are of great importance – many information systems fail and exhibit the *productivity paradox* (Brynjolfsson & Hitt, 1998). This paradox refers to the fact that investment in Information Technology appears to be unrelated to increased outputs. One explanation of the productivity paradox is that some organizations do not pay sufficient attention to processes within their organization when introducing new technology. If organizational change is not implemented well, and work processes not redesigned, the new systems do not lead to gains in productivity. Organizations that gain in productivity appear to be those in which there is a restructuring of the organization and flatter, less hierarchical structures with decentralized decision-making.

Thus, it is necessary to consider change and processes of change as well as structure. The authors have a particular view of organizational change. This view is that change is "emergent." Change is not solely "technology led" or solely "organizational/agency driven." Change arises from a complex interaction between technology and the people in an industry or organization (Markus & Robey, 1988).

The conceptual model developed here is based on the structurational theory of information technology of Orlikowski and Robey (1991). This model posits four relationships: (1) information technology is a product of human action; (2) information technology is an influence on human action; (3) organizational properties are an influence on human interactions with information technology; and (4) information technology is an influence on the organization. The model is extended to include the market, technological and societal influences from the external environment that affect an organization.

So what are the implications of the online world for industry structure and process? Barriers to participating in electronic transactions are decreasing. Rather than having networks only link existing trading partners in a tightly coupled environment, new electronic markets can easily include larger numbers of buyers and sellers (Malone, Yates & Benjamin, 1987).

On the other hand there is evidence for hierarchical arrangements supported by electronic networks, with firms in many industries reducing the number of their suppliers, and entering into contractual arrangements for the supply of goods. These arrangements constitute *supply chain management*. The arguments from economic theory for the changes in market structures are complex. Holland and Lockett (1994) propose an *"anything goes"* or mixed-mode hypothesis where firms develop different forms of market and hierarchical relationships that are maintained simultaneously. The interrelationships and interdependencies of governance structure, asset specificity, market complexity and coordination strategy will determine interorganizational arrangements (Klein, 1998).

A value chain consists of the movement of components through various stages of production and distribution as they are transformed into final products. A firm can decide to produce each of the goods and services needed along the value chain in-house or to outsource it. There is a view that greater use of interorganizational networks will lead to vertical disintegration and greater outsourcing. For example, instead of an organization having its own IT department, it may outsource this function to a specialist IT service provider. However, evidence to support this view is still being collected (Steinfeld, Kraut & Chan, 1998). Some expect disintermediation to occur, where intermediaries are removed because of the ease with which they can be bypassed on electronic platforms. For example, retailers and wholesalers can be bypassed by the customer placing orders online directly with the manufacturers. It is not clear, however, that disintermediation will always occur. Instead, different forms of intermediaries may emerge; e.g., a cybermediary such as Amazon.com which to some extent replaces the traditional intermediaries, namely, book shops.

It appears that maximum benefit is obtained from e-business when it is integrated with other applications in the organization. This integration can require re-engineering of the way in which the organization does business. E-business reduces the costs of handling paper-based information. For example, the cost to the U.S. Federal government of a paper check was 43 cents compared to two cents for an electronic payment (Turban, McLean & Wetherbe, 1999). Small companies can use the Internet for marketing and compete against firms globally at comparatively little expense. Employees can work from home or from different parts of the globe. Teams can be linked with electronic communication.

To summarize, the implications of the online world for industry include: market transformations, the need for alliances, changes in outsourcing behavior, and changes in the role and type of intermediaries. In addition, the need for re-engineering and the manner in which organizational change is approached must be considered carefully.

What are the implications for higher education?

CHANGING UNIVERSITIES

Universities and the higher educational sector face similar challenges to other industries in the online world.

Universities are due for a radical restructuring. After centuries of evolutionary changes, they are faced with carving out new roles and methods to get there. Today the predominant model is still the combination of traditional teaching and academic research as mapped out by Wilhelm von Humboldt in the last century. The guiding principles of Humboldt's vision of the university are forschung und lehre *(research and teaching) and of professors,* einsamkeit und freiheit *(solitude and freedom). But change is unavoidable and pressure for change is increasing from the public, the media, and political groups. This change is mainly driven by the new technological possibilities and the new learning environments they enable.*

(Tsichritzis, 1999, p.93)

Specific implications for universities can be drawn from the conceptual model based on the structurational theory of information technology of Orlikowski and Robey (1991):

- Organizational change arises from a complex interaction between technology and the people in the organization. For example, information technology makes possible new learning environments and changed work practices for university staff.
- Information technology can influence changes in organizational structure. The improved communication options offered by advances in information technology support the formation of alliances and the "unbundling" of the functions of the university (content, packaging and presentation). This vertical disintegration, in which functions are differentiated and either outsourced or dealt with by partners in strategic alliances, creates new intermediaries in the learning/teaching network.

There is evidence of organizational change arising from the interaction of technology and people in some universities. In Australia, online and videoconferencing systems are being developed as alternatives to face-to-face communication where the people are physically dispersed. These methodologies require both staff and students to change existing work practices and to acquire new literacies (Wallace & Yell, 1997). The new technological possibilities (and new learning environments that arise from the interaction between technology and the people) include: the Internet (facilitating synchronous and asynchronous interactions between learners); videoconferencing (facilitating tutorials comprising distributed groups of students, and also remote access to live lectures); digital libraries (as knowledge repositories); computer simulation (substitutes for laboratories); etc. Overall, the interaction of these new technologies with the people creates a learning environment in which learners, tutors and learning resources can all be networked.

These same technological possibilities also permit new working environments for those responsible for the facilitation of learning. Thus lecturers can use the Internet for synchronous and asynchronous communication with colleagues, videoconferencing for meetings, digital libraries for research. The interaction of these new technologies with the people creates a teaching environment in which lecturers, tutors and teaching resources can all be networked.

There is also evidence of changes in organizational structure that have been influenced by information technology. Traditionally, universities have carried out all the functions relating to the provision of higher education: content production; packaging content; credentialing programs; presentation to students; marketing; registration, payment and record keeping; and assessment. In the online world, these functions can more readily be "disintegrated" and the university can specialize in those functions which it regards as its "core business," forming alliances for other functions or outsourcing to new intermediaries in the value chain.

The marketing of a university's programs can be outsourced to a company that specializes in researching the market and promoting the university. Recruitment can be better accomplished close to the student, and in the case of international students, in the student's mother tongue by agents overseas. Library facilities could be provided by new intermediaries close to the students or provided online by cybermediaries. Fee payment, especially online payment, can similarly be outsourced to a cybermediary. If an institution is offering on many sites and many countries, then outsourcing invigilation and related examination administration is necessary. Sylvan Learning Systems (2001) is an example of an organization specializing in the function of assessment in the education value chain. Based in the USA, it offers computer-based testing services to educational institutions, for example the Graduate Management Aptitude Test (GMAT) and the Test of English as a Foreign Language (TOEFL).

Research, of course, can be conducted by others outside universities, so there is really no reason why this activity couldn't be outsourced. But it could be argued that there is a nexus between research and teaching in universities that is essential for higher education.

The functions of course development and materials development are perhaps the ones seen as most likely to remain with universities. But there are those who even suggest the need for outsourcing and alliances for the performance of these functions. Gibbons (1998, p.61) predicts that universities "will learn to make use of intellectual resources that they don't own fully. This is the only way that they will be able to interact effectively with the distributed knowledge production system."

In the higher education industry there is an increasing number of instances of institutions delivering the content of others. UNext is an internet-based distance learning 'university' which utilizes content developed by the London School of Economics, the University of Chicago, Colombia, Stanford and Carnegie Mellon Universities, and delivers Master of Business Administration (MBA) degrees to the corporate sector. UNext also handles the global marketing and management of the programs (UNext, 2001). Western Governors University (WGU) was formed in 1996 by the governors of the western USA to share higher education distance learning resources. It offers online access to over 500 distance education courses from over 40 higher education institutions. It assesses students and awards degrees, but its programs are produced and delivered by the participating institutions (WGU, 2001).

Gibbons (1998, p.61) suggests that a university should be regarded as "a sort of 'holding institution' in the field of knowledge production, perhaps limited to accrediting teaching done primarily by others while in research doing their part by forming problem-solving teams that work on fundamental issues." This view sees the core business of the university as participating in knowledge production and credentialing the teaching programs of others. But if so many functions are outsourced, then an important new function must be added to the work of the university – the function of organizing the learning space – bringing all the outsourced functions together to facilitate learning by the students. Indeed, one could say that the organization of the learning space perhaps becomes the central function of the university.

As the various functions of the higher education process are differentiated, so too the *nature of work* and the *workforce* change (Coaldrake & Stedman, 1999). The authors now consider a case study that illustrates this change.

CASE STUDY OF CENTRAL QUEENSLAND UNIVERSITY IN AUSTRALIA

Central Queensland University (CQU) is a regional university in Australia that is responding to the challenge of the online world. With 15,000 students, CQU is now Australia's fastest growing university in terms of international students. Only 25% of its students were in grades 11 and 12 in Australia during the last two years; the remainder are mature-aged or international students. In other words, CQU has a diverse student population quite unlike that of "traditional" universities.

In Central Queensland, CQU's traditional catchment area, Rockhampton is the location of the main campus; Mackay campus 350 kilometres to the North; Gladstone campus 120 kilometres to the South; Emerald campus 280 kilometres to the West; and Bundaberg campus 330 kilometres to the South. A key component of this integrated network of campuses is the Interactive System-Wide Learning (ISL) system – a synchronous video link that facilitates networked learning. Thus, on these campuses, classes are taught using combinations of synchronous video delivery of live lectures, videoconferencing to connect distributed groups of learners, web-delivery, synchronous and asynchronous computer-mediated discussions, and face-to-face classes.

CQU has been a distance education provider since 1974. Distance education students are serviced with a combination of printed, CD-ROM and web-delivered material, as well as electronic asynchronous communication for class discussion and mailing lists.

CQU formed an alliance with a commercial partner, Campus Management Services, to establish campuses at Sydney in 1994, Melbourne in 1996 and more recently in Brisbane and the Gold Coast. At these campuses the students are mostly of international origin. In addition, there are campuses operating in Singapore, Hong Kong and Fiji. At all these campuses, the CQU programs are tutored by locally appointed academic staff, specifically employed for teaching rather than research. The mode of delivery is face-to-face for tutorials and lectures, supported by the distance education resource materials produced by the CQU academic staff in Central Queensland.

Inherent in the CQU educational partnership with Campus Management Services is a model in which the function of content production has been detached from other functions traditionally carried out by the university (for example, lecturing). This vertical disintegration, in which functions are differentiated and either outsourced or dealt with by partners in strategic alliances, creates new intermediaries in the value chain.

For both on-campus and distance education modes, CQU has moved to a networked learning paradigm, using communication and information technologies to link learners and learning resources. But it has also moved to a networked teaching paradigm that links lecturers, tutors and teaching resources.

There are inherent dangers, however, in globalization coupled with the facility to network all teachers and learners. Inappropriate structures and processes for this global network have the potential to create stress for the individuals at the CQU campuses. When becoming more global, it is important to take care that the models used for teaching are scalable—for example, one coordinator in Rockhampton should not be dealing with a mailing list comprising one thousand students from all over the world.

There are also fears that the globalization of higher education could lead to a global western academic homogeneity—yet another wave of cultural imperialism. But the fear that global higher education will destroy indigenous cultures fails to acknowledge that other forms of communication between cultures have existed for hundreds of years, and the fact that cultures survive such transculturation is evidence of cultural 'resistance' and 'adaption' (McQuail, 1994).

> *The intensifying of worldwide social relations sets up dialectical ties between the global and local, such that what happens in any particular milieu is an expression of, but also can often stand in contradistinction to, distanciated social forms.*

> (Giddens, 1991, p. 210)

So, when becoming more global, it is important to take care to create a system which does not seek to undermine cultural 'resistance' and 'adaption,' but which instead is responsive to the knowledge, culture and needs of the local learners. One aspect of this process is the "internationalising" of the curriculum to allow local knowledge and culture to be incorporated and valued.

To overcome the dangers mentioned above, it is important to move to a "glocal" meta-model in which the staff in each faculty of CQU are responsible for the organization of the global learning environment whilst the educational partners are responsible for the organization of the local learning environment (see Figure 1). Hence the portmanteau expression "glocal" – it is global and local at the same time.

Figure 1: The "Glocal" model of networked learning

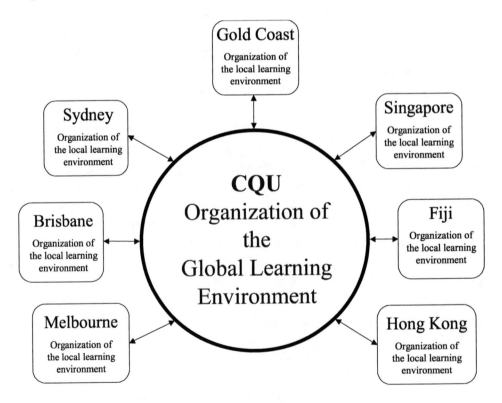

CASE STUDY OF THE "GLOCAL" META-MODEL: CQU GOING ONLINE IN SINGAPORE

Let us consider the specific example of CQU facilitating learning in Singapore.

CQU was originally offering programs in Singapore using distance education (DE) materials together with local tutorial support – a sort of "supported DE delivery." This was the original "glocal" model, viz., global learning resources with local learning support/mediation provided by local tutors employed by our Singaporean partner. The penetration of communication and information technology in Singapore is considerably higher than in most of the other CQU learning locations and so it was natural to make this the first location for CQU to offer its programs online.

The first, and perhaps most important point to make about the Singapore online project is that it was the result of emergent change. In an evolutionary fashion, CQU added online interactivity and support to what it was already offering in Singapore. Thus, the online programs in Singapore are not offered in a pure online mode of delivery – instead they are offered in "supported online mode," i.e., with some printed DE materials, some face-to-face tutorials and other campus-based support. This "supported online mode" is simply an example of the flexible learning paradigm embraced by the University, or more specifically, an example of the "glocal networked learning paradigm."

The communication and information technologies which enable us to create the networked learning environment for the student also enable us to create a networked education system in which lecturers, tutors and teaching resources are all linked. In the CQU/Singapore network, a CQU academic development team is responsible for the collection of the resources, the creation of the materials and the development of the "global core" for the supported online course. The global core is then electronically delivered to the local partner in Singapore.

The local partner in Singapore is responsible for adding the local education interface to the global core (see Figure 2). Thus, the online component of the global core is mirrored on our partner's server in Singapore and the local partner then creates a website with the required local online "look and feel." The CQU academic development team works electronically with the local development team to maintain quality control of this locally added component.

Figure 2: The "Glocal" resource development process

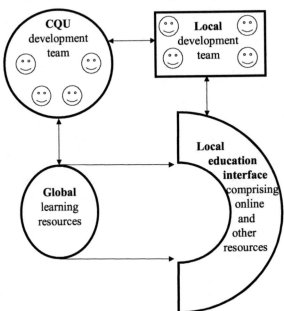

As regards the facilitation of learning during the running of a particular course, a lecturer on one Central Queensland campus is designated as the coordinator of a particular unit (course), and that person, together with the administration multi-campus support team, coordinates the activities of the learning facilitators/tutors on all the other campuses on which that particular course is taught. Thus, rather than dealing directly with a thousand students on campuses all over the world, the CQU coordinator deals with the in-country tutors who in turn facilitate the learning of the students. The local campus/centre acts as a hub – a local network – as shown in Figure 3.

Through the coordinator, CQU is responsible for quality control of the facilitation of the learning process. The usual quality control mechanisms are used, including moderation of assignments, marking of examination scripts, and site management visits.

CONCLUDING REMARKS

In this chapter, the authors have identified forces leading to change in industries in the online world, including increasing global competition, increasingly powerful consumers and rapid changes in technology, especially those related to telecommunications. Implications for industry include market transformations, the need for alliances, changes in outsourcing behavior, the need for re-engineering, and changes in the role and type of intermediaries.

Figure 3: The local learning network linked to CQU

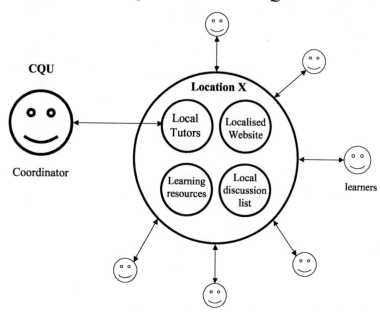

In the higher education industry, pressures for change include global competition and technology-facilitated learning. Outcomes are evolving, but include the formation of alliances, outsourcing and re-engineering of systems and work practices. In particular, the communication and information technologies that facilitate networked learning also link lecturers, tutors, and teaching resources to create the possibility of networked education.

The particular "glocal" networked education paradigm that the authors have outlined separates out four functions:

1) Development of the global core of learning resources;
2) Development of the local education interface;
3) Coordination of the learning facilitation on a specific occasion; and
4) Local learning facilitation.

An important distinction here for CQU is the separation of the development and the teaching functions. By embracing this separation, CQU has been able to develop ways of working which allow the creation of a scalable and flexible model. In this model, however, the work of the university academic is changed considerably.

The authors have shown how the online world tends to lead to vertical disintegration in universities and results in the differentiated functions being performed by alliance partners or being outsourced. In the same way, the functions traditionally performed by a single university academic are differentiated in the CQU "glocal" networked education paradigm and are performed by a network of learning facilitators. The distinction between academic and nonacademic university staff blurs as both take on more "learning management" roles, for example, management of learning facilitators and management of learning resources. In this scenario, university academics may find themselves responsible for the learning of hundreds of students. They may never, however, find themselves face-to-face with a single student.

REFERENCES

AVCC. (2000). *Australian Vice Chancellors Committee: Key Statistics Internationalisation*. Canberra: AVCC. Available on the World Wide Web at: http://www.avcc.edu.au/australias_unis/statistics/internationalisation/.

Brynjolfsson, E. and Hitt, L. M. (1998). Beyond the productivity paradox. *Communications of the ACM,* 41(8), 49-55.

Coaldrake, P. and Stedman, L. (1999) Academic Work in the Twenty-first Century: Changing roles and policies. *Department of Education, Training and Youth Affairs (DETYA)*, Commonwealth of Australia: Canberra. Available on the World Wide Web at: http://www.detya.gov.au/highered/occpaper.htm.

Duderstadt, J. J. (1999). Can colleges and universities survive in the information age? In Katz, R. N. & Associates (Eds.), *Dancing With the Devil-Information Technology and the New Competition in Higher Education*. San Francisco: Jossey-Bass.

Gibbons, M. (1998). Higher education relevance in the 21st century. *UNESCO World Conference on Higher Education*, Paris, October 5-9.

Giddens, A. (1977). *Studies in Social and Political Theory*. London: Hutchinson.

Giddens, A. (1984). *The Constitution of Society*. Cambridge: Polity Press.

Giddens, A. (1991). Structuration theory: Past, present and future. In Bryant, C. and Jary, D. (Eds.), *Giddens' Theory of Structuration: A Critical Appreciation*. Chapter 8. London: Routledge.

Gregor, S. and Johnston, R. B. (2000). Developing an understanding of interorganizational systems: Arguments for multi-level analysis and structuration theory. In Hansen, H. R., Bichler, M. and Mahrer, H. (Eds.), *Proceedings of the 8th European Conference on Information Systems,* Vienna, 3-5 July, 1, 575-582.

Gregor, S. and Johnston, R. B. (2001). Theory of interorganizational systems: Industry structure and processes of change. *Thirty-Fourth Hawaii International Conference on System Sciences (HICSS-34)*. January. To appear.

Holland, C. P. and Lockett, G. (1994). Strategic choice and interorganizational information systems. In Nunamaker, J. F. and Sprague, R. H. (Eds.), *Proceedings 27th HICSS, vol IV, Collaboration Technology, Organizational Systems and Technology*. Los Alamitos, CA: IEEE Computer Society Press, 405-413.

Johnston, R. B. and Gregor, S. (2000). A structuration-like theory of industry-level activity for understanding the adoption of interorganizational systems, In Hansen, H. R., Bichler, M. and Mahrer, H. (Eds.), *Proceedings of the 8th European Conference on Information Systems,* Vienna, 3-5 July, 1, 567-574.

Klein, S. (1998). The diffusion of auctions on the Web. In Romm, C. and Sudweeks, F. (Eds.), *Doing Business Electronically*. London: Springer, 47-63.

Malone, T., Yates, J., and Benjamin, R. (1987). Electronic markets and electronic hierarchies: Effects of information technology on market structure and corporate strategies, *Communications of the ACM,* 30(6), 484-497.

Markus, M. L. and Robey, D. (1988). Information technology and organizational change: Causal structure in theory and research. *Management Science,* 34(5), 583-598.

McQuail, D. (1994) *Mass Communication Theory: An Introduction.* 3rd ed., London: Sage.

Orlikowski, W. J. and Robey, D. (1991). Information technology and the structuring of organizations, *Information Systems Research*, 2(2), 143-169.

Rose, J. (1999). Frameworks for practice: Structurational theories of IS, *Proceedings of the European Conference on Information Systems*.

Steinfeld, C., Kraut, R. and Chan, A. (1998). The impact of interorganizational networks on buyer-seller relationships. in Romm, C. and Sudweeks, F. (Eds.), *Doing Business Electronically,* Springer, London, 7-26.

Sylvan Learning Systems. (2001). Sylvan Learning Systems. Available on the World Wide Web at: http://sylvanlearning.com/home.html.

Tsichritzis, D. (1999). Reengineering the university, *Communications of the ACM,* 42(6), 93-100.

Turban, E., McLean, E. and Wetherbe, J. (1999). *Information Technology for Management,* Wiley, New York.

Unext. (2001). Unext.com. Available on the World Wide Web at: http://www.unext.com/.

Wallace, A and Yell, S. (1997). New literacies in the virtual classroom. *Southern Review*, 30(3). Available on the World Wide Web at: http://

www.infocom.cqu.edu.au/Staff/Susan_Yell/Teaching/fmctl/liter.htm.

WGU. (2001). Western Governors University. Available on the World Wide Web at: http://www.wgu.edu/wgu/index.html.

Chapter III

The Potential Attraction of Online Distance Education: Lessons from the Telecommuting Literature

Geoffrey N. Dick
University of New South Wales, Australia

Distance education involves both the student and the instructor in various tasks associated with learning and testing the absorption of that learning. In this chapter, parallels are drawn between educational and workplace tasks— the understanding of prescribed material, assignments, experiences and acquisition of knowledge on one hand and the components of a job on the other. It draws on the telecommuting literature as it relates to telecommuting's attraction to the worker, the organization and the community, the importance of the task, the technology required, the role of the supervisor and the individual attributes one needs to be a successful teleworker. These are brought together in a model aimed at providing a guide to the possible adoption of distance education and enabling administrators to assess its potential and some of the pitfalls that may be encountered.

INTRODUCTION

Distance education, particularly online distance education is attracting considerable attention from both providers of education and potential students. There are many similarities between this form of education and telecommuting. From the employer (or provider) perspective, there is the attraction of a wider pool of potential recruits (read potential students), savings on facilities and organizational infrastructure, meeting demand and changing work practices. From a student perspective, the telecommuting advantages of reduced travel, flexibility and the time to devote to other commitments (work, family, etc.) are at least initially attractive.

The objective of this chapter is to review the telecommuting literature and put forward a model that outlines the potential influences affecting the adoption of distance education for use by academic institutions in their decisions related to this area. Such a model may be helpful for research into distance education too.

CHAPTER OVERVIEW

This chapter begins with a review of the benefits, costs and risks associated with telecommuting (Gray et al., 1993; Turban & Wang, 1995; Ford & McLaughlin, 1995; Ellis & Webster, 1997) for each of the three components of the telecommuting arrangement–the individual, the organization and the community, and suggests that several of the matters relevant here have direct relevance to the distance education decision. In essence, these issues form part of the drives and constraints which need to be present or absent to some degree for telecommuting to take place. Other drives and constraints include the suitability of the task, the attitude of the supervisor, etc. This theme is continued by an examination of the enablers (Mokhtarian & Salomon, 1994; Tung & Turban, 1996) which provides some insight into the technological factors that are likely to influence the acceptance and potential use of this form of education.

Using a theoretical task model to encompass the component, coordinative and dynamic themes of complexity (Wood, 1986), the task characteristics of uncertainty and equivocality (Daft and Macintosh, 1981) and the organizational issues of resources and scheduling of work (Thompson, 1967), a set of attributes for educational tasks is developed. It is suggested that this model forms a central component of an overall model for the evaluation of the suitability of educational tasks to distance education. In addition the task model provides a firm basis for consideration of the appropriateness of the attributes associated with various distance education tasks and the suitability of those tasks.

Studying and learning from home will require particular student attributes: some familiarity with computing and communications technologies, the ability to organize one's self, and time management skills are all likely to help the potential student. These personal attributes of the individual have parallels in the telecommuting literature too. These are most likely to be in the areas of personal characteristics such as the ability to get information required, knowing when advice is needed, the ability to solve one's own problems and good self-management (Venkatesh & Vitalari, 1992; Gray et al., 1993; Wheeler & Zackin, 1994; Mokhtarian & Salomon, 1996a) and the home environment (Yap & Tng, 1990; Mannering & Mokhtarian, 1995).

For many potential telecommuters, the supervisor is an important figure in the decision to work from home. To some extent the role of the Professor is analogous with that of the supervisor. As the supervisor controls allocation, timing and resources for tasks (Starr, 1971), the Professor controls task content, timing and the required resources. Accordingly, this literature, as it relates to telecommuting, offers some assistance in studies of distance education.

Telecommuting literature also provides some pointers to demographic influences on the preference to telecommute: age, gender, time in the workplace, job type, education, transport, presence of small children, and the number of cars in the household (Mokhtarian and Salomon, 1997; Belanger, 1999; Dick and Duncanson, 1999). Some of these seem to have relevance to the decision to engage in distance education.

The chapter concludes with a discussion of the adoption model proposed, relating it to a series of issues presently being encountered in distance education.

ADVANTAGES AND DISADVANTAGES

For the Individual

The telecommuting literature (Olson, 1983; Rice, 1987; Ford & Butts, 1991; Gray et al., 1993; Mokhtarian & Salomon, 1994; McQuarrie, 1994; Turban & Wang, 1995) suggests the following as potential advantages and disadvantages of telecommuting–each item is discussed with a view to its applicability to the student undertaking distance education, assuming that some form of information and communications technology will be used to aid him in the associated tasks.

The Advantages
- Reasons associated with travel to work, such as reduction in commuting stress, saving money and time and helping the environment. There is at

least some relevance here to distance education; not having to attend on a regular basis may reduce travel costs for the student, particularly if long distance travel is involved. In this context it should be noted that reduction of living costs may be a significant factor for the potential student. Also, this area might be broadened to include those for whom travel would be impossible, such as those living abroad or in remote areas.

- Better able to manage one's own affairs; e.g., more independence, flexibility, control of the physical working environment, to study or pursue personal interests. This factor has particular relevance (perhaps a very strong relevance to the postgraduate student, or the mature-age student) in the sense of being better able to manage work commitments.

- To be able to work if sick, disabled or to look after a sick child or other dependent. This potentially increases the possibility of education for those who may be disabled or extensively involved in the care of dependent children or other relatives.

- To reduce the stress experienced in the office. Relevant perhaps to those who might find the campus environment threatening or intimidating.

- To spend more time with one's family. A similar advantage for distance education students.

- To get more work done. Campus life offers many distractions for the student; while these are mostly seen as an advantage, some students may benefit from the possibility of removing themselves from these distractions. On the other hand, many of the activities available to, and experienced by, undergraduates on campus are part of the getting of wisdom and their being unavailable may render the educational experience a poorer one.

The potential advantages get generally high exposure in the distance education literature: accessibility, convenience, international (or recognized) instructors and a "consumer orientation" (Alavi et al., 1997; Emmons, 1999), allowing students to remain in a familiar environment, and the possibility of advancing the emergence of global software development and discussion (Passerini & Granger 2000), and the ability to continue education or keep up to date while having only limited time available due to heavy work commitments (Jana, 1999; Boisvert, 2000).

The Disadvantages
- More difficult to work at home due to less help available, motivational problems, increased family conflict and distractions. One might expect these to be serious impediments to distance education for many people,

requiring particular personal attributes for them to be overcome.

- Viewed negatively by management, being "out of sight and out of mind." If we interpret "management" to mean faculty, there could well be a feeling among distance students that those with physical access to the faculty and university resources get enhanced help and assistance.
- Exploitation by management–missing out on overtime or having to work extra time to cover peak periods. "Management" in this sense could be interpreted as the university administration that supplies resources and occasional casual work to supplement student incomes.
- Travel time can be used productively, to run errands, or provide a break between home and the office. Travel is seen as a time for completing assignments, reading, study, etc.
- The office is nicer/better equipped than a home office would be. A significant issue for potential distance students may be the need to equip a home study area with a PC and appropriate software, telephone line and communications software, although there is a recent move among University administrations to require students to purchase laptops and the appropriate software.
- The social interaction found at the conventional workplace and missing out on the extracurricular activities that take place on campus could be viewed by many as serious disadvantages to distance education.
- The professional interaction found at the conventional workplace–getting to know one's fellow students, easy access (formal and informal) to faculty. At a more strategic level, a diminished educational experience may result.

Many of these potential disadvantages are echoed in the distance education literature to date. There is broad support for the notion that an educational program is far more than a curriculum and that there are benefits from a "surround interaction" between the students, the instructor and the lectures. This rich variety of interaction is likely to be lost (Bertagnoli, 2001). Others include not learning the skills to think on one's feet, the absence of support and help, longer to develop a rapport between student and Professor and cost issues related to tuition and technology (Emmons, 1999). Attempts to measure satisfaction with distance education have been sporadic, other than the measure of enrollments and the growth in the number of institutions offering some form of distance education. One recent approach using the service industry as a base (Long et al., 2000) based the assessment largely on immediate application in the workplace—not an invalid measure, but perhaps only one of many.

For the Organization

Advantages to the organization from telecommuting normally center around productivity, better use of an employee's time, a wider pool of recruits on which to draw, saving on conventional office space and an extension of working hours (Katz, 1987; DuBrin, 1991; Gray et al., 1993; Hamblen, 1999). Similar advantages could accrue to universities offering distance education. Increasing staff workloads and the ability to offer courses outside conventional hours may appeal to university administrations; the wider pool of students, with the associated revenue (Keohane, 2000) is already seen as a major driving force; there could also be savings in lecture halls, tutorial rooms, laboratories and other on-campus facilities. Indeed there is evidence that this is already happening (Chellappa et al., 1997; Kirk & Bartelstein, 1999; Bertagnoli, 2001). In addition, there is at least circumstantial evidence that computer-based learning is less costly than classroom instruction (Mottl, 2000).

Disadvantages of telecommuting from an organizational perspective are largely to do with changing the way organizations work and function, duplicating equipment costs, absence of key personnel from the conventional workplace, morale problems and security (Ford & Butts, 1991; Filipczak, 1992; Li & Gillespie, 1994; Tamrat et al. 1996; Orlikowski, 1996; Dick & Duncanson, 1999). Re-skilling faculty (not just those who are keen to experiment with technology) and changes to more traditional ways of teaching may present significant problems. There will be additional costs (Herther, 1997) in supporting students' online access, and the absence of students from the conventional classroom may diminish the teaching standing of the university, due to the potential reduction in the student-professor interaction. Research may suffer too, due to the high demands of distance education in course preparation, rewriting and overhead associated with student contact (Chan, 1999).

Again distance education literature suggests that university administrations are already trying to cope with these issues (Theakston, 1999). The standing of the course is a matter for serious concern. A not uncommon perception of distance education is that it is a lesser experience and of lesser academic standing, partly as a result of it largely being offered by low-quality correspondence schools in the past (Emmons, 1999). While the analogy of takeout Chinese food compared with a restaurant dinner (Kling, 2001) seems a little unkind, this remains an issue for university administrations.

For the Community

Potential reduction in the demand for transport infrastructure, reduction in pollution and benefits to local or rural communities are often cited as possible effects of telecommuting (Blanc, 1988; Mokhtarian et al., 1995; Nilles, 1996). There is some scope for these benefits from distance education; perhaps the most significant may be the reduction in the subsidies required for public transport. As a rather bizarre example of the attraction of such an issue, there was a move after the Olympic games in Sydney to remove the stands at either end of the Olympic stadium, thereby reducing its capacity (empty seats do not look good on television), a move supported by the State Government as each person travelling to and from the stadium involves a public transport subsidy.

Another potential benefit to some communities and institutions is that the provision of distance education may provide the opportunity to leapfrog more established universities and colleges with their established (and perhaps difficult to change) infrastructure, in distance education, all institutions are on the starting blocks (Gregg, 1997).

Against this, business activity in the city centres and university towns may fall, travel may increase in outlying areas, and energy consumption in the home may rise (Gray et al., 1993).

ENABLERS

There is a long list of electronic enablers that facilitate telecommuting: PCs and laptops, printers, modems, copiers, fax machines, cellular telephones, answering machines, high-speed communications links and access to e-mail and the Internet (Hotch, 1993; Tung & Turban, 1996). While clearly not all are required for all tasks, this list is a useful starting point for the types of electronic assistance that would facilitate online distance education. At present much of this equipment is made available free of charge to students in the traditional campus environment. Considerable expense would be incurred by the student in equipping himself with such technology. On the other hand many universities expect students to have such technology available at home.

TASK SUITABILITY

The following model, constructed from the telecommuting and task literature, outlines various aspects of task properties that make a task suitable for telecommuting.

Figure 1: A task model

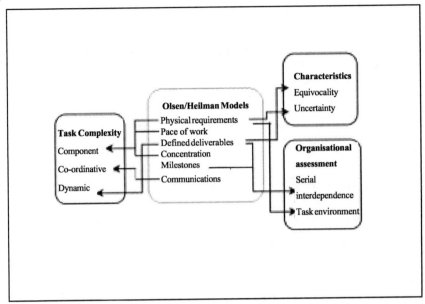

Based on original models of task suitability for telecommuting (Olson, 1983; Huws et al., 1990), the model suggests support for these properties from the task-related literature.

The original telecommuting models suggested that tasks may lend themselves to telecommuting if:

- physical requirements (for resources and equipment) are kept to a minimum,
- the staff member is in a position to control the pace of his work,
- the work has defined deliverables,
- the work required concentration,
- the work has specific milestones set, and
- there is minimal need for communications with one's supervisor or fellow employees.

There are obvious parallels here to those tasks that are likely to be part of distance education: assignment writing, research, understanding course notes and lecture material, and examination preparation.

In general terms, as the degree of task complexity rises, the task becomes less suitable (or more difficult) for telecommuting (Wood, 1986). The same may be said of distance education. Component complexity is a function of the number of distinct acts that are required to perform the task and the number of information cues to be processed in performing these acts. Component complexity is also affected by the task being dependent on completion of other tasks. The type of task may have relevance here too. Some concepts may be difficult to explain or demonstrate without "hands on" experience, for example, dissection, modeling and instrument operation. Coordinative complexity refers to the form and strength of relationships and the sequence of inputs. Wood suggests that the more complex the timing, frequency, intensity and location requirements, the greater the knowledge and skill the individual must have to be able to perform the task. Changes in the acts and information required or in the relationships between inputs and products, Wood calls dynamic complexity; an example could be a change in the desired output due to variations requested by a client. This too can create shifts in the knowledge or skills required.

To illustrate the potential impact of task complexity in a distance education environment, if we consider component complexity, tasks with minimal component complexity may be those such as reading a study guide, notes or a textbook and answering a series of "review" questions. At the other end of the scale, research using multiple resources, including hard copy and electronic journals, textbooks and the Internet, discussions with a colleague and writing up a summary of the research may present difficulties for the distance education student. Likewise coordinative complexity could range from one person completing an assignment, to working as part of a team with each member responsible for various components and then the team having to link them together to produce a final product.

Distance education today is largely conducted in an asynchronous mode (it does not require the students to be working together either at the same location or at the same time). This is part of its attraction in that this flexibility answers the drive of being better able to manage one's own affairs and commitments. However, where coordinative complexity is concerned, one person's time to complete a task may not suit another. Consider the case (typically used in IS courses) of building a web site and sending it to another student to critique before submitting it for grading. In the campus environment, many classmates could undertake the critiquing task if one's first choice was unavailable immediately. The student in a distance education environment may wait several days to discover his colleague is away, unable to master the technology required, or simply hasn't read his email. By this time, the assignment may be late, incurring penalties, etc.

Another example (again from the IS environment): one team member may develop program specifications, two or three others do the programming, and another tests the finished product. Software, hardware, and understanding another's work all become more difficult to manage at a distance, requiring extra overhead in management and control of the task.

The above examples illustrate a potential danger. In order to have such courses available for distance education and in an attempt to overcome such obstacles the instructor may be tempted to omit such coordinatively complex tasks from the course, meaning a lesser education experience may result.

The task characteristics of equivocality (ambiguous meanings or instructions) and uncertainty (about what is required or how to go about it) are also particularly relevant to tasks involved in distance education (Daft & Macintosh, 1981; Daft et al., 1987). Considerable difficulty might be expected to be experienced by the student if tasks are not clearly explained without ambiguity and specified to reduce uncertainty. In such an environment, a student may easily become frustrated and annoyed and may be more willing to question the value added by the instructor. There is a fine line to tread here. On one hand the course has to be challenging and enable the student to develop his skills and knowledge to their full potential. On the other hand, in the campus environment, many tasks are developed and modified on the fly (Kling, 2001) and give the instructor the opportunity to modify tasks for a particular student by changing requirements. If students are having trouble locating a particular resource, for example, the instructor may suggest alternatives or make it available by another means. Many assignments are set in such a way as to encourage the student to explore one of several options. Such amendments and vaguely worded assignments, without the likelihood of immediate remedy, can cause significant problems in the distance education environment and lead to the frustration and annoyance mentioned above.

In the campus environment too, the student enjoys access to a range of support groups of which the professor is only one part. Other groups include past students living in the college, current colleagues the student has established relationships with due to class contact, and formal administrative support groups such as counseling and tutorial services. All of these might be expected to be less readily available to the distance student. This requires the professor to be particularly careful in setting work and may influence the standard of such work.

Similarly, the environment in which the tasks take place (Thompson, 1967) may have some relevance to their suitability. Serial dependence refers to the need to wait on others (professor or student) in order to commence or complete one's own work. Also relevant is the degree of "networking" and team building that educational tasks are designed to include.

PERSONAL ATTRIBUTES

Successful telecommuters display certain traits (Gray et al., 1993). According to the authors, these traits are:

- the ability to make sound decisions, know where to get the information that leads to the decision-making process or the completion of the task and to know when they need advice;
- the ability to solve their own problems. This might require a knowledge of the organization, the tasks or the technology and an analytical approach to problem solving; and
- good self management; i.e., self motivation, time management, the ability to assess their own work and to be able to put these skills together to deliver quality work on time.

There is considerable support for these traits in the literature (see also, Venkatesh & Vitalari, 1986; Mokhtarian & Salomon, 1996b; Lewis, 1998). Confidence in working within the electronic community may also be an important attribute (Venkatesh & Vitalari, 1986; Hesse & Grantham, 1991; Trevino & Webster, 1992). The telecommuter is isolated from "help" and runs the risk of being seen as incapable of working with the required tools or being seen as incompetent if he/she does not hold the necessary skills.

Other aspects identified in various studies by Mokhtarian and others include the need for self discipline, household interaction problems, and aversion to risk (Mokhtarian & Salomon, 1994), susceptibility and aversion to stress (Mokhtarian & Salomon, 1997; Trent et al., 1994) and the desire to get more work done (Mokhtarian et al., 1994).

For the distance student, knowing where to get relevant information and when to seek advice would seem to have particular importance, as does the ability to solve his own problems: The added reliance on information technology and communications equipment gives this aspect added weight. Undergraduates are perhaps more likely, than their postgraduate counterparts, to have motivational problems and will need to develop time management skills to enable work of an appropriate quality to be delivered on time. On the subject of the household environment, the telecommuting issues of presence of small children, number of people in the household and family orientation may also have some effect on the preference to undertake education at a distance (Mannering & Mokhtarian, 1995).

THE SUPERVISOR

The supervisor has an enigmatic role in telecommuting. On one hand, without the supervisor's approval of individual instances, telecommuting is unlikely to take place, while on the other, the attitude of the supervisor does not seem to affect the preference to telecommute (Dick, 2000). Nevertheless, if we align the role of the supervisor with that of the professor, some issues do arise. It has already been noted that one of the disadvantages of telecommuting to the organization relates to changes in the way of working. Faculty will need to learn new skills, particularly IT-related ones. They will need to be prepared to "formalize" presentations and the learning experience imparted to a considerable degree and to correspond with students by the, perhaps unfamiliar media of email, "chat rooms" and "bulletin boards." These changes will not be easy and are likely to involve universities in considerable upheaval.

AN ADOPTION MODEL

The above suggests that the following model (Figure 2) may be useful in the evaluation of online distance education as an alternative for students and universities. The model is an attempt to identify the various influences on the possible acceptance of online distance education by universities, staff and students. As such it may provide some assistance to those evaluating the provision of distance education as a viable model, an understanding to those considering undertaking distance education of the issues, pitfalls and attractions involved, and potential researchers with a body of literature from a related field adapted to the topic.

CONCLUSION

Many education institutions are considering, or have already implemented, distance education programs, using some form of online delivery.

There is some temptation for academic institutions, attracted by the possibility of dramatically increased student numbers (often paying full fees), the apparently relatively easy conversion of current lecture material into online study guides, and a proliferation of software for online teaching to follow a "build it and they will come" approach. This is not likely to work.

So what can we learn to help in distance education from the telecommuting research? First, it should be noted that there are a complex set of factors that work together in consideration of such programs. This means that distance education is not likely to be suitable (or even attractive) to all; some courses and some components of courses are not likely to be suitable to distance education, and distance education may not be suitable for an entire educa-

Figure 2: An adoption model

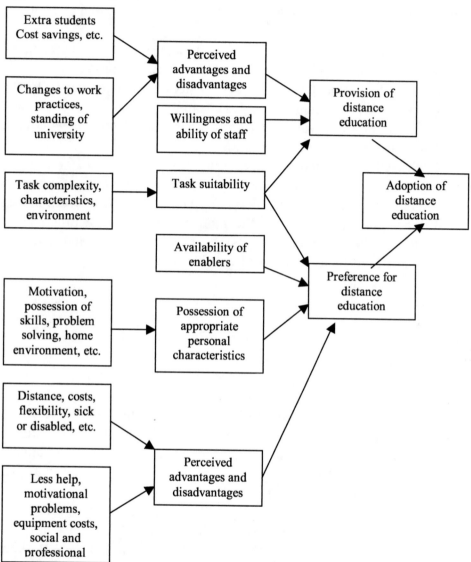

tional program. There seems little doubt that much academic work will be modified from the campus environment in its translation to the distance education one. Several possibilities arise here. One, there will be a proliferation of institutions offering low-quality tertiary education, much of which would be better offered as online training. Two, the large start-up costs associated with establishing any form of distance education will be lost as students eventually shy away from degrees "that everybody passes." Three, for the better administered and developed courses, faculty will be required to put in considerable extra effort to make the course available in a distance mode, which at least in the short term may mean less research and a lower academic standing for the university.

Modification to the work practices of faculty and the tasks to be completed by students will not come without some disruption to the university environment. In the long term it is possible that these changes may be for the good; however, telecommuting research would suggest that the programs will work best where they fit neatly into current organizational work practices and match student desires and abilities.

The varying approaches to telecommuting over the last 20 years and the way these approaches have been modified by such things as careful selection of telecommuters, the recognition that full-time telecommuting is often not good practice, and the modification of work practices to accommodate telecommuting suggest that careful planning and an evaluation of all of the factors involved will be required for any measure of success to be achieved.

Research on these programs is just beginning. There is a need for the evaluation of such programs against a sound research model. An important contribution of this chapter is to bring the telecommuting-related literature together in a manner that allows the development of a preliminary research model for studies of the provision of distance education from the educational institution perspective and for the desire to partake in distance education from an individual perspective. The model brings together the tasks (and the related issues of scheduling and control of work), personal characteristics of the individuals, the perceived advantages and disadvantages of undertaking a course of study in this way and the necessary underlying technology.

An important element in any form of education is the partnership between the instructor (or professor) and the student. On the face of it, the imposition of any form of technology between these two partners is likely to erect a barrier rather than facilitate learning. Accordingly, technologies and procedures must be found and implemented that enhance the learning experience.

REFERENCES

Alavi, M. A., Yoo, Y. and Vogel, D. R. (1997). Using information technology to add value to management education. *Academy of Management Journal,* 40(6), 1310-1333.

Belanger, F. (1999). Workers' propensity to telecommute: An empirical study. *Information and Management*, 35, 139-153.

Bertagnoli, L. (2001). Education reservation. *Marketing News*, 35(4), 4.

Blanc, G. (1988). Autonomy, telework and emerging cultural values. In Korte, W. B., Robinson, S. and Steinle, W. J., (Eds.), *Telework: Present Situation and Future Development of a New Form of Work Organization*, 189-200. Amsterdam: Elsevier Science Publishers. B.V. (North Holland).

Boisvert, L. (2000). Web-Based Learning: The anytime, anywhere classroom. *Information Systems Management,* 17(1), 35-40.

Chan, Y. E. (1999). Creating Canada's first privatized MBA program. *Academy of Management Executive,* 13(2), 100-105.

Chellappa, R., Barua, A. and Whinston, A. B. (1997). An electronic infrastructure for a virtual university. *Communications of the ACM*, 40(9) 56-58.

Daft, R. L., Lengel, R. H. and Trevino, L. K. (1987). Message equivocality, media selection and manager performance: Implications for information systems. *MIS Quarterly,* 355-366.

Daft, R. L. and Macintosh, N. B. (1981). A tentative exploration into the amount and equivocality of information processing in organizational work units. *Administrative Science Quarterly*, 26, 207-224.

Dick, G. N. (2000). Telecommuting in Australia and Singapore. *Proceedings of The Fifth International Workshop on Telework*. Stockholm.

Dick, G. N. and Duncanson, I (1999). Telecommuting: Does it work in the long term?. *Proceedings of the 32nd Hawaii International Conference on System Sciences*, January, Hawaii. IEEE.

DuBrin, A. J. (1991). Comparison of the job satisfaction and productivity of telecommuters versus in-house employees: A research note on work in progress. *Psychological Reports*, 68, 1225-1234.

Ellis, T. S. and Webster, R. L. (1997). Information systems managers' perceptions of the advantages and disadvantages of telecommuting: A multivariate analysis. *Proceedings of the 30th Hawaii International Conference on System Sciences*, Hawaii, IEEE.

Emmons, N. (1999). E-Degrees. *Legal Assistant Today*, January-February.

Filipczak, R. (1992). Telecommuting: A better way to work?. *Training,* 53-61.

Ford, R. C. and Butts, M. A. (1991). Is your organization ready for telecommuting?. *SAM Advanced Management Journal*, 56, 19-23.

Ford, R. C. and McLaughlin, F. (1995). Questions and answers about telecommuting programs. *Business Horizons*, 38, 66-72.

Gray, M., Hodson, N. and Gordon, G. (1993). *Teleworking Explained.* New York: John Wiley & Sons.

Gregg, J. (1997). As 'distance learning' takes off, US lags behind, *Christian*

Science Monitor, 89(121), 19.

Hamblen, M. (1999). Merrill trains staff to work at home. *Computer World* 33(17), 50.

Herther, N. K. (1997). Distance learning and the information professional. *Online*, September-October, 63-72.

Hesse, B. W. and Grantham, C. E. (1991). Electronically distributed work communities: Implications for research on telework. *Electronic Networking: Research, Applications and Policy*, 1.

Hotch, R. (1993). Managing from a distance. *Nation's Business*,81(10), 24-26.

Huws, U., Korte, W. B. and Robinson, S. (1990). *Telework: Towards the Elusive Office*, Chichester: John Wiley & Sons.

Jana, R. (1999). *Getting the Most Out of Online Learning*. September 13, 119. Available on the World Wide Web at: http://www.infoworld.com.

Katz, A. I. (1987). The management, control and evaluation of a telecommuting project: A case study. *Information & Management*, 13, 179-190.

Keohane, N. O. (2000). Going the distance. *Educause Review*, 35(4), 10.

Kirk, E. E. and Bartelstein A. M. (1999). Libraries close in on distance education. *Library Journal*, 1, April.

Kling R. (2001). Education Reservation. In Bertagnoli, L. (Ed.), *Marketing News*, 35(4), 4.

Lewis, B. J. (1998). Tapping into the benefits of telecommuting. *Journal of Management in Engineering*, 14, 9-10.

Li, F. and Gillespie, A. (1994). Team telework: An emergent form of work organization. In Baskerville, R., Smithson, O., Ngwenyama, O. and DeGross, J. I. (Eds.), *Transforming Organization with Information Technology*, 397-418. Amsterdam: Elsevier Science Publishers (North Holland).

Long, P. D., Tricker, T., Rangecroft, M. and Gilroy, P. (2000). Satisfaction with distance education: Evaluation of a service template. *Total Quality Management*,11(4-6), S530-S536.

Mannering, J. S. and Mokhtarian, P. L. (1995). Modeling the choice of telecommuting frequency in California: An exploratory analysis. *Technological Forecasting and Social Change*, 49, 49-73.

McQuarrie, F. A. E. (1994). Telecommuting: Who really benefits?. *Business Horizons*, 37, 79-83.

Mokhtarian, P. L., Handy, S. and Salomon, I. (1995). Methodological issues in the estimation of the travel, energy and air quality impacts of telecommuting. *Transportation Research A*,29A, 283-302.

Mokhtarian, P. L. and Salomon, I. (1997). Modeling the desire to telecommute: The importance of attitudinal factors in behavioural models. *Transpor-*

tation Research A, 31, 35-50.

Mokhtarian, P. L. and Salomon, I. (1996a). Modeling the choice of telecommuting 2: A case of the preferred impossible alternative. *Environment and Planning A*, 28, 1859-1876.

Mokhtarian, P. L. and Salomon, I. (1996b). Modeling the choice of telecommuting 3: Identifying the choice set and estimating binary choice models for technology-based alternatives. *Environment and Planning A*, 28, 1877-1895.

Mokhtarian, P. L. and Salomon, I. (1994). Modeling the choice of telecommuting: Setting the context. *Environment and Planning A*, 26, 749-766.

Mokhtarian, P. L., Salomon, I., Saxena, S., Sampath, S., Cheung, P., Le, K. and Bagley, M. N. (1994). Adoption of Telecommuting in Two California State Agencies. *unpublished work*.

Mottl, J. N. (2000). *Distance Learning*. January 3, 75-78. Available on the World Wide Web at: http://www.informationweek.com.

Nilles, J. M. (1996). What does telework really do to us?. *World Transport Policy and Practice*, 2, 15-45.

Olson, M. H. (1983). Remote office work: Changing work patterns in space and time. *Communications of the ACM*, 26, 182-187.

Orlikowski, W. J. (1996). Improvising organizational transformation over time: A situated change perspective. *ISR* 7, 63-92.

Passerini, K and Granger M. J. (2000). Information technology-based instructional strategies. *Journal of Informatics Education and Research*, 2(3), 37-44.

Rice, R. E. (1987). Computer-mediated communication and organizational innovation. *Journal of Communication*, 37, 65-94.

Starr, M. K. (1971). *Management: A Modern Approach*, New York: Harcourt Brace Jovanovich.

Tamrat, E., Vilkinas, T. and Warren, J. R. (1996). Analysis of a telecommuting experience: A case study. *Proceedings of the 29th Annual Hawaii International Conference on System Sciences*, Hawaii, USA.

Theakston, C. (1999). How technology might aid distance-learning MBA students: Using Durham University Business School as a case-study. *International Journal of Information and Management*, 19, 413-417.

Thompson, J. D. (1967). *Organizations in Action: Social Science Bases of Administrative Theory*, New York: McGraw-Hill.

Trent, J. T., Smith, A. L. and Wood, D. L. (1994). Telecommuting: Stress and social support. *Psychological Reports*, 74, 1312-1314.

Trevino, L. K. and Webster, J. (1992). Flow in computer-mediated communication: Electronic mail and voice mail evaluation and impacts. *Communication Research*, 19, 539-573.

Tung, L. L. and Turban, E. (1996). Information technology as an enabler of telecommuting. *International Journal of Information Management*, 16, 103-117.

Turban, E. and Wang, P. (1995). Telecommuting management: A comprehensive overview. *Human Systems Management*, 14, 227-238.

Venkatesh, A. and Vitalari, N. P. (1992). An emerging distributed work Arrangement: An investigation of computer-based supplemental work at home. *Management Science*, 38, 1687-1706.

Venkatesh, A. and Vitalari, N. P. (1986). Computing technology for the home: Product strategies for the next generation. *Journal of Product Innovation Management*, 3, 171-186.

Wheeler, M. and Zackin, D. (1994). Telecommuting. *Work-Family Roundtable*, 4, 2-14.

Wood, R. E. (1986). Task complexity: Definition of the construct. *Organizational Behaviour and Human Decision Processes*, 37, 60-82.

Yap, C. S. and Tng, H. (1990). Factors associated with attitudes towards telecommuting. *Information & Management*, 19, 227-235.

APPENDIX: CONCEPTS AND TERMS

Telecommuting	Normally working from home, but may include working from a site office or community centre, using some form of telecommunications and computing equipment to communicate with one's colleagues and the normal work place.
Drives and Constraints	Telecommuting can be attractive to some, unattractive to others. The strength of the presence of the "drives" (eg. to be better able to manage one's own affairs) and the weakness of potential constraints (eg. the difficulty of working from home) affect the desire for telecommuting.
Task suitability	A complex relationship between task complexity, task characteristics and the organisational environment in which the task is performed, in order to determine its suitability for telecommuting.
Personal attributes	Not all people make suitable telecommuters – telecommuting demands skills such as time management and the ability to make decisions, seek out information and be self-reliant.
Relationship to distance education	Distance education uses many of the same technologies and has similar drives and constraints to telecommuting. There are similarities in the tasks performed (at least at a theoretical level) and in the personal attributes required. *Prima facie* many of the lessons learnt in telecommuting have relevance to distance education programmes.

Chapter IV

The Future of Distance Learning in the Traditional University

Gary Saunders
Marshall University, USA

The growth in college and university offerings of Internet courses has been phenomenal and, as that growth accelerates, some writers have predicted that the university, as we now know it, will cease to exist. There is little doubt that distance learning with Internet courses will have an impact on the traditional university and a very important question is, will Internet courses represent a new and significant improvement over traditional pedagogy for educating students or just a lessening in the rigor of academic programs? This chapter presents the attitudes of accounting department chairpersons and College of Business (COB) deans on Internet courses. Ninety-four accounting chairpersons and 66 COB deans returned E mail questionnaires. In the view of the nearly 65% of the chairs and almost half of the deans. Internet courses are simply correspondence courses presented with new technology.

SYNOPSIS

For decades universities have delivered instruction over long distances through correspondence courses. During the decade of the 1990s developments in technology offered new delivery vehicles for correspondence courses. Internet courses, where the interaction between faculty and student occurs primarily over the Internet, represent a substantial departure from the traditional learning model. The growth in college and university offerings of Internet courses has been phenomenal and, as that growth accelerates, some writers have predicted that the university, as we now know it, will cease to exist. There is little doubt that distance learning with Internet courses will have an impact on the traditional university and a very important question is, will Internet courses represent a new and significant improvement over traditional pedagogy for educating students or just a lessening in the rigor of academic programs?

This chapter presents the attitudes of accounting department chairpersons and College of Business (COB) deans on Internet courses. In the view of the nearly 65% of the chairs and almost half of the deans, Internet courses are simply correspondence courses presented with new technology. Those who agree that Internet courses are correspondence courses are more negative on offering Internet courses in university programs or offering degrees through the completion of only Internet courses.

Results of this research suggest that, while the traditional university will face some challenges from the distance learning revolution, its survival will not be in jeopardy. Rather, the challenge may well be integrating the new technology without significantly diminishing the quality of the educational process.

INTRODUCTION

Distance learning is not a new instructional model for universities, only the delivery techniques are evolving. For decades universities have delivered instruction over long distances through correspondence courses. Typically these courses required a student to finish a specific program of relatively independent study and successfully complete one or more exams. These exams were, almost universally, proctored by an independent third party. Although correspondence courses have been offered by a number of universities, the percentage of universities offering these courses is relatively small. Additionally, correspondence courses have never obtained the same degree of acceptance as traditional on-campus courses requiring a student's attendance and participation. Perhaps that is why they have not been a threat to the traditional on-campus model of instruction. Schools that have offered a degree completely by correspondence have typically not been mainstream colleges and universities, but tend to have offered paraprofessional degrees.

During the 1990s developments in technology offered new delivery vehicles for correspondence courses. With the rapid spread of the Internet and email, universities seemed to sense a source of previously untapped revenue, offering courses to anyone in the world who had a computer and an Internet connection. Some jargon had to be added to describe the new environment so terms like, "distance learning" and "Internet courses" were added to the academic lexicon. Distance learning, where an instructor is in a location remote from that of the student, could apply to a number of different delivery schemes. New technology has allowed students to complete a course from a remote site using a telephone line or a satellite uplink. Television (TV) courses were available previously but they were not interactive. New technology allows the faculty and student to communicate, both verbally and visually, in real-time. Internet courses represent an even greater departure from the traditional learning model by allowing a student anywhere in the world to complete a course by using the Internet and Email. Universities have an initial investment in the development of an Internet course but the continuing cost of repeatedly offering the course is small compared to the potential revenue. Unless the course is revised the incremental cost to the university for offering the course to additional students is primarily to compensate the instructor. A virtually unlimited number of students can be added with minimal utilization of investment in additional fixed assets.

Problems with Internet Courses

Some of the traditional controls available with correspondence courses are not as easily implemented with Internet courses. Proctoring of exams has been the norm with university correspondence courses and with television courses. With TV courses a technical person is usually required at each site to keep the equipment functioning, so proctoring is typically not a problem. However, with Internet courses proctoring becomes much more difficult. One real advantage of Internet courses is bringing education to persons in extremely remote locations, and this poses problems in locating certifiable proctors. Traditionally, proctors have been credentialed educators who were neutral with respect to the student. In population centers this type of proctor is not too difficult to locate, but in the frozen tundra of Alaska or the sweltering outback of Australia, it may be impossible. In effect, when a university offers an Internet course with no required campus visits, it gives up virtually all of the traditional controls over the course and accepts on faith that the student receiving credit for the course is the same person who completes the assignments.

Perhaps to a greater degree than for correspondence courses, Internet courses are appropriate only for students who are highly motivated and capable of working independently with a minimum of personal instruction. Smith (2000) discussed some of the advantages and disadvantages of Internet courses and pointed out, among others, the following disadvantages:

1. Internet courses are not for all students.
2. Students must have the requisite computer skills to complete an Internet course.
3. Face-to-face interaction is missing.
4. Courses must be prepared in detail and approved before being offered and are rather unyielding to change.
5. Communications must be very precise and many students and faculties are not proficient at communicating explicitly.

Growth of Internet Courses

Given the challenges that Internet courses present, colleges and universities would be expected to proceed cautiously and test carefully before implementing Internet courses and degree programs. To the contrary, however, they have activated courses and programs at a surprising rate. The 1993 Peterson's College Guide listed 93 'cyberschools' and the 1997 Distance Learning Guide lists 762. That represents a phenomenal growth of more than 700 percent. Forbes reports that "in December 1999, the National Center for Educational Statistics (NCES) of the U.S. Department of Education (USDE) released a national survey on what it calls 'distance learning' in higher education. In 1997-98 almost 44% of all higher education institutions offered distance courses. Larger institutions were moving faster; 87% of those with more than 10,000 students offered distance classes, while only 19% of institutions with fewer than 3,000 students did so. Total enrollment in post-secondary, credit-granting distance learning courses in 1997-98 was 1,363,670; the number has grown considerably since, although as yet there are no firm figures" (Forbes, 2000). The American Federation of Teachers indicated that "distance education is one of the fastest-growing developments in higher education. Seventy percent of the nation's 4,000 two- and four-year colleges offered online courses in 2000, up from 48% in 1998" (Black Issues in Higher Education, 2001). There is little doubt that the number of colleges and universities offering electronic courses (Internet courses) is growing rapidly.

Projections call for 2.2 million students to be enrolled in Internet courses by 2002 and by 2005 it is expected to be a $46 billion business. Small wonder that universities, not wanting to be seen as followers, are abandoning their traditionally conservative approach and rushing headlong to cash in on the lottery. Their actions are reminiscent of the avaricious appetite of the dot-com investors in 1999 before the bubble burst in 2000.

As the phenomenal growth in college and university offerings of Internet courses continues and more institutions offer Internet degrees completely through the Internet, some writers have predicted that the university, as we now know it, will cease to exist. In his article *Electronics and the Dim Future of the University*, Noam (1996) says that:

> *Instead of prospering with the new tools (communications technologies), many of the traditional functions of universities will be superseded, their financial base eroded, their technology replaced and their role in intellectual inquiry reduced.*
>
> *There is little doubt that offering E-courses and E-degrees represents a dramatic departure from the traditional university teaching model. The new direction may be fueled by fiscal and political considerations rather than educational...If the university's dominance falters, its economic foundations will erode.*

Distance learning, utilizing Internet courses, may or may not represent the future for universities, but there can be little doubt that Internet courses will have an impact on the traditional university. Perhaps the conventional wisdom is to embrace the trend in the hope of surviving as a viable institution.

As researchers speculate on the impact that Internet courses and programs will have on the traditional university, there is a very important question that is rarely asked aloud. That question is, "Do Internet courses represent a new and significant improvement over traditional pedagogy for educating students or just a lessening in the rigor of academic programs?" Substantial research is needed to answer that question over a time frame of several years. In the shorter term, faculty and administrators of universities will have a major influence on whether Internet courses will be an improvement or a detriment to the educational process. They will play a vital role in crafting Internet courses and programs for their respective universities and their attitudes may provide a glimpse of the future impact of distance learning on the traditional university.

Attitudes of Accounting Chairpersons and COB Deans

In order to determine the attitudes of accounting department chairpersons and College of Business (COB) deans, an email questionnaire, containing 17 statements relating to Internet courses, was sent to 341 university accounting department chairpersons and 334 COB deans in the U. S. The questionnaire contained 17 statements, relating to Internet courses, with five Likert-type response categories ranging from "Strongly Agree" to "Strongly Disagree." The questionnaire sent to the deans contained two additional questions, with "yes and no" response categories, that related to whether the school currently offered, or planned to offer, Internet courses. No effort was made to slant either questions or response categories in a direction that might influence responses and no effort was made to detect any response bias from the question arrangement or the direction of the response categories. In this study the terms "Internet course" and "E-course" were considered interchangeable.

Questionnaires were sent via email over the Internet and three different response modes were suggested. Thirty-six of the questionnaires sent to chairpersons were undeliverable because of email address problems that could not be resolved, resulting in 305 valid questionnaires sent. A total of 94 usable responses was received, 18 from the web site, 9 through the post office, and 67 directly from the respondent on the Internet. Most of the responses that were received via the U.S. Postal Service were mailed in an envelope with the university's return address on it.

Eighty of the questionnaires sent to COB deans were undeliverable resulting in 254 questionnaires delivered to the deans. Sixty-six of the 254 deans who received a questionnaire responded, 23 on the web site, 22 through the United States Postal Service (USPS), and 21 via email. Most of the responses that were received via the USPS were mailed in an envelope with the university's return address on it. Apparently, with both chairpersons and deans, anonymity was not the major motivation in using this mode of response. The 94 responses from chairpersons yielded a response rate of 30.8% and the 66 responses from deans yielded a response rates of 26.0%.

Offering Internet Courses

Table 1 contains the questions and the percentage of responses in each response category for chairpersons and deans. The "Strongly Agree" and "Agree" categories and the "Strongly Disagree" and "Disagree" categories were combined in order to make the data easier to comprehend. Also, a one-way ANOVA was run on the data to determine if the responses of the two groups differed significantly. Table 2 contains the questions, the ANOVA results, and the percentage of responses in each combined response category.

The first statement said that "Except for the delivery medium E courses are essentially correspondence courses," and almost 65% of chairpersons and 42% of deans agreed or strongly agreed. Only 25% of chairpersons and 48%

Table 1: Chairpersons' and Deans' response percentages

| Chairpersons - n = 94, Deans - n = 66 | % Responses in Each Category | | | | | |
| | Chairpersons | | | Deans | | |
Scale: 1-Strongly Agree, 2-Agree, 3-Neutral, 4-Disagree, 5-Strongly Disagree	SA & A	Neu-tral	SD & D	SA & A	Neu-tral	SD & D
1. Except for the delivery medium E courses are essentially correspondence courses.	64.9	9.9	25.2	42.2	9.4	48.4
2. E courses should be offered in Accounting programs.	36.3	26.3	37.4	56.9	32.3	10.8
3. E courses should be offered in Business programs.	45.6	38.0	16.4	67.7	26.1	6.2
4. E courses should be offered in non-business programs.	52.2	37.0	10.8	63.0	30.8	6.2
5. A student should be able to obtain a degree in Accounting by taking only E courses.	5.5	3.2	91.2	16.9	12.3	70.8
6. A student should be able to obtain a degree in Business by taking only E courses.	7.6	1.1	91.3	15.4	12.3	72.3
7. A student should be able to obtain a degree in non-business programs by taking only E courses.	7.6	9.8	82.6	15.4	26.2	58.4
8. When E courses are offered, they should be available to on-campus as well as off-campus students.	68.5	23.9	7.6	89.3	6.1	4.6
9. When E courses are offered, SOME exams should be proctored by an independent person.	66.0	19.8	14.2	69.3	15.4	15.3
10. When E courses are offered, ALL exams should be proctored by an independent person.	49.0	27.2	23.8	50.8	29.2	20.0
11. When E courses are offered, the student should be required to come to campus at LEAST ONCE during the course.	49.5	23.1	27.4	33.8	32.3	33.9
12. When E courses are offered, the student should be required to come to campus MORE THAN ONCE during the course.	41.1	27.8	31.1	31.2	34.4	34.4
13. The student-to-student and the student-to-instructor interaction that is missing in E courses makes them less valuable to the student.	82.3	4.4	13.3	46.9	9.4	43.7
14. As the number of E courses grows, the importance of the formal university will diminish.	36.3	12.1	51.6	12.5	12.5	75.0
15. If the importance of the formal university diminishes, society will benefit.	2.3	6.9	90.8	10.8	6.2	83.0
16. As the number of E courses grows, the importance of the university professor will diminish.	34.0	11.0	55.0	18.4	9.2	72.4
17. If the importance of the university professor diminishes, society will benefit.	4.4	6.6	89.0	4.7	4.7	90.6

of deans disagreed or strongly disagreed. Between 9% and 10% of the chairpersons and the deans were neutral on the issue. Obviously, a substantial majority of the accounting department chairpersons view Internet courses as essentially correspondence courses delivered over the Internet while COB deans are about evenly split on the issue. In the minds of those chairpersons, any baggage that correspondence courses carried is apparently attached to Internet courses.

Responses to the second statement that "E courses should be offered in accounting programs" were almost evenly split for the chairpersons and in strong agreement for the deans. Slightly more than 36% of the chairpersons and more than 56% of the deans indicated that Internet courses should be offered in accounting programs. A relatively large portion, 26% and 32% of the chairpersons and the deans respectively, chose the neutral response.

Table 2: ANOVA results and the percentage of responses for accounting chairs and college of business deans

	ANOVA Signif.	% of Responses in Each Category					
		SA & A		Neutral		SD &D	
		CH	DN	CH	DN	CH	DN
1. Except for the delivery medium E courses are essentially correspondence courses.	**.018**	64.9	42.2	9.9	9.4	25.2	48.4
2. E courses should be offered in accounting programs.	**.000**	36.3	56.9	26.3	32.3	37.4	10.8
3. E courses should be offered in Business programs.	**.003**	45.5	67.7	38.1	26.1	16.4	6.2
4. E courses should be offered in non-business programs.	.154	52.1	63.0	37.0	30.8	10.9	6.2
5. A student should be able to obtain a degree in accounting by taking only E courses.	**.000**	5.5	16.9	3.2	12.3	91.3	70.8
6. A student should be able to obtain a degree in Business by taking only E courses.	**.001**	7.6	15.4	1.1	12.3	91.3	72.3
7. A student should be able to obtain a degree in non-business programs by taking only E courses.	**.001**	7.6	15.4	9.8	26.2	82.6	58.4
8. When E courses are offered, they should be available to on-campus as well as off-campus students.	**.005**	68.4	89.3	24.0	6.1	7.6	4.6
9. When E courses are offered, SOME exams should be proctored by an independent person.	.742	66.0	69.3	19.7	15.4	14.3	15.3
10. When E courses are offered, ALL exams should be proctored by an independent person.	.488	49.0	50.8	27.1	29.2	23.9	20.0
11. When E courses are offered, the student should be required to come to campus at LEAST ONCE during the course.	.244	49.5	33.8	23.0	32.3	27.5	33.9
12. When E courses are offered, the student should be required to come to camppus MORE THAN ONCE during the course.	.333	41.1	31.2	27.8	34.4	31.1	34.4
13. The student-to-student and the student-to-instructor interaction that is missing in E courses makes them less valuable to the student.	**.000**	82.3	46.9	4.4	9.4	13.3	43.7
14. As the number of E courses grows, the importance of the formal university will diminish.	**.001**	36.3	12.5	12.0	12.5	51.7	75.0
15. If the importance of the formal university diminishes, society will benefit.	**.012**	2.3	10.8	6.9	6.2	90.8	83.0
16. As the number of E courses grows, the importance of the university professor will diminish.	**.019**	34.1	18.4	10.9	9.2	55.0	72.4
17. If the importance of the university professor diminishes, society will benefit.	.836	4.4	4.7	6.6	4.7	89.0	90.6

When the same statement was posed relative to business programs, chairs' opinions shifted toward the agree end of the scale. Almost 46% of the chairpersons and almost 68% of the deans agreed or strongly agreed with the statement that "E-courses should be offered in Business programs," while only 16% of the chairs and 6% of the deans disagreed or strongly disagreed.

A further shift is found in responses to the statement related to offering Internet courses in nonbusiness programs. In response to the statement that "E courses should be offered in nonbusiness programs," 52% of the chairpersons and 63% of the deans either agreed or strongly agreed, and only 10% of the chairpersons and 6% of the deans disagreed with the statement.

Opinions of accounting department chairpersons are about evenly split on the subject of offering Internet courses in accounting programs but are more tolerant of offering them in non-accounting programs. In fact, a majority of the respondents believed they should be offered in nonbusiness programs. Whether these views stem from a belief that accounting topics are less amenable to being mastered over the Internet or whether it is simply a "not in my area" reaction is not known. Independent study courses typically lack the structure, deadlines, and regular face-to-face student-instructor interaction that traditional courses possess. Most would agree that some topics are more easily learned through independent study than are others. Perhaps all that the respondents are conveying is that structure, deadlines, and student-faculty interaction is more important in accounting and business topics than in other areas.

As can be seen in Figure 1, the data indicate that COB deans have a significantly (at the 0.018 level) more favorable view of Internet courses than do accounting department chairpersons. This difference may be attributable to the different concerns of deans and accounting chairs. Deans are undoubtedly more concerned with the financial aspects of offering courses and might, therefore, more strongly support new enrollments and new sources of revenue. Accounting chairs might be more concerned with the quality of the courses being offered.

Accounting chairpersons move from being split on offering Internet courses in accounting programs to supporting their offering in business programs to more strongly supporting them in nonbusiness programs. The support of deans, however, is stronger for offering Internet courses in business programs than for offering them in nonbusiness programs. Apparently, 4.7% of the deans moved from supporting Internet courses in business programs to being neutral on offering them in nonbusiness programs. This may indicate a hands-off attitude toward programs in other colleges.

Overall, deans support offering Internet courses in accounting and business degree programs more strongly than do accounting chairs. These

Figure 1: Data indicating that COB deans have a significantly more favorable view of Internet courses than do accounting department chairpersons

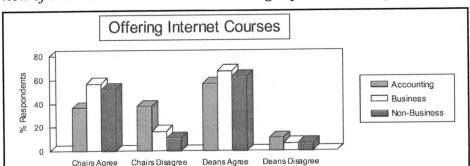

differences were significant at the 0.000 and the 0.003 level for accounting and business programs respectively. The opinions of chairs and deans on offering Internet courses in nonbusiness programs were not significantly different at the 0.05 level.

Offering Degrees Solely Through Internet Courses

The next area considered dealt with the question of awarding degrees based solely on completion of Internet courses. In response to the statement that "A student should be able to obtain a degree in Accounting by taking only E courses," an overwhelming 91% of chairpersons and 70% of deans disagreed or strongly disagreed. A surprising 72%, almost three quarters of the accounting chairpersons, and 41% of deans strongly disagreed with the statement.

Responses were not much different regarding the offering of degrees in business or in nonbusiness programs based solely on the completion of Internet courses. More than 90% of chairpersons and 72% of deans disagreed or strongly disagreed that business degrees should be offered solely over the Internet. On offering degrees in nonbusiness areas with all courses completed over the Internet, 82% of the chairs and 58% of deans disagreed or strongly disagreed while only 7% of the chairs and 15% of deans agreed or strongly agreed. The only noticeable shift in responses to the three statements is a move of about 14% of the deans from the disagree to the neutral category when considering Internet degrees in nonbusiness programs compared with accounting and business programs.

As vividly illustrated in Figure 2, accounting chairpersons are solidly opposed to universities offering degrees in any academic discipline totally through the Internet. They apparently believe that the campus experience gives the student a component of education that should not be left out of the degree experience. Deans are somewhat less opposed, and signifi-

Figure 2: Accounting chairpersons are solidly opposed to universities offering degrees in any academic discipline totally through the Internet

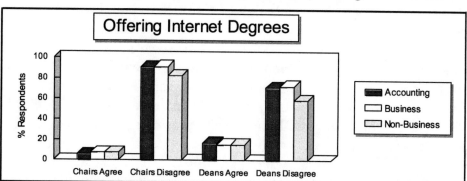

cantly less opposed than are accounting chairs, to offering degrees totally through Internet courses but a solid majority still does not believe that Internet degrees should be offered in any academic area. Little doubt exists that a degree that does not contain the campus experience is different from one that does. Whether it is better or worse is a question left for time and experience to answer.

Enrolling On-Campus Students and Proctoring of Exams

One complication that universities face with Internet courses is that of on-campus students registering for courses and causing regular on-campus courses to have low enrollments. Because Internet courses are normally paid as an overload course, this shift in enrollment may result in less efficient use of one of the university's most costly resources, professors' class time. This issue was addressed by the statement: "When E courses are offered, they should be available to on-campus as well as off-campus students." A substantial majority of respondents, 68% of chairs and 89% of deans, agreed that on-campus students should have the same access to Internet courses as off-campus students.

Another issue that faces designers and instructors of Internet courses is the proctoring of exams. Two statements addressed this issue. The first stated, "When E-courses are offered, SOME exams should be proctored by an independent person." Sixty-six percent of the chairpersons and 69% of deans agreed. Only 14% of chairs and 15% of deans disagreed with this statement. A companion statement, "When E courses are offered, ALL exams should be proctored by an independent person," had 49% of the chairs and 50% of deans in agreement. Less than one-fourth, 23% of chairs and 20% of deans disagreed with the statement.

As Figure 3 illustrates, the support of deans for making Internet courses available to all students was significantly stronger than that of the chairs. Perhaps accounting chairpersons and COB deans view this issue from a perspective of fairness; when Internet courses are offered they believe that all students should have equal access to them. Also, some independent confirmation of the level of student learning with Internet courses is essential. By more than a four to one margin, proctoring of some exams is considered essential and the proctoring of all exams is preferred by more than a two to one margin. The attitudes of chairs and deans on the proctoring of exams were not significantly different.

Figure 3: The support of deans for making Internet courses available to all students was significantly stronger than that of the chairs

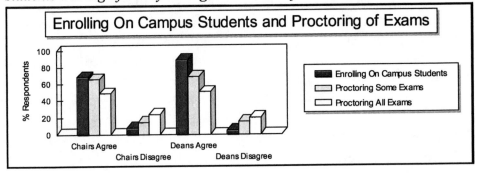

Visiting Campus

Some universities that offer degrees solely through completion of Internet courses require students to come to campus for some of the classes during a term. Three statements were included that referred to that facet of Internet courses. When asked if students completing an Internet course should be required to come to campus at least once during the course, 49% of the chairs and 33% of deans agreed. An interesting note is that of the 33.8% of deans that agreed, 24% strongly agreed, and only 9% of the 34% that disagreed, strongly disagreed.

The second question related to requiring more than one campus visit during the course. A slightly smaller percentage of respondents, 41% of chairs and 31% of deans, agreed with this statement than agreed with the previous statement. The third statement relating to visiting campus asked, "If more than once, how many times in a three-semester hour course?" and 39 of the 92 chairs (42%) entered a number. The average number of campus visits indicated by respondents for students completing Internet courses was 5.54 times during the course. For deans who entered a number of campus visits (43 of the 66 responding, 65%) the average number of visits indicated was 2.77 for a three-hour course.

There should be little disagreement that the student-to-student and the student-to-instructor interaction is less in Internet courses than in traditional courses. A valid concern is whether this reduced interaction makes them less valuable to the student. By a more than six to one margin (82% to 13%) accounting chairs agreed that the reduced level of interaction in Internet courses makes them less valuable to students. Deans were about evenly split on the issue with 47% agreeing and 43% disagreeing.

As the graph shows, by almost a two to one margin (49% to 27%) accounting chairs believe the campus experience is a valuable component of a university course and that it should not be left completely out of Internet courses, while COB deans are about evenly split on the issue. Chairpersons favor requiring more than one visit, although by a slimmer margin, and deans shift slightly against requiring more than one campus visit. Accounting chairpersons strongly believe that a course that contains less student-to-student or student-to-instructor interaction is a move in the wrong direction and the course is less valuable to the student; deans do not share this view. The difference in the views of chairs and deans on this question was significant at the 0.000 level.

Figure 4: Chairpersons favor requiring more than one visit, although by a slimmer margin and deans shift slightly against requiring more than one campus visit

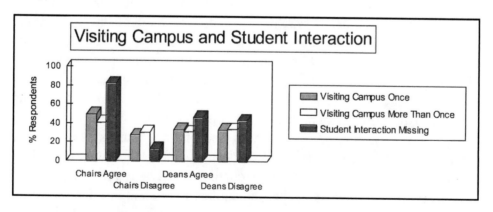

Impact of Internet Courses on the University

The last two questions dealt with the perceived impact of Internet courses on the formal university. Regarding the statement, "As the number of Internet courses grows, the importance of the formal university will diminish," 51% of chairs and 75% of deans disagreed with the statement. Neither accounting chairpersons nor COB deans appear to share Noam's view of the Internet's impact on the "traditional university."

Responses to a similar statement, "As the number of E-courses grows, the importance of the university professor will diminish," were very similar to those relating to the university. Agreeing with the statement were 34% of the chairs and 18% of deans, while 55% of the chairs and 72% of deans disagreed with it. As with the university, neither accounting chairpersons nor COB deans are very apprehensive about any negative effects of expanded Internet course offerings on university professors. However, chairs were significantly more concerned about the impact of Internet courses on the university and on the professor than were deans.

Significant Relationships

Pearson correlations were run and significance levels determined for the relationships between responses to each of the 17 different statements for both the chairs' and the deans' responses. Responses of the chairs to the first statement that likened Internet courses to correspondence courses were significantly related to nine of the other sixteen statements. For the deans, Statement One responses were significantly related to five other statements. That relationship was negative, and significant, for Statements Two through Six for the chairs and Two through Four for the deans. Those results indicate that when chairs and deans tended to agree that Internet courses were "essentially correspondence courses," they also tended to disagree that universities should offer Internet courses in accounting, business, or nonbusiness programs. In other words, respondents who thought Internet courses were essentially correspondence courses were more inclined to believe that Internet courses should not be offered in university programs. Accounting chairpersons who viewed Internet courses as correspondence courses also tended to believe that students should not be able to obtain degrees in accounting or business by taking only Internet courses.

Additionally, chairpersons who viewed Internet courses as essentially correspondence courses also tended to believe that all exams should be proctored for Internet courses, that students should be required to come to campus more than once, and that the student-to-student and instructor-to-student relationships that are missing make the courses less valuable to students. As the respondents view Internet courses more like correspondence courses, their opinion of Internet courses appears to be lower and more restrictive.

Deans who considered Internet courses to be correspondence courses did not believe that all exams should be proctored, that students should be required to come to campus more than once, or that the missing student-to-student and instructor-to-student relationships make the courses less valuable to students any more than deans who did not view Internet courses as correspondence courses. They did, however, tend to believe more strongly that "As the number of E-courses grows, the importance of the university professor will diminish" and "If the importance of the university professor diminishes, society will benefit" than did deans who did not see the Internet course/correspondence course connection.

One interesting observation is, as chairs and deans tended to agree with the statement that "the student-to-student and the student-to-instructor interaction that is missing in E-courses makes them less valuable to the student," they tended to disagree that Internet courses and Internet degrees should be offered in accounting, business, or nonbusiness programs. Two exceptions to this general observation are that, for deans, the relationships for offering Internet courses in accounting and offering Internet degrees in nonbusiness programs, and the interaction that is missing were only significant at the 0.059 and 0.098 levels respectively.

A surprising result was that deans who believed Internet courses were essentially correspondence courses also tended to believe that "As the number of Internet courses grows, the importance of the university professor will diminish," and "If the importance of the university professor diminishes, society will benefit." Chairs did not display that same tendency.

Difference in COB Deans' Opinions of Internet Courses Then Their Institutions Offer Internet Courses

The questionnaire sent to the deans included Questions 18 and 19 which relate to the offering of Internet courses in each dean's college. Question 18 asked "Does your college or university currently offer E-courses?" Forty of the deans responded in the affirmative (60%), 23 answered "no" (34%), and 3 did not indicate an answer.

Deans of COBs where Internet courses were currently being offered believed more strongly that Internet courses were not essentially correspondence courses with a different delivery medium. They also tended to agree more strongly that "E-courses should be offered in nonbusiness programs," that "A student should be able to obtain a degree in Business by taking only E-courses," and that "A student should be able to obtain a degree in nonbusiness programs by taking only E-courses." Additionally, deans at schools that offer Internet courses disagreed more strongly with the notion that "When E-courses are offered, the student should be required to come to campus MORE THAN ONCE during the course."

COB deans at institutions that did not offer Internet courses were very strongly opposed to offering Internet degrees. In fact, 81% were opposed to offering Internet degrees in Accounting, 95% opposed offering them in Business, and 77% opposed offering them in nonbusiness areas. Roughly two-thirds of those opposed were strongly opposed to offering Internet degrees in the different areas. Those percentages compare with 65% of COB deans at institutions offering Internet courses opposed to offering Internet degrees in Accounting, 60% opposed to offering them in Business, and 47% opposed to offering them in nonbusiness areas. These differences could be a reflection of additional familiarity with and knowledge of Internet courses possessed by deans whose institutions offer Internet courses. On the other hand, they could reflect an acceptance and tacit endorsement of events occurring at their schools. Whichever is the case, the answer is beyond the scope of this data.

Question 19 asked, "If no, (to Question 18) do you plan to offer E-courses in the next three years?" Of the 23 deans whose schools did not offer Internet courses at that time, 12 planned to offer them within the next three years and 11 indicated no plans to do so. Significant differences of opinion existed between those who planned to offer Internet courses and those who did not on only two questions. Deans who did not plan to offer Internet courses believed more strongly that a student should NOT be able to obtain a degree in Business by taking only Internet courses. They also tended to agree more strongly that "When E-courses are offered, the student should be required to come to campus MORE THAN ONCE during the course." Apparently, deans who do not plan to offer Internet courses within the next three years are more skeptical about Internet courses. That is consistent with the differences based on responses to Statement 18, deans who do not currently offer Internet courses were more skeptical than those who do.

SUMMARY

Opinions of accounting department chairpersons are about evenly split on the subject of offering Internet courses in accounting programs but are more tolerant of offering them in non-accounting programs. In fact, a majority of the chairpersons believed they should be offered in nonbusiness programs. COB deans, on the other hand, weigh in heavily in favor of offering Internet courses in accounting, business and nonbusiness programs. Whether the chairs' views stem from a belief that accounting topics are less amenable to being mastered over the Internet or whether it is simply a "not in my area" reaction is not known. Deans may be viewing the question more from the standpoint of attracting students to their degree programs. Both chairs and deans strongly rejected the concept of offering degrees, in any academic discipline, entirely over the Internet.

Independent study courses, such as Internet courses, typically lack the structure, deadlines, and regular face-to-face student-instructor interaction that traditional courses possess. Most would agree that some topics are more easily learned through independent study than are others. Perhaps all that the respondents are conveying is that structure, deadlines, and student-faculty interaction are more important in accounting and business topics than in other areas.

Respondents can be grouped by whether or not they agree that "except for the delivery medium Internet courses are essentially correspondence courses." Roughly 2 1/2 times as many chairs agreed with the statement as those who disagreed (64.9 % to 25.3%), while the deans were about evenly split. Those who agree with this statement are more negative on offering Internet courses in university programs or offering degrees through the completion of only Internet courses. They are also more restrictive with Internet courses, favoring the proctoring of exams and requiring students to come to campus as part of the Internet course. The average number of campus visits recommended by the 39 chairs (42% of total) who responded to that statement was 5.54 visits per course. The 43 deans who entered a number (65% of the 66 responding) recommended an average of 2.77 campus visits for a three-hour course. Those who viewed Internet courses as correspondence courses also tended to agree that "the student-to-student and the student-to-instructor interaction that are missing in E courses makes them less valuable to the student."

If the view of the nearly 65% of the chairs and almost half of the deans is accurate and Internet courses are simply correspondence courses presented with new technology, then will they be more successful in the university paradigm than correspondence courses have been? Experience teaches that successful completion of correspondence courses requires a level of dedication that many do not possess. Degree programs in technical areas have been available from some colleges for decades, and they have not challenged the existence of the formal university. Technical knowledge can usually be best learned in a do-it-yourself environment, such as that provided by a vocational-technical school. If the objective is to simply gain technical knowledge, probably few professors would assert that a university setting is either required or is necessarily the best setting.

Traditionally, universities have awarded degrees to students who satisfied "educational" requirements by successfully completing courses in a broad-based curriculum. Universities are challenged to develop students' interpersonal and group skills and to teach students how to "think critically." Meeting these particular challenges would seem to be next to impossible when a student never has direct, face-to-face contact with either an instructor or other students, as in the pure Internet course degree program. That is not to say that Internet courses may not have a role to play in complementing the traditional university degree program, just as correspondence courses have had, but supplanting the traditional university, hardly.

On the basis of the current research, Noam's view of "the dim future of the university" may be more hype than substance. Surely universities will change, such is called evolution. Surely the new technology will be integrated into the university paradigm, but it is unlikely that "this system of higher education [that has] remained stable for more than 2,500 years" (Noam, 1996, p. 7) will be discarded to be replaced by the Internet. At least accounting chairpersons and COB deans don't seem to think so. That conclusion is supported by the results of a study (Hagan & Omolayole, 2000) of 3,600 business professors teaching in various colleges in the US. They appear to recognize Internet courses as correspondence courses delivered over the Internet.

The question may well be, "are Internet courses simply correspondence courses in new packaging?" Have universities taken an academic concept that garnered limited acceptance in the past, wrapped it in the glitzy attire of Internet technology, and presented it as the pedagogical discovery of the century? By more than a 2 1/2 to 1 margin (64.8 % to 25.3%) the accounting chairpersons responding to the survey appear to think so. Almost half of the COB deans responding appear to agree.

While the traditional university will face some challenges from the distance learning revolution, evidence suggests that its survival will not be in jeopardy. Rather, the challenge may well be integrating the new technology without significantly diminishing the quality of the educational process. Proctored exams and noting on the transcript which courses or degrees have been completed as distance learning courses may be essential.

A Bible story relates that men do not put new wine in old bottles because the aging process will burst the bottles. Instead, new wine is placed in new bottles to preserve the wine. There is little doubt that Internet courses represent new bottles, a new delivery system. The question remains, however, "are Internet courses old wine in new packaging?" Have universities taken an academic concept that garnered limited acceptance in the past, wrapped it in the glitzy attire of Internet technology, and presented it as the pedagogical discovery of the century?

REFERENCES

Carnevale, D. (2000). Turning traditional courses into distance education. *Chronicle of Higher Education*, August, 46(48), A37-39.

Carr, S. (2000). A university moves to require distance courses. *Chronicle of Higher Education*, October, 47(8), A48.

Gaskin, J. E. and Calera, R. E. (2000). Virtual learning struggling to make the grade. *Inter@active Week*, August, 7(4), 28-29.

Hagen, A. and Omolayole, O. (2000). The impact of technology mediated distance learning on American business colleges: An empirical investigation. *Proceedings of the OOICTL-Business 2000 International Conference*, September, 143-146. Shreveport, LA.

Hereford, L. (2000). Virtually no consistency in online college courses. *Community College Week*, March, 12(15), 8-9.

McCartney, L. (1996). Virtual MBA: Going back to school doesn't have to mean sitting in a classroom again. *Informationweek,* November, 32-36.

New AFT report proposes standards for online programs. (2001). *Black Issues in Higher Education*, February, 17(5), 43.

Noam, E. M. (1996). Electronics and the dim future of the university. *American Society for Information Science. Bulletin of the American Society for Information Science*, 22(5), 6-11.

Oblinger, D. and Kidwell, J. (2000). Distance learning: Are we being realistic? *Educause Review*, May-June, 35(3), 30-37.

Oppermann, O. (1995). E-mail surveys: Potentials and pitfalls. *Marketing Research*, 7(3), 29-33.

Roach, R. (2001). The army marches into online learning. *Black Issues in Higher Education*, January, 17(24), 32-3.

Schuldt, B. A. and Totten, J. W. (1994). Electronic mail vs. mail survey response rates. *Marketing Research*, 6(1), 36-41.

Smith, W. (2000). The advantages and disadvantages of online delivery of accounting courses: Pitfalls to avoid. *Presented at the Fiftieth International Economics Conference*, October. Charleston, SC.

Svetcov, D. (2000). The virtual classroom vs. the real one. *Forbes*, September, 166(7), 50-52.

Vasarhelyi, M. A. and Graham, L. (1997). Cybersmart: Education and the Internet. *Management Accounting*, August, 32-36.

Vazzana, G. and Bachmann, D. (1994). Fax attracts. *Marketing Research*, 6(2), 18-25.

Section II

Faculty, Student and Program Challenges

Chapter V

Faculty Perceptions and Participation in Distance Education: Pick Fruit From The Low-Hanging Branches

Kim E. Dooley and Jane Magill
Texas A&M University, USA

The environment for higher education has become much more dynamic and even more complex with the recent development of new digital technologies (Hanna, 1999, p. 25).

Motivating faculty members to teach at a distance has been a challenge for most colleges and universities. What will be the impact of teaching using technology on faculty responsibility? Is teaching students through any or all distance education methods really nothing more than adapting traditional classroom approaches? What are the attitudes and barriers to using technologies often associated with distance education? In this chapter the authors present data obtained from an extensive survey of faculty opinions on teaching at a distance, as well as several case studies describing incentives and training made available for distance education. To enhance participation in distance education, faculty must have the competence, attitude that distance education is important and valuable, and infrastructure available to facilitate the additional time and effort to convert courses. Faculty training programs cannot be "one-shot" and should include personnel in close proximity to faculty, preferable on their own equipment. Release time is an important incentive to encourage participation.

INTRODUCTION

In 1989, Connie Dillon addressed the perceptions of faculty participation in instructional telecommunications. Her study provided insight into the factors that influence the integration of telecommunications teaching within the higher education system. A decade has passed and many higher education institutions are still struggling to integrate and utilize distance education technologies. The technologies have changed, but faculty attitudes often remain the same.

To prepare students successfully for today's digital marketplace, educators should incorporate the use of information technologies. "Educators must help all students become adept at distanced interaction, for skills of information gathering from remote sources and of collaboration with dispersed team members are as central to the future American workplace as learning to perform structured tasks quickly was to the industrial revolution" (Dede, 1996, p. 30). Students learn from competent instructors who have been trained how to communicate effectively through the technology. Thomas Cyrs (1997) identifies areas of competence important to a distance education environment: course planning and organization, verbal and nonverbal presentation skills, collaborative teamwork, questioning strategies, subject matter expertise, involving students and coordinating their activities at field sites, knowledge of basic learning theory, knowledge of the distance learning field, design of study guides, graphic design and visual thinking (Cyrs, 1997). Lacina-Gifford and J.-Kher-Durlabhji (1996) emphasized that instructors must be part of a change process in their role as instructors if distance learning is to be successful. The authors also mentioned that the students attributed the success of the program to user-friendly technology and the promptness of the instructor in communicating with the students.

Linda Wolcott (1997) conducted an analysis of the institutional context and dynamics of faculty rewards at research universities. She discovered that 1) distance education occupies a marginal status, 2) distance teaching is neither highly valued nor well-rewarded as a scholarly activity, 3) distance teaching is not highly related to promotion and tenure decisions, and 4) rewards for distance teaching are dependent on the academic unit's commitment to distance education. Faculty barriers stem for the lack of perceived institutional support (faculty rewards, incentives, training, etc.) for course conversion to distance education formats (Dillon & Walsh, 1992; McKenzie, Mims, Bennett, & Waugh, 2000; Wolcott, 1997; Olcott & Wright, 1995). Part of this support may include release time for course preparation. Reports indicate that teaching at a distance takes more time than teaching a traditional course (NEA, 2000; McKenzie, Mims, Bennett, & Waugh, 2000; Rockwell, Schauer, Fritz, & Marx, 1999; Visser, 2000).

The need for a change and modification of the faculty role in teaching at a distance has been recognized (Dillon & Walsh, 1992; Layzell, 1996; Plater, 1995; Purdy & Wright, 1992; Schifter, 2000). "It is not that the technology underpinning distance education drives the system but rather that fundamental changes in teaching style, technique, and motivation must take place to make the new 'classrooms' of the present and future function effectively" (Purdy & Wright, 1992, p. 4).

Despite the fact that much of the literature in distance education discusses the importance of faculty, this group has been largely neglected by the research (Dillon & Walsh, 1992; Beaudoin, 1990). Beaudoin (1990) observes that:

> [t]he emergence of increasingly student-centered learning activities in the 1970s facilitated by new instructional technology introduced in the 1980s is contributing to a dramatic evolution in faculty roles, and raises fundamental questions within the professoriate about how it will contribute to the teaching-learning process in the 1990s and beyond. (p. 21)

As indicated by Moore (1997) in his comparison of distance education, programs with a commitment to faculty support and training result in higher quality. Institutions that are involved in, or currently moving into the realm of distance education can benefit from the discussions in this chapter. As the complexity continues and the desire to integrate distance education programs expands, attention must be given to faculty training and support.

In consideration of this incredible growth and increased complexity, what will be the impact of teaching using technology on faculty responsibility? Is teaching students through any or all distance education methods really nothing more than adapting traditional classroom approaches? What are the attitudes and barriers to using technologies often associated with distance education?

This chapter is divided into two major sections. The first provides a glimpse of faculty perceptions about teaching at a distance based upon several research studies conducted at Texas A&M University. The second section will provide case studies of actual faculty training, support, and incentives that were implemented to encourage faculty to participate in teaching at a distance—some that worked and some that didn't.

FACULTY PERCEPTIONS OF TEACHING AT A DISTANCE

The changing student population, rapid technological advances, and the economic issues facing higher education are creating an accelerated demand for learning anytime, anyplace. The ability of an organization to adapt to these changes will be influenced by at least three factors: a) the knowledge, skills, and abilities of its faculty/staff, b) the amount of importance placed on distance learning technologies to accomplish teaching and learning, and c) the availability of high-quality facilities, equipment, technical support, and training.

At Texas A&M University, distance education began in the early 1990s with the development of the Trans-Texas Videoconference Network (TTVN). There are now over 100 interactive video sites across the state and in two international locations (Mexico City, Mexico and San Jose, Costa Rica). The network initially was a means to connect all the components of the Texas A&M University System administratively. By the mid 1990s, faculty who had been teaching in off-campus programs began teaching courses on the network and today there are six Masters degrees and one Joint Doctor of Education degree offered entirely at a distance. Additionally, the university adopted WebCT in 1998 and faculty began to include more web-based components in their courses and degree programs.

In the College of Agriculture and Life Science, there is currently a Master of Agriculture Degree with three content options (Natural Resource Development, Interdisciplinary Science, and Agricultural Development) and the Joint Doctor of Education in Agricultural Education degree offered with Texas Tech University. Recent studies were conducted to provide baseline data for faculty perceptions of electronic technologies used in teaching and to determine the rate of adoption of distance education as an innovation (Dooley & Murphy, 2001; Dooley & Murphrey, 2000; Murphrey & Dooley, 2000; Poe, 2000). The studies include both quantitative and qualitative data collection procedures and analysis, and provide the basis for recommendations to encourage faculty participation in distance education.

In the Dooley and Murphy study (2001), all teaching faculty in the College of Agriculture and Life Science (15 departments) were surveyed (N=315). The instrument used to collect data was a three-part questionnaire designed by the researchers. Part I of the questionnaire was designed to identify the characteristics and level of involvement of the respondents in technology-mediated instruction. Part II was designed to measure faculty competence, value and quality of infrastructure with a five-point Likert response scale. Part III consisted of three open-ended questions designed to provide an opportunity for the respondents to add their comments concerning the improvement of their use of distance education technologies.

In all, 263 survey instruments were returned for a final response rate of 84%. Survey and follow-up procedures were in accordance with those outlined by Dillman (1978). Descriptive statistics were calculated for each variable. Frequencies and percentages were used to summarize agreement or disagreement with each of the statements related to competence, value, and quality of infrastructure. An attempt to control non-respondent error was made by comparing the data from early and late respondents as suggested by Miller and Smith (1983). No significant differences were found between the groups.

The constant comparative method was used for the open-ended, qualitative data analysis (Lincoln & Guba, 1985). Colored markers were used to differentiate respondent themes so that the data would remain in context and provide visual indications of emerging categories. Delimiting the construction occurred as the data sources became saturated and the categories were integrated.

In this study, over one-half the faculty members reported having a website related to their course. Of these, 84% were described as simply enhancing the course, 15% were described as a required component of the course, and .7% (1 course) was described as being completely delivered via the website.

Almost exactly half the faculty with a course website administer that site themselves. Less than one-quarter assign a graduate assistant to the task. Almost as many (21%) use professional support staff. Most of these course websites reside administratively near the faculty members on their departmental servers (62%), and on university servers (21%). Faculty members were almost evenly split on the software used to edit these websites, with 32% using a text editor, and 28% using Microsoft Word. Only 5% use Microsoft FrontPage, while 23% report using "other" software.

While many of the teaching faculty had websites, few had experience teaching learners at a distance. Only 1% had taught a course at a distance more than ten times. Another 10% had taught at a distance between two and ten times, while 9% had taught at a distance once. Almost 80% of the faculty members responding to the survey indicated that they had never taught a class to learners at a distance.

Eleven items on the questionnaire were used to measure the perceived level of competence that respondents possessed in the use of electronic technologies often associated with distance education. The faculty indicated that they were able to use many of these technologies. Almost two-thirds of the faculty indicated they agreed or strongly agreed that they could create their own presentation graphics, while less than a quarter disagreed or strongly disagreed. A clear majority of the faculty members (84%) agreed or strongly agreed that they used email for "almost all of my correspondence," while 29% agreed or strongly agreed that they would send their "most important or confidential" documents through email." A majority of the faculty members (59%) agreed or strongly agreed that they could "scan photographs into digital files," while 29% disagreed or strongly disagreed. Nearly one-half agreed or strongly agreed that they were able to "connect a computer to the various output devices available (LCD projector, TV, etc.)." By a narrow margin, the faculty members agreed that they could "manipulate digital images" (46% agreed or strongly agreed vs. 43% disagreed or strongly disagreed). Slightly over one-half agreed or strongly agreed that they could "confidently deliver my course over the videoconferencing equipment."

While many of the faculty members were fairly confident in their ability to use presentation software, email, and digital images in their teaching, they also identified areas in which they were not as confident. Over one-half of the faculty members disagreed or strongly disagreed that they could create their own web page. Only a handful agreed (7%) or strongly agreed (3%) with the statement, "I am able to record and use digital sound in my presentations." Nearly two-thirds disagreed or strongly disagreed with the statement, "I could confidently deliver my course on the web."

Faculty members had much more confidence in their technical competence than they did in their methodological ability to use these technologies in their teaching. Over one-half of the respondents disagreed or strongly disagreed with the statement, "I am familiar with the teaching methods appropriate for distance learning."

Nine items were used to measure value, i.e., the importance of the role respondents believed these technologies have or will have to teaching agriculture. An overwhelming majority of the faculty members strongly agreed and agreed with the statement, "The Internet/WWW are convenient ways to access information." Nearly half agreed or strongly agreed with the statement, "Participation in listservs, threaded discussion groups, chats and other electronic communications offers great benefits." The respondents agreed (40%) and strongly agreed (18%) that most course materials could be improved by incorporating multimedia. They agreed (40%) and strongly agreed (18%) that "Animated graphics increase student interest and retention." Almost exactly two-thirds of the respondents agreed or strongly agreed that "Students today prefer a more visual learning experience." Over three-quarters of those responding agreed or strongly agreed that "Electronic information technologies provide students with instantly available supplemental course and research materials." Over one-half agreed or strongly agreed that "It is important that I incorporate electronic information technologies in the courses I teach."

Faculty opinions were mixed concerning the effect of these technologies. While they clearly agreed (38%) or strongly agreed (32%) with the statement, "Electronic communications and information drastically alter how we teach in the next five years," they did not support the statement, "Electronic communications and information will drastically alter what we teach in the next five years" (46% disagreed or strongly disagreed).

Ten items were used to measure the perceived availability of equipment, facilities, and training to determine the extent to which the campus environment supported the use of technologically mediated instruction on- and off-campus. Concerning the availability of equipment, 92% of the teaching faculty members indicated they were connected to electronic mail in their office and 72% indicated they were connected at home. More than one-third agreed or strongly agreed that "The equipment needed to produce and display multimedia course materials is readily available to me." More than one-half agreed or strongly agreed that they were aware of "the necessary procedure to secure electronic presentation equipment for classroom use within the university." Over half of the faculty members agreed or strongly agreed that that they "have access to a classroom designed to support the use of multimedia teaching aids."

Teaching faculty members perceived training and assistance in the use of instructional technologies to be less available than equipment. More than one-third disagreed or strongly disagreed that "there are ample opportunities to secure faculty development on using multimedia and videoconferencing equipment" while 27% agreed or strongly agreed. While 44% indicated they were neutral on the question, 11% strongly disagreed with the statement, "There are enough faculty development workshops regarding videoconferencing" while 7% strongly agreed. Over half the faculty members disagreed or strongly disagreed that they were "aware of the procedure, office, and personnel responsible for scheduling videoconference classes/sessions for the college."

The respondents did not believe that the climate was supportive of the use of these technologies. Almost one-half of the respondents (43%) disagreed or strongly disagreed that "The time spent developing course materials is valued by my department."

In general, faculty agreed that electronic technologies could make a valuable contribution to the learning process, that they should be used in all classes, and that technology will change how we teach in the next five years. About one-half of the respondents reported having a course website, but most lacked experience in teaching learners at a distance, and were much more confident in their technical competence than in their methodological ability to use modern technologies. All respondents perceived training and assistance in the use of instructional technologies to be less available than equipment and facilities. For a view of patterns for competence, value, and quality of infrastructure, see Figure 1.

Dooley and Murphy (2001) discovered through the open-ended responses that faculty were currently using distance education technology in the following ways: 1) web-based tracking simulations, 2) PowerPoint presentations for in-class, videoconferences, and web-based courses, 3) other multimedia, such as animation, 4) course webpages with features such as an ability to check grades, download lecture outlines, class notes, handouts, course assignments, and course syllabi, and 5) email and threaded discussion for increased communications and interaction between faculty and students. Virtual library resources and the capability to conduct research online were providing access to dispersed students and faculty. Faculty also mentioned the use of interactive video for guest speakers, including international connections, and for final defenses.

When faculty were asked, "What would significantly improve your use of the electronic technologies often associated with distance education?" Answers fell into six categories: 1) *Support Resources* (technical and course conversion personnel, including funding student workers/graduate students, 2) *Faculty Rewards/Recognition* (release time/faculty development to learn to use technologies, recognition for tenure and promotion, etc., 3) *Training* (to improve comfort and familiarity with equipment), 4) *Access to State-of-the-Art Equipment*, 5) *Quality Assurance* (through research, success at other peer institutions, and continuity in format and procedures), and 6) *Availability of an Audience Base* (to sustain and make the effort worthwhile).

Many faculty perceive a lack of "Real SUPPORT from the department and university, including recognition that its development in my program is as important and valued as developments in my research. This recognition would need to be accompanied by time for necessary TRAINING and the ready access to equipment (respondent emphasis)." Additional time was most frequently mentioned as a factor to improve use. "Having enough time to develop the materials needed, and to practice developing and using the materials. One-shot training programs....leave me frustrated...." Overall, there is a perception that these six areas must be addressed prior to faculty adoption of distance education technologies.

Dooley and Murphy (2001) also asked faculty, "What components should be present in an effective course delivered using electronic technologies?" There were five primary response categories: 1) *Interactions/Feedback*, 2) *Systematic Instructional Design*, 3) *Multimedia Components*, 4)

Figure 1: Patterns in competence, importance and quality of infrastructure

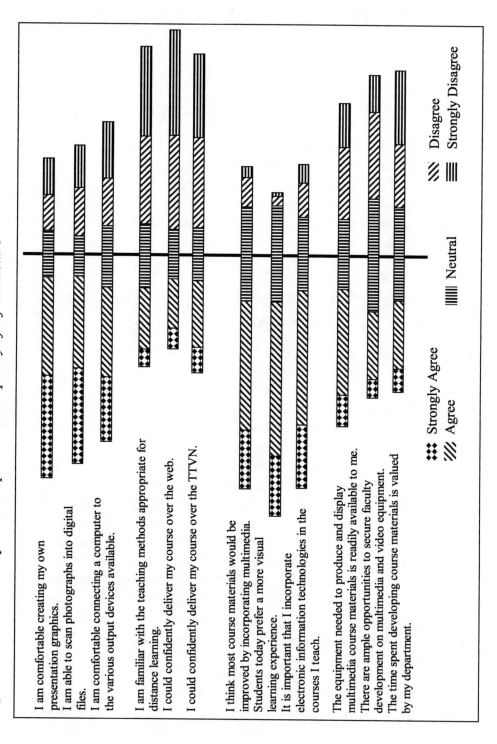

Simple and Reliable Delivery System (that is supported and easily accessible), and 5) *Strong Content/Supplemental Materials*. Faculty again mentioned the importance of time and money to create and fully utilize computer technology. There was a strong view that the components of effective instruction for distance learning are the same as "traditional" courses. Most emphasized the importance of interaction (mentioned 60 times). "The professor must be able to 'connect' with each and every student during the lecture and students must have unhindered access to the professor."

Faculty perceived that "technology is a tool similar to a chalkboard or overhead—all tools have advantages and disadvantages over all other tools available. There is no 'perfect' teaching philosophy or tool, only varying degrees of effectiveness with various audiences." "Development of high quality courses for distance education requires significant investments of time and resources."

WHAT SHOULD (CAN) BE DONE TO ENHANCE FACULTY PARTICIPATION

Faculty recognize that these technologies are—and will be—an important part of the instructional process. Faculty members also perceive that support and training are less available than equipment. Resources must be directed to the provision of adequate levels of support and training such that electronic technologies are used for the benefit of students, and not as doorstops.

While faculty recognize the potential, intervention strategies are necessary to alter how people perceive and react to distance education technologies. It is apparent that steps must be taken to increase faculty training and support. Three major areas require consideration: 1) support, 2) training, and 3) incentives. Support extends beyond "verbal" to providing the support/professional staff to assist faculty. Training should not only include technology exposure, but instructional design, pedagogy/andragogy, and "cookbook" strategies and "how-to" manuals. By providing incentives such as release time, mini-grants, continuing education stipends, and recognition in the promotion and tenure process, faculty will have more than "verbal" encouragement to continue, or begin, using distance education technologies and will have the reason to do so (Murphrey & Dooley, 2000).

If you think of an analogy of a fruit tree, faculty must be encouraged to pick the low-hanging fruit first. It may be the case that faculty members simply want to put their syllabi in a word processing document, save it as an Adobe

Acrobat (PDF) file and post it on a homepage. Eating that "apple" may initially fill them up! They may want another piece of fruit (like email or the ability to put students' grades on the website), but the training required for each application is relatively simple compared with a complete conversion to distance education format (trying to pick from the top of the tree). Both of the authors of this chapter teach courses at a distance and provide assistance to other faculty teaching at a distance through the Office of Distance Education for the Agriculture Program. In the following sections the authors will describe actual scenarios (successes and failures) intended to support, train, and provide incentives for faculty teaching at a distance.

Workshops and Training

Case One: A faculty member who uses the Mac OS went to a workshop for PowerPoint. She had used the very basic features of PowerPoint and wanted to learn more. In the workshop, the participants used relatively old PCs (no MACs) with Windows and the newest version of PowerPoint that was unfamiliar to this faculty member. When she returned to her Power Mac 8500 computer with PowerPoint 3.0, the differences between the computers and the versions of PowerPoint were so great that when she tried to duplicate what she had been taught in the workshop, she could not. The menus were different; many of the commands were different; the whole face of the program had changed it seemed. The differences were so great she became frustrated and gave up.

A major problem in conducting workshops for faculty members is getting them out of their offices and to the training site! An equally difficult problem lies in using computers that are unfamiliar and software versions different from what the faculty member has on his/her own computer. To address the problem of faculty reluctance to leave their offices to learn new computer skills, the Office of Distance Education for the Agriculture Program (ODE-AG) started a program whereby any teaching faculty members who wanted to learn PowerPoint could request that someone come to their offices and teach them on their own computer. One requirement of each faculty member was that they have a legal copy of the software. Initially, two undergraduates were hired who were very knowledgeable about PowerPoint and comfortable with teaching faculty. In following years, ODE-AG recruited talented undergraduates, who were trained by the Coordinator of Distance Education. This program has worked quite well. In a follow-up questionnaire, most of the faculty members who learned in this way used PowerPoint in their teaching and some have gone on to teach at a distance.

Even though there are some problems inherent in using workshops to provide training for faculty, there are also many potential benefits, including improving the technical (and sometimes, instructional) competence of faculty. But, the survey of teaching faculty in our college (Dooley & Murphy, 2001) indicated that many faculty have the competence, but lack the *desire* (and time) to make this a priority. Training programs should include research about how the use of technology impacts the teaching and learning process, rather than "this is how you do this." Additionally, faculty may respond to training programs designed in "small chunks" rather than a half-day program. To teach faculty to use WebCT for example, Texas A&M University provided three consecutive days of half-day workshops. Very few faculty could commit to this training format. The trainers altered the workshop format which is now "tool" specific and in a one to two hour format. Faculty participation in these workshops has increased.

Why Faculty Choose to Participate

Case 2: Professor A teaches a popular course in environmental sciences at the sophomore level. In fall of 1996, she was concerned that the course was filled and more than 20 students remained on the waiting list. Since she had participated in delivering a web-based course the preceding semester, she decided to add a new section to the environmental science course, one that would be web-based. She had already developed a website for her courses and had put all course materials on the web for her residential students anyway, so there was relatively little extra work to do for the added web section. The students were required to have an email address and to interact with the instructor weekly by answering content-related questions or finding relevant websites. At the end of the semester, the grades for the students in the web-assisted section, 30 in all, were slightly higher (on the same exams) than the students in the traditional section, approximately 100. However, the evaluations from the web-assisted section rated all aspects of the course higher than the overall evaluations of students in the traditional section.

Case 3: Professor L teaches a required senior level course for nutrition majors. He converted his course materials to electronic format and put them onto the web so students could come to class or not as they chose. At the beginning of the semester one student, a graduating senior called and tearfully told this instructor that she had just come out of surgery and must return home to Dallas to convalesce for four weeks, making it impossible to take this required course. She was scheduled to graduate at the end of the semester and thought she would have to come back for one more semester. Professor L suggested that she take the course from her bed in Dallas, which she did. She was well enough to take exams to pass the course and graduate on time.

Case 4: Professor B teaches an ecology course at the graduate level. He is a well-known researcher in his area and frequently is invited to give lectures, seminars and symposia at other universities in the United States and abroad. He was offered the opportunity to spend four weeks participating in a research project at a university in Australia during the fall semester of 1999 but that meant he could not teach his graduate course. His department head urged him to teach his course on the web and use mostly email to communicate with the students during the time he was away. He had never taught a web-based course, but he had already put most of his course materials on the web for the benefit of his residential students. With the promise of some additional support from his department head, he accepted the opportunity in Australia and successfully taught part of his course from there. This support consisted mostly of partial funding for a web-savvy graduate student in the same area of expertise to develop a better website, convert a few remaining course materials to electronic format and to transfer those additional files.

Case 5: Professor M saw how his colleague had used interactive practice tests and simple animations accessed on the web to help students understand some difficult concepts in biochemistry. He worked with the same educational technologist to develop interactive practice tests for his residential genetics course and put them on the web. The students really appreciated the interactive exercises and animations that were available at all times on the web. Professor M then converted all his course materials to the web and has developed more practice tests. Last semester, he decreased the number of lecture periods in his residential course from three to one per week and added several assignments on the web. The students were uniformly enthusiastic about the decreased lecture time and the average grade appeared the same as previous semesters. After Professor M saw how effectively the technology could be used in teaching the course, he plans to try teaching the course completely web-based in summer of 2001.

Most of the College of Agriculture and Life Science faculty who teach at a distance began as a direct result of using a few tools of distance education to solve existing residential problems. Some of the problems include a lack of space in residential courses, students with an illness or permanent disability unable to access a residential course, students unable to fit a required course into their lecture schedules, and the need for instructor flexibility with travel and research programs. Once courses and course sequences were available via distance education technology, geographically dispersed students needing access to a degree program were able to participate. Using distance education effectively adds "new bricks and mortar" to expand the school's capacity, and for some students, shorten their time (and monetary investment) in school. The faculty chose to participate in distance education for *intrinsic* reasons—providing access to their students.

Use of Support and Training as Faculty Incentives to Teach at a Distance

Case 6: An excellent teacher in the College of Liberal Arts was offered several thousand dollars and a lap-top computer to deliver his course at a distance to teachers pursuing their Masters degrees. The faculty member who received the incentives had no experience in teaching at a distance. Although he had some help, the use of the videoconferencing equipment was frustrating for him. Since he had no prior experience adapting course materials for a website (or by any other distance methods), delivering some of the information to the distant students proved to be challenging and time-consuming. He was not given any release time from his other courses nor from his research commitments, and therefore he could not spend the extra time needed to master the technology. Unfortunately, this excellent teacher had a frustrating experience that left the students frustrated as well. This award-winning faculty member has not taught another course at a distance.

Case 7: Professor Q teaches a course in education that many teachers would like to take. He was offered the use of a full-time graduate student to help him prepare his course for the web, providing he agreed to teach the web-based version within the next six months. Unfortunately, Professor Q was not given any release time and taught two other courses during the semester he had the use of the graduate student. He could not find enough time to convert the course to a web-based version and has yet to teach the course on the web.

Several faculty and administrators have suggested that more faculty would teach at a distance if given significant incentives beyond adequate support and training. In the authors' opinion, the use of specific incentives has not been effective in convincing resistant faculty members at our institution to embrace distance education. This comment is not meant to discount the importance of release time and a belief that this is time well spent as previously mentioned in the section above. Many universities have been successful with monetary incentives to encourage participation. It takes a considerable investment of time to teach at a distance and it must be compatible with existing reward structures. This can be a problem in building a sustainable, critical mass of faculty to participate in distance education.

Depending on the institution, the *extrinsic* motivations will vary. The authors have found that an effective way to assist faculty in course conversion is to hire undergraduates as student workers who will work directly with the faculty member. Hiring a student who has taken the course being converted has many advantages to the faculty member. First and perhaps most important, the individual responsible for conversion has some knowledge of the content area. Secondly, many undergraduates are much more familiar with computer programs required for course conversion than faculty. Thirdly, cost of undergraduate student labor is quite low. In fact, at most institutions undergraduates earn minimum wage for most jobs. Thus, an undergraduate working ten hours per week for one semester would cost the university approximately $800. Most undergraduates benefit greatly from this employment because they generally earn an outstanding letter of recommendation from the professor. Students can also register for independent study options, thus making this affordable and a learning experience for the student and faculty member. Contrast this with assigning a graduate student on an assistantship to the task of converting course materials. Graduate assistantships typically pay approximately $5000 or more per semester. Hiring a technical person to convert course materials is even more costly.

SUMMARY

Texas A&M University (and specifically the College of Agriculture and Life Science) has been the authors' test bed. But through the search of the literature and providing training and consulting services at other higher education institutions, the authors believe that implications from our research and case studies can provide "lessons learned" for other universities striving to encourage faculty participation. Rockwell and associates (1999) also found that the primary incentives for faculty were *intrinsic* or personal rewards, including the opportunity to provide innovative instruction and apply new teaching techniques. Other incentives included extending educational opportunities beyond the traditional institutional walls, and release time for faculty preparation. That study also determined that the major obstacles were related to time requirements, developing effective technology skills, and assistance and support needs. Monetary awards for faculty were not seen as incentives or obstacles (Rockwall et. al., 1999). McKenzie and her research team (2000) also found similar conclusions.

According to Olcott and Wright (1995),

The accelerated development of distance education programs across American higher education will require a renewed commitment to its most important resource . . .faculty. Advances in technology afford institutions unique opportunities to deliver education.... However, responsibility for instructional quality and control, the improvement of learning, and the aggregate effectiveness of distance education still rests with the faculty.

If faculty are going to participate in distance education, they must have the competence, attitude that distance education is important and valuable, and quality of infrastructure available to facilitate this participation. It is indeed true that faculty roles and responsibilities must change to accommodate the use of these technologies, and that teaching at a distance does require a different set of competencies. Yet faculty members' attitudes, and the barriers created by the lack of institutional support, must be addressed to integrate more fully these technologies into the teaching and learning process. Training programs cannot be "one-shot" and may include the use of undergraduate students or other personnel, on their own equipment, in the faculty office space. Release time is probably the most important incentive to encourage participation.

Back to the analogy, faculty will be more willing to participate if they can pick the "low-hanging fruit." A first step may be putting the lecture notes into some presentation form, e.g., PowerPoint or a word processing program. Once converted digitally, the next step may be creating a course website. Faculty need to see that course conversion can be incremental and that the technology tools they might choose for distance education can also serve to increase interaction and communications (and improve teaching effectiveness) for their on-campus students as well. Go ahead. Take a bite!

REFERENCES

Beaudoin, M. F. (1990). The instructor's changing role in distance education. *The American Journal of Distance Education*, 4(2), 21-29.

Cyrs, T. (1997). *Teaching at a Distance with Merging Technologies: An Instructional Systems Approach*. Las Cruces, NM: Center for Educational Development, New Mexico State University.

Dede, C. (1996). The evolution of distance education: Emerging technologies and distributed learning. *The American Journal of Distance Education*, 10(2), 4-36.

Dillman, D. A. (1978). *Mail And Telephone Surveys: The Total Design Method*. New York: John Wiley & Sons.

Dillon, C. L. (1989). Faculty rewards and instructional telecommunications: A view from the telecourse faculty. *The American Journal of Distance Education*, 3(2), 35-43.

Dillon, C. L. and Walsh, S. M. (1992). Faculty: The neglected resource in distance education. *The American Journal of Distance Education*, 3(6), 5-21.

Dooley, K. E. and Murphy, T. H. (2001). College of agriculture faculty perceptions of electronic technologies in teaching. *Journal of Agricultural Education,* 42(2).

Dooley, K. E. and Murphrey, T. P. (2000). How the perspectives of administrators, faculty, and support units impact the rate of distance education adoption. *The Journal of Distance Learning Administration*, 3(4). Available on the World Wide Web at: http://www.westga.edu/~distance/jmain11.html.

Hanna, D. E. (1999). *Higher Education in an Era of Digital Competition: Choices and Challenges*. Madison, WI: Atwood Publishing.

Lacina-Gifford, L. and J.-Kher-Durlabhji, N. (1996). Preparing to Teach a Class by Internet. *College Teaching*, 44, 94-95.

Layzell, D. T. (1996). Faculty workload and productivity: Recurrent issues with new imperatives. *The Review of Higher Education*, 19(3), 267-281.

Lincoln, Y. S., and Guba, E. G. (1985). *Naturalistic Inquiry*. Newbury Park, CA: Sage.

McKenzie, B. Mims, N., Bennett, E. and Waugh, M. (2000). Needs, concerns and practices of online instructors. *Online Journal of Distance Learning Administration*. Available on the World Wide Web at: http://www.westga.edu/~distance/ojdla/fall33/mckenzie33.html. Accessed March 22, 2001.

Miller, L. E. and Smith, K. L. (1983). Handling nonresponse issues. *Journal of Extension*, 21(5), 21-23.

Moore, M. G. (1997). Quality in distance education: Four cases. *The American Journal of Distance Education*, 11(3), 1-7.

Murphrey, T. P. and Dooley, K. E. (2000). Perceived strengths, weaknesses, opportunities, and threats impacting the diffusion of distance education technologies for Colleges of Agriculture in land grant institutions. *Journal of Agricultural Education*, 41(4), 39-50.

National Education Association. (2000). *A Survey of Traditional and Distance Learning Higher Education Members*. Available on World Wide Web at: http://www.nea.org/he/abouthe/dlstudy.pdf. Accessed March 2001.

Olcott, D. and Wright, S. J. (1995). An institutional support framework for increasing faculty participation in post-secondary distance education. *The American Journal of Distance Education*, 9(3), 5-17.

Plater, W. M. (1995). Future work: Faculty time in the 21st century. *Change*, 27(3), 22-33.

Poe, M. E. (2000). Factors affecting attitudes of participating and non-participating graduate faculty toward use of two-way audio/two-way video as a primary instructional delivery system in Texas A&M University classes. *Unpublished dissertation.*

Purdy, L. N. and Wright, S. J. (1992). Teaching in distance education: A faculty perspective. *The American Journal of Distance Education*, 6(3), 2-4.

Rockwell, S. K. Schauer, J., Fritz, S. M. and Marx, D. B. (1999). Incentives and obstacles influencing higher education faculty and administrators to teach via distance. *Online Journal of Distance Learning Administration*, 2(4). Available on the World Wide Web at: http://www.westga.edu/~distance/rockwell24.html.

Schifter, C. C. (2000). Faculty motivators and inhibitors for participation in distance education. *Educational Technology*, 40(2), 43-46.

Visser, J. A. (2000). Faculty work in developing and teaching web-based distance courses: A case study of time and effort. *The American Journal of Distance Education*, 14(3), 21-32.

Wolcott, L. L. (1997). Tenure, promotion, and distance education: Examining the culture of faculty rewards. *The American Journal of Distance Education*, 11(2), 3-18.

Chapter VI

The Challenge of Teaching Effectively From a Distance

Valerie E. Polichar and Christine Bagwell
University of California, San Diego, USA

Distance learning has the potential to be as powerful at successful instruction as conventional classroom learning. To take advantage of this potential, planners and educators should apply known principles of perception and learning gleaned from cognitive, behavioral, educational, and perceptual psychological research. These principles include those of elaborative encoding, interactive learning, reinforcement and the spacing effect. These principles and their relationship to human learning are presented. Applications of these principles in conventional distance learning packages are discussed, including Web page development, course-in-a-box software, chat rooms, MUD/MOO environments, bulletin boards and real-time online lectures. Suggestions are provided to guide the course designer in developing effective instructional tools.

Janet, a student in a traditional classroom, is taken on a field trip as part of her studies of the history of her hometown. She goes on a walking tour of the downtown area with a guide. They stop to read plaques on important buildings, and Janet asks questions about some of the strange architecture she sees. Her guide points out aspects of the geography of the area that affected the development of the urban area; Janet looks up a street and sees the steep hill leading to an old church, and notices the smell of sea air in the still-bustling market center. After the tour, Janet is assigned a project: building a model of one of the buildings she has seen.

David is taking an online course in local history offered by his city's community college Website. Each week he connects and reads the latest chapter of the online text. He looks at online pictures of famous local buildings. Every six weeks, he takes an online "midterm." If he passes two midterms and a final, he will pass the class and earn credits.

Most educators would probably agree that Janet's experience was "richer." But while one might suspect that it was also more effective for learning and retaining information about the subject, it might not be clear precisely why this is so. In fact, it is likely that her experience would lead to longer retention and better comprehension of the subject matter. This is not, however, an inherent disadvantage of distance learning. Rather, it is a difference in pedagogical approaches. With care, an online course can be made equally effective—even if not always equally sensually engaging. (It's hard to smell the sea through the computer screen!)

Instructors are spending increasing amounts of time and energy converting their courses into distance education. They create Web-based classes and local public broadcasting courses, and make use of packaged courseware, "drill-and-practice" software, and tools to enhance traditional face-to-face teaching environments. Students are beginning to embrace the new formats, but how certain can an instructor be that her students are truly learning the material? If she runs into one of them a year later, what will he be able to tell her about the subject matter? Will the student be able to translate and transfer what he has learned into his life, his work, his understanding of the world?

Much of the research into technology education has focused on the hurdles of attracting and keeping students' attention, interest and participation. For example, the TLT Group's respected Flashlight Program (1999; 2000; 2001) focuses on analysis of accessibility, technology barriers, and tracking use of educational technology installations. An article on "The effects of electronic classrooms on learning English composition" (Stinson & Claus, 2000) contains many references to aspects of the class that students "liked" or "disliked," and focuses on faculty/course evaluations as a method of evaluating technology enhancement success or failure. In the 1990s, a successful educational product was one that kept students involved and motivated to use it for the largest number of hours and the longest stretch of weeks. The research and applications focus has been, understandably, on assessing and improving student participation.

As educational technology moves into its next decade, practitioners and planners are beginning to evaluate whether or not a product successfully teaches (see, Smith & Warren, 1999), notes Patti Harvey, a consultant quoted in Geith (1999), "Faculty start to question what is working. We are now focusing on what learning is, how we describe it, and what that means for current approaches to how we measure for learning." Developing successful distance learning programs is going to require careful attention to, and incorporation of, successful conventional instructional methods, appropriate application of conventional and new student assessment methods (such as testing), and an organized empirical approach. In addition to all that, it will require a re-examination of what is known about perception, learning, memory, and the brain, and the incorporation of that knowledge into instructional design.

The development of educational curriculum and teaching methodology is most successful when it is informed by educational research. Educational research, in turn, is most specific and accurate when informed by psychological research—especially work in the areas of behavioral, perceptual, cognitive and educational psychology. Classroom methods tend to incorporate *ad hoc* methods into the mix—things that a particular instructor has found or believes to be effective. Often, these discoveries are shared in workshops and books developed for face-to-face instructors, and are subsequently analyzed in terms of their psychological effectiveness.

Such work has not, however, been applied as frequently to educational technology design. In fact, careful study of many of the educational products available for developers of distance courseware reveals influences from a wide range of non-research sources. Such sources include video games, early Internet communication technologies (that in turn drew on community communication metaphors, such as the newspaper and public bulletin boards), and old-fashioned "drill-and-practice" teaching techniques that are no longer heavily practiced in a modern, live classroom. In addition, developers of course websites and other courseware unthinkingly may convert bad or ineffective classroom practices into bad online practices, simply because they are familiar.

As much as there is still to be learned about the human mind and human learning, what is known provides powerful suggestions about effective teaching. With the rapid growth of distance learning, it's timely to look at some of the most important psychological principles of learning and see how they might be exploited to create the most effective possible distance learning environment.

ELABORATIVE ENCODING

The most basic element of learning is probably the storage of information in long-term memory. From research in cognitive psychology, it is known that elaborative encoding—using information to be remembered in a creatively constructed, meaningful way—vastly increases memory for that information at a later time. The more meaningful the construction, the greater is the likelihood of retention over the longest period of time (Bradshaw & Anderson, 1982).

Most computer-based instruction programs make some attempt to incorporate elaborative encoding into their structure. Some are more successful than others (and some are successful purely by accident). In many interactive self-paced training and instructional programs, students are encouraged to attempt to "fill-in-the-blank" to provide the missing term in a sentence. This technique is especially popular in some of the early multimedia-rich training CD-ROMs—an intermediate step between the traditional classroom and online instruction. In many of these, the student either is asked to "guess" what might be coming next in the lecture (that is, the needed information cannot be derived from the preceding text), or to regurgitate something, in a prescribed form, that has recently been presented. This is not the most effective elaboration; it is fairly shallow processing and may not lead to lasting memory.

Yet this type of exercise is still very popular in corporate and professional computer-based training. It is even found in academic environments, especially in the context of staff development training.

"Course-in-a-box" software packages provide a simple way for faculty or teaching assistants to construct a course website without programming knowledge. These applications can be used from anywhere on the Internet, rather than past modes of needing software in a particular lab or relying on CD-ROM-based instructional aids. Tools such as a bulletin board or chat room can be added with a "point and click." Other commonly included tools are password protection, grade posting, image databases, and glossary tools. Administrative departments such as health and safety are often anxious to leverage such institutional instructional technology investments to reduce personnel costs for training. Rather than using the packages in a meaningful way, however, they convert old "fill-in-the-blank" quizzes to an online format, and remove some of the valuable aspects of classroom instruction (such as interaction with instructors) without looking for online replacements.

But many "course-in-a-box" applications, such as WebCT, offer an excellent opportunity for elaborative encoding: they have the capability to permit the student to develop his or her own Web page. If the student creates a website to present to others some aspect of the material that she has studied, learning can be enhanced. The process of reorganizing information in order to teach others is intensely elaborative.

This facility is extremely valuable—more so than less structured offerings such as chat rooms. Conventional classroom teachers have realized for years that creative constructions using course material are incredibly effective. Like a book report, a science fair project, and the seminar-style class (typical of graduate studies, where each student in turn presents new material to his fellow students), the creation of a website gives the student an opportunity to meaningfully encode the material he has been taught.

At Mount Union College in Alliance, Ohio, Jim Phillips takes the elaborative online assignment one step further. He asks students in his instructional design courses to develop full-blown online tutorials that instruct others on a topic they are studying. This causes the students not only to use learned material in an elaborative way, but to examine in depth their logic and grasp of the subject by asking and anticipating questions from their own audience (J. Phillips, personal interview with C. Bagwell, 2000).

MUD/MOO text-based virtual environments are becoming increasingly popular in educational applications. MUDs are modeled after 1970s text-based computer adventure games such as Adventure and Zork. They place the user in a virtual world, where he can navigate from room-to-room and interact with objects found there using plain English-style commands. MUDs, however, provide access to multiple users at the same time, and permit users to interact with each other in the virtual environment (for example, users in the same virtual "pub" may chat, order beers for each other, and look around at an identical text-based scene). MUDs also have features that, more than simple chat rooms, allow the creative educator to develop ideal environments for elaborative encoding. There are several aspects of MUDs/MOOs that enable elaboration:

- context–rich conversational environments
- the ability to develop relevant yet appealing educational "adventures" or "quests," where students must use both their knowledge of the subject matter and their reasoning and problem-solving skills to work their way through a process. (MUD "quests" resemble interactive experience-based problem-solving/teaching games such as the Learning Company's Carmen Sandiego (2001).)
- "'Bots" (programs that interact with students as if they were simply another participant). These can be programmed to converse with the student on the topic of interest, to provide feedback and reinforcement for discussion of relevant subject matter, and to offer hints, more advanced information, and explanations in response to creatively phrased questions from the student.

Mike O'Brien of the Aerospace Corporation used MUD technology to create an Egyptology quest, known as TinyLondon. The quest provides participants with an exciting and mentally challenging text-based adventure game—and, in the process, teaches them several aspects of the Middle Egyptian language.

The adventurer wanders through the Nile Valley, collecting scraps of parchment ostensibly written by Herodotus, the Greek historian. For example, you see a bit of vellum on the ground and look at it:

look vellum
```
"For whatever reason, these Ancients appeared never to
vary their verbs, as we do, so that commands and statements
sounded alike in their ears, and past, present and future
were but ill-distinguished. Thus, J3I, to cross a stream
or river, has no other forms or conjugation."
```

Later, you sit at the bank of the Nile, which you'd like to cross. You see a boat:

look boat
```
There is a boat here, with no one in it. It is made out
of woven papyrus reeds, and bobs gently against the bank
of the river.
```
Get into boat
```
You climb into a rickety-looking, shaky boat made out of
papyrus reeds.
In a Boat(#9538R)
The boat is sound, though seemingly fragile. It does not
move, but you sense that it could take you where you wish
if you expressed yourself properly.
```
You might try a few English commands with no effect:

cross
```
Huh? (Type "help" for help.)
```
Go across
```
* You can't go that way.
```
Take me across
```
* I don't see that here.
```
Finally, you remember that scrap of vellum you read about Middle Egyptian verbs, and its casual reference to crossing streams. You say:

J3I
```
The boat hears your command, and you are whisked quickly
and silently across the breadth of the Nile.
```
(M. O'Brien, personal interview with V. Polichar, September, 1999).

A great deal of potential exists in the use of MUDs/MOOs for education. One early adopter of this technology is Reed Riner, a professor of anthropology at Northern Arizona University (NAU) who for many years in the early

1990s taught a class in futures anthropology using a MUD (Riner & Clodius, 1995). Remote participants included not only the students at NAU, but also sister classes at the University of Dayton (under John Bregenzer) and other schools and advisors scattered around the U.S. and Canada.

ONLINE INTERACTIVE DISCUSSION

Work by Frase and Schwartz (1975) indicates that having students work together, taking turns asking and answering questions about course material, improves subsequent test performance. A bulletin or discussion board offers an excellent structured environment for such discourse, and can be an effective learning tool for online courses. As opposed to a chat room or a MUD/MOO, a discussion board offers students an asynchronous forum for communication. A discussion board gives students as much time as needed to formulate their thoughts and questions. It forgives slow typing, and provides a forum for the shy and for those less adept with English. (The inherent time delay between question and answer in this environment may also be beneficial, if students go on studying other material in the interim; this useful effect will be discussed later in the chapter.)

Chat rooms are a popular enhancement to online courses, but have the potential to be a dead end for learning. Students may chat about anything and everything—and not necessarily course material. (At the authors' home university, chat rooms have become known as "Hey, babe!" rooms.) Worse, chat rooms may lead to both elaboration and reinforcement of mistakes and incorrect understandings of course material.

For faculty who want students to interact, but who want control over where the discussion leads, discussion board systems (such as DISCUS, WebBoard or facilities in Blackboard's CourseInfo or WebCT) are preferable. Message-queuing features offer moderators the option to post or reject messages, so that faculty or TAs can ensure that messages are on target, concepts are being explained accurately, and facts being shared are correct. The interactive quality of these systems makes them nearly as appealing to students as chat rooms, but usually more pedagogically appropriate. (Alternatively, in a MUD or MOO environment, TAs, faculty, or even "Bots" can remain present in real-time to guide the discussion or answer questions.)

Chat rooms can be useful if tightly controlled. Teaching assistants at the University of California-San Diego, use them to provide virtual office hours prior to exams. A 9–11 p.m. on-campus study session is often impractical for working and married students. However, offered online, virtual office hours provide students with an opportunity to have critical questions answered in the comfort of their own homes.

Some programs, such as WebCT, allow for review of the chat room logs. Care must be taken, however, not to violate local privacy policies, especially in the university environment. It may also foster an atmosphere of distrust that could lead to decreased use of the environment. Finally, when an instructor corrects a student's misconception based on a log, the correction is received long after the concept has been voiced, and encoded, by the student. It is entirely likely that the misunderstanding will be what is remembered, unless the instructor requires an elaborative task to be performed along with the receipt of the correction.

Other skills are learned in the educational process besides the specific topic at hand. Carol B. MacKnight points out that students "need coaching and practice in how to carry on online discussions. Initially, faculty must step in and support disciplined discussions... in monitoring discussions or group work activity, faculty must engage in a line of questioning that will continue to drive an idea, thus helping students develop and apply critical thinking skills." These "critical skills" are important for elaborative encoding, and hence for learning (MacKnight, 2000). Theodore Groves, of the University of California-San Diego, would agree. He found it initially challenging to accept student questions via electronic mail without returning the exact answer immediately. Ideally, in a face-to-face office hours situation, an instructor would not simply give out an answer but instead guide students into arriving at solutions themselves by giving hints, supplying leading information and asking the students questions. It takes extra attention to apply this technique in an asynchronous medium, be it electronic mail or a bulletin board, but it is necessary to take full advantage of the value introduced by the technology (T. Groves, personal conversation with C. Bagwell, 2000; Knowlton, Knowlton & Davis, 2000). Effective use of teaching technology will help the student "go beyond being exposed to content to the point of critically interacting with it" (MacKnight, 2000).

REINFORCEMENT

Reinforcers help to increase the likelihood that a given behavior will happen again (Thorndike, 1898). More colloquially, rewarding a person's action makes the person likely to repeat that action. Many educational software developers have incorporated this notion into their programs. For example, in an addition drill program for children, successful completion of the presented math problem might result in a song being played.

There are several challenges in using reinforcement to enhance learning, but one of the most compelling is that it is not always effective. The very first question you must ask when seeking to incorporate reinforcement into your courseware is *what is a reinforcer for my audience?* (A secondary, but also important question, is *what is a punisher for my audience?*) Only with this information can you create courseware that does not skirt its intended purpose, or, worse, frustrate the user to the point where they cease to use it.

For many students, especially children and young adults, simply working with a computer is a reinforcer. Doing *anything* on a computer may be more appealing than participating in class activities, sitting in a large crowd, or even driving to campus. In fact, the experience of searching for a parking place on a crowded college campus may act as a punishment for driving to school! This effect will drive many students to choose a distance learning option, whether or not it is effective, and whether or not they use the courseware in the manner the instructor intended.

It's important for course designers to be aware of this inherent reinforcement effect for two reasons. First, developers must be certain that any reinforcer in the program is both dependent upon desired behavior, *and* more powerful than the other pleasures of interacting with the machine or program, or it will not increase learning. This is true whether the reinforcer is one they have deliberately inserted, or one that unexpectedly emerges during testing.

Sharon Polichar, a San Diego elementary-level English as a Second Language (ESL) educator, has used Davidson & Associates' Falling Fruit software to help her students learn punctuation. An unpunctuated sentence appears on the screen; students are asked to position a colorful toucan under the piece of falling fruit that contains the appropriate punctuation mark. If the punctuation is correct, the toucan gets to eat the fruit. If it is incorrect, the fruit explodes onto the toucan's head.

Polichar found that, instead of attempting to select the right answer, students were moving the toucan at random. The sight of the toucan getting whacked on the head with exploding fruit was much more entertaining than the sight of him eating! The most powerful reinforcer in the program was one the designers had clearly intended as a punisher. The planned reinforcer had little or no effect (S. Polichar, personal conversation with V. Polichar, 2000).

In addition to ensuring that reinforcement is appropriately affecting behavior, it's important to remember that simply getting to use a computer for a class is *not* a reinforcer for all students. It is critical for computer-based instruction to be compelling, or some students will cease to participate.

One generally effective reinforcer for self-paced online or disk-based courses is the inclusion of frequent, short quizzes with the score displayed prominently (along with a message such as, "Congratulations, you scored 82%! You have passed this chapter!"). The frequency and brevity help ensure that the student will succeed; their placement at the end of a section of study ensures that the student has worked through the chapter. These quizzes should *not* be confused with actual tests that measure learning. Most students will complete the test using short- and medium-term memory. However, the process of taking the quiz may assist in elaborative encoding, and the notice of *passing* the quiz provides reinforcement to study and to elaborative work. Moreover, Graham (1999) has found that administering pop quizzes significantly enhanced scores on subsequent exams and increased student motivation to study.

Many courseware programs offer quizzes. In most cases, however, they can be taken at any time, whether or not a chapter has just been completed, and taking the quizzes is not inherently part of completing a chapter. This decoupling somewhat lessens the positive effect that might otherwise be obtained. In the worst cases, as in some web-based "driver education" classes that are offered for U.S. drivers who have received speeding tickets, students have the ability to complete all the quizzes without even clicking through the pages containing the training information.

Reinforcement in the computer-based segment of a course can enhance the face-to-face segment as well. David Perlmutter at the University of California-San Diego uses spaced quizzes to encourage in-class participation and attendance, and to compel students to keep up with the reading. He requires students in his "Sign Language and Culture" courses to take a weekly online pass/fail quiz. He decided to add this online supplement because of a copying delay. On the day of a scheduled midterm, the exam was not ready to be distributed. When he announced his intention to give a lecture in place of the exam, half the class got up and left the room. By ambitiously and successfully implementing the online weekly quizzes, which are graded automatically, he has effectively provided motivation for lecture attendance. The automated nature of this tool permits him to provide this motivation for over 250 students (D. Perlmutter, personal conversation with C. Bagwell, 1999).

Reinforcers can be powerful learning tools when training any skill, such as playing basketball, knitting, or soldering. The principles of operant conditioning teach us that progressively reinforcing closer and closer approximations to a desired physical task, or "shaping," will effectively train a subject to perform a task with great accuracy.

It's less clear how reinforcement is useful in learning conceptual materials, such as understanding the political motivations behind a historical event. While one can reinforce correct answers to test questions, this has the effect of improving test scores. It is not necessarily clear that it will improve understanding.

However, reinforcers can be extremely useful in keeping students on task, especially reluctant ones. Faculty who anticipate difficulty in getting students involved in online participation can circumvent the problem by offering incentives to students who post and respond to questions. Incentives might include class participation grade points or public "Good job!" messages. Stanley Chodorow, at the University of California-San Diego, assigns his Humanities students points based on their participation on the class message board (S. Chodorow, personal conversation with C. Bagwell, 2000).

THE "SPACING EFFECT"

A final important psychological principle is the spacing effect. When an item to be committed to memory is studied for a while, put away for a longer period (which can be weeks or even months), and then taken out and restudied, later recall for the item is more effective than if the same total study time is spent in one session (Reder & Anderson, 1982; Greene, 1989). Self-paced learning naturally exploits this phenomenon, but it can be enhanced by careful course structure.

Interspersing topics is a useful technique. It creates natural breaks between periods of study of a given topic; also, it has been found that information retrieval is strengthened when information to be learned is related to information already stored (Singh et al., 1994). Deft interrelating of different topics, as well as course segments that build on segments that come before, can enhance this effect.

Increasing specialization of training has made it tempting to create single-subject or sub-subject course segments that can "stand alone." The practical value of such a segmented course to the student is partially offset by the fact that topics are no longer interrelated or built on each other. To take advantage of the Singh effect, courses need not be entirely incremental. Students can be asked to apply knowledge and techniques learned in one segment as they approach a second topic. Alternatively, the students themselves may be asked to create the relationship in their creative efforts (e.g., "Develop a Web page that shows how you might apply these principles of long-term memory storage to what you learned in the last chapter about visual perception").

Finally, self-paced may not be the best pace. It's possible to avoid this problem by scheduling some real-time events (such as an online guest speaker in the MUD/MOO or chat room, or an upcoming television documentary to be watched when it airs) and activities (such as a creative project, a trip to a local museum, or an exploration of a community resource) into a course. Introduction of time structure into a distance course has two positive effects.

First, it helps keep the student working at a realistic pace. "Cramming" is notoriously ineffective at true instruction (Fulkerson & Martin, 1981; Brethrower, 1982), and a self-paced class makes this practice more likely if some structure is not also present. Secondly, it creates an opportunity to take advantage of the spacing effect to improve overall learning.

NEW AREAS FOR RESEARCH

The isolation effect, generally attributed to von Restorff (1933), demonstrates that memory for a unique type of item in a list of otherwise similar items will be enhanced. This discovery has spawned a great deal of research into the possible mechanisms for this enhancing effect, but the effect itself is potentially useful in instructional design.

More research is needed in this area, but the possible applications are interesting. For example, one way of making sure students get the critical point of a discussion might be to embed it in a presentation of a different type of information. If the date of one particular Civil War battle is critical to understanding a political decision process, a list of locations of Civil War battles might be presented, with a date appearing by only one. A discussion of export products of Australia might include a note about the geology of the country, since that country's unique geology is a driver of many of these products. Even if the student can't remember the list of battles or the list of products, they might recall that a critical battle took place before a particular presidential decision, or might be able to reconstruct the exports by remembering the great mineral resources of an ancient, flat continent.

It is well known that short-term memory can only hold 7 ± 2 "chunks" of information at one time, and information must remain in short-term memory long enough to be encoded if it is to be transferred to long-term memory. Given this, dense, information-packed hour-plus lectures make it difficult for most students to absorb much of the material at the time of presentation. The typical college student takes copious notes, doesn't try to digest any of the material at the time of presentation, and depends on later processing and interpretation—but often notes are not sufficient for complete understanding. Older-style distance learning, where students watched lectures on television in series, compounded the problem, as it was not possible to ask the instructor even to pause for a question. New technology can help avert this problem for distance learners.

Streamed audio and video presentations are becoming very popular as information delivery methods. Stanley Chodorow used to bring in slide carousels for his traditional-classroom lower division Humanities courses.

Now, using Real Presenter, Microsoft PowerPoint and a Real streaming server, he records his voice coordinated with the slideshow, creating an online presentation. In addition to making these presentations available to students for on-demand and multiple viewings, this method permits Chodorow to break up his lectures into five- to ten-minute segments. Such a segment is much more digestible to students than an hour-long lecture, permitting information to remain in their short-term memory long enough to be encoded and stored. Studying in segments of this sort also permits students to take advantage of the spacing effect. And students like the new format. Though the presentations are not interactive, a surprising side effect was that many students felt they were, in the sense that it felt as if the professor was speaking directly to the individual student (S. Chodorow, personal interview with C. Bagwell, 2000).

Finally, a new effort in research should be directed at measuring, as much as possible in the real online instructional environment, the real effects on learning and memory of the above-mentioned techniques. Without this validation, extrapolation from psychological findings will quickly fall into the same "pop psychology" realm that drives so much traditional classroom development. The first step is to make the link between psychological research and effective learning. The second is to find ways to realize these connections to make distance learning more effective. The third is to evaluate the effectiveness of implementations and to make appropriate changes. As more continues to be discovered about the brain and how humans learn, distance learning can be refined to be as effective as—perhaps even more effective than—traditional classroom instruction.

Claire is a student in a new distance learning class on local history. Each week, she spends some time interacting with her fellow students in an online MUD that represents her hometown as it was 100 years ago. Her special assignment for the semester is to work with her fellow students to develop a method of delivering water to new residents, whose homes are progressively further away from the river. To improve her ability to negotiate online with other students responsible for the metal works, labor animals, land rights and other relevant areas, she is given suggestions on places to visit in real life. She stops by the town waterworks and talks to the foreman, who has been there for many years. At the library, she finds photographs and plans of the first municipal sewer system. Online at the town's utilities company Web page, she watches an animation of city water delivery and learns about capacities and costs of the system.

In addition to her personal project, Claire is learning about local political, architectural, economical and agricultural history. She watches streaming video and public broadcasting specials. She reads short texts and responds to questions at the end of them, receiving instant feedback to confirm that her understanding is correct. She connects to an online chat room during office hours and talks to her instructor. She takes part in group discussions on the MUD, takes exams online, and even submits her final "paper"—a multimedia presentation analyzing her successes and failures in the virtual MUD environment—via electronic mail.

A year in the future, who do you think will be able to answer your questions about their own town's history, David, Janet or Claire?

Strategic application of what is known about how humans learn to the distance learning environment can produce instruction that is as effective as, or even more effective than, traditional classroom teaching. Encouragement of student processes that cause elaborative encoding to occur, careful use of reinforcers and targeted interrelation of topics and time intervals to take advantage of the spacing effect, combined with appropriate use of interactive online discussion, will add power to courseware. Further research will help identify additional psychological factors that can be used to strengthen distance learning, and will help establish these effects empirically.

REFERENCES

Bradshaw, G. L. and Anderson, J. R. (1982). Elaborative encoding as an explanation of levels of processing. *Journal of Verbal Learning & Verbal Behavior*, 21, 165–174.

Brethower, D. M. (1982). Teaching students to be scholars. *Journal of Learning Skills*, 2, 3-10.

Ehrmann, S.C. (1999). Shining a Flashlight on teaching, learning and technology. *Presentation/abstract in EDUCAUSE 99*.

Ehrmann, S.C. (2000). The Flashlight Program—evaluating instructional uses of the Web. *Syllabus*, September, 38-42.

Frase, L. T. and Schwartz, B. J. (1975). Effect of question production and answering on prose recall. *Journal of Educational Psychology*, 67, 628-635.

Fulkerson, F. E. and Martin, G. (1981). Effects of exam frequency on student performance, evaluations of instructor, and test anxiety. *Teaching of Psychology*, 8, 90-93.

Geith, C. (1999). Assessment shaping technology use and learning. *Converge*, November, 20-22.

Graham, R.B. (1999). Unannounced quizzes raise test scores selectively for mid-range students. *Teaching of Psychology*, 26, 271-273.

Greene, R. L. (1989). Spacing effects in memory: evidence for a two-process account. *Journal of Experimental Psychology: Learning, Memory and Cognition*, 15, 371–377.

Knowlton, D. S., Knowlton, H. M. and Davis, C. (2000). The whys and hows of online discussion. *Syllabus*, June, 54-58.

Learning Company's Carmen Sandiego (2001). Available on the World Wide Web at: http://www.carmensandiego.com/ [Accessed 6/2001].

MacKnight, C. B. (2000). Teaching critical thinking through online discussions. *Educause Quarterly*, 23(4), 38-41.

Reder, L. M. and Anderson, J. R. (1982). Effects of spacing and embellishment on memory for the main points of a text. *Memory & Cognition*, 10, 97-102.

Riner, R. and Clodius, J. (1995). Simulating future histories: the NAU solar system simulation and Mars settlement. *Anthropology and Education Quarterly*, 26, 95-104.

Singh, S., Mishra, S., Bendapudi, N. and Linville, D. (1994). Enhancing memory of television commercials through message spacing. *Journal of Marketing Research*, 31, 384-392.

Smith, K. L. and Warren, B. (1999) *Evaluating Performance: Strategies for a Technology-Enhanced Learning Environment*. Handouts, worksheets, technology models and guidelines distributed as part of a presentation at *EDUCAUSE 99*. Available on the World Wide Web at: http://reach.ucf.edu/~fctl/fac_support/faculty_support__resources.htm [Accessed 6/2001].

Stinson, B. M. and Claus, K. (2000). The effects of electronic classrooms on learning English composition. *T.H.E. Journal*, February, 98-103.

Thorndike, E. L. (1898). Animal intelligence: An experimental study of the associative processes in animals. *Psychological Review Monograph Supplement*, 2, 8.

TLT Group (2001). *Flashlight Program*. Available on the World Wide Web at: http://www.tltgroup.org/programs/flashlight.html [Accessed 6/2001].

Chapter VII

A Preliminary Exploration of Social Needs in Distance Education

William B. Martz, Jr. and Morgan M. Shepherd
University of Colorado at Colorado Springs, USA

This chapter explores the concern for social needs in distance education. As a foundation, the chapter discusses the evolving learning environment and stakeholder expectations that distance education must address as it grows in prevalence. In addition, technology is a key enabler of any distance learning program. This chapter analyzes several theories that integrate learning and technology for potential insights applicable to distance learning. These insights lead to an exploratory study to compare the "need for affiliation" between students working in groups for distance classes (virtual groups) and students working in groups for on-campus classes (actual groups). The preliminary results of the study indicate that some issues concerning socialization do exist between the two groups. Ultimately, the study points to the need for more formal and definitive measures of the social aspects of group work in distance education.

INTRODUCTION

Distance education is struggling to identify what it should be. Clearly, there are many stakeholders vested in the results of the ultimate definition. State organizations want to efficiently use taxpayer dollars for education;

instructors want to efficiently present course topics for effective learning; students want to optimize their learning process to maximize their careers. It is safe to say that, ultimately, all parties want the best outcome; the biggest problem is that no one is sure of all the parts that need to be considered.

For the purpose of this discussion, distance education is defined as creating a learning environment that facilitates structured learning without the traditional practice of face-to-face interaction in an on-campus environment. This means that the practice of rural teachers who traveled between settlements to educate students in their homes meets the spirit of the definition. However, in today's world, distance education usually implies some sort of technological support through the Internet, email or videoconferencing.

As distance education becomes more viable for undergraduate education, the education industry should understand into what learning environment it is trying to assimilate. The practice of traditional education is changing quickly also. One pedagogical model receiving significant attention is called Learning Centered Education (LCE). This concept "places learning and learners at the core of the educational process" (Bilimoria & Wheeler, 1995). Essentially, a learning partnership is created whereby the teacher identifies what needs to be learned and the students help identify the means by which their own learning occurs. The concept works because it realizes that there are obligations on both sides of this partnership; the teacher facilitates and the student participates.

In summary, distance education is not a new concept. However, the unprecedented growth in technology and pedagogical changes in education power its growth. Internet, email, videoconferencing, etc., are enabling distance education to take a firm hold technically. The evolving model of Learning Centered Education provides one pedagogical perspective from which to view distance education.

BACKGROUND ON LEARNING

One of the fundamental concerns remaining in learning is when it is that learning actually occurs. John Locke (Chaplin & Krawiec, 1960) believed that humans start with a blank slate – *tabula rasa* – and that we, as human beings write our experiences on that slate throughout life. These experiences are what we have learned. Early researchers in the field of psychology picked up on this notion and tried to measure learning quantitatively: How much was being added to the *tabula rasa*. Ebbinhaus (1913) conducted several experiments from which he derived a famous retention curve to show how well individuals learned nonsense syllables over time. Gulliksen (1934) and Hull

(1943) created formulas to measure learning by differences in what has been attained (learned) and what is left to attain (learn). Carr (1931) took a less quantitative approach and organized learning into several classes of general laws. One such class was that learning is an adaptive activity and individuals learn by going through a series of activities and noting the responses from their environment. These activities and corresponding responses become learned as they are retained over time, in memory.

More recently, researchers (Papert, 1980; Bandura, 1977; Hills & Francis, 1999) argue that "real learning" requires a social context. Seymour Papert (1980) makes his case in his book, *Mindstorms*, as he relates teaching computer programming logic to children. Social Learning Theory (Bandura, 1977) emphasizes the interaction of people both with other people and with the environment. The level of social presence, the perceived "consciousness of another person in an interaction," (Tu, 2000) is described as the main driver in learning. Hill and Francis (1999) conducted their research with respect to computer-based training (CBT). Somewhat paradoxically, their findings showed that CBT environments were more successful when they included more social context

Much like CBT, which is generally "a solitary experience which takes place away from the real job," the distance environment will be required to take into account the social aspects of learning. Hogan and Kwiatkowski (1998) report on the social aspects of teaching in large groups in the United Kingdom. Their argument includes the premise that technology can handle the activity of teaching to large groups, but that the emotional aspects of this teaching method have been ignored. Similar concerns are raised in Australia, where technology has been supporting distance teaching for many years. Hearn and Scott (1998) argue that before adopting technology for distance teaching, technology must acknowledge the social context of learning.

The issues around implementing distance education are not just conceptual. There are stakeholders with very pragmatic needs. The students want to obtain skills for better jobs, and employers want to obtain graduates with better skills. Can distance education serve these needs? In a research study comparing recruiter and student perceptions of key skills necessary for employment and career advancement, several of the top skills required social interaction (Martz & Landof, 2000). Teamwork, project management and leadership skills ranked in the top five characteristics desired by recruiters. The fact that these skills require significant interaction with others to be successful means that they are "socially driven." If true, this means that learning development may suffer in the distance education environment.

One such problem is environment-driven. Haythornthwaite et al., (2000) coin a term, "fade back," to describe students & do not participate in the distance class. They point out that the "fading back" is accomplished easier in distance learning environments where the number of social cues is reduced. These cues include text without voice, voice without body language, class attendance without seating arrangements, students signing in without attending (Haythornthwaite et al., 2000). This implies that in similar classes, with similar levels of student interests, the likelihood of students "fading back" is greater in distance learning classes than in face-to-face classes.

Real learning seems to have a significant social component. As distance education evolves, it must be able to recognize and incorporate this component. There are stakeholders with pragmatic requirements that must be addressed. Employers want employees with both technical skills and skills that are "socially driven." Finally, into this mix an appropriate level of technology is added with the desire to remove the student from the physical confines of the classroom. This leads one to consider how technology and people interact.

HOW TECHNOLOGY AND PEOPLE INTERACT

As one thinks about distance education, it must be acknowledged that distance education incorporates many factors such as how individuals are motivated to learn and how individuals interact with technology. Looking at theories from each of these areas can help guide our investigation. First, there are a set of theories that have developed around the individuals and how individuals learn. These are labeled *foundation theories* because motivation to learn must exist before distance learning can be effective. Second, as technology has become more and more necessary to enable distance education, theories have been developed about how individuals and groups interact with technology. These theories are classified as *technology interaction theories* because they predict how individuals and groups interact with technology. These theories grow from the technology-oriented areas such as group support systems and collaborative work. Here researchers have been studying how people interact productively with technology. Commonalities across these foundation theories and technology interaction theories can help understand some of the issues faced by distance education.

Foundation Theories

Foundation theories, such as Field Theory, Social Exchange Theory, and Needs Theory, try to explain the various behaviors exhibited by individuals

Table 1: Technology Interaction and Foundation Theories

Technology Interaction
Media Richness Theory
Social Information Processing Theory
Adaptive Structuration Theory
Foundation Theories
Field Theory
Social Exchange Theory
Needs Theory

in groups. Briefly, Field Theory (Lewin, 1951) looks at the group dynamics caused by how individuals behave to overcome barriers as they try to achieve a goal. Lewin relates learning to this motivation (Chaplin & Krawiec, 1960). In groups, the large number of possible interactions complicates this behavior. Social Exchange Theory describes behavior in terms of its rewards and costs. "Rewards are pleasurable outcomes associated with particular behaviors; costs include such things as mental effort, anxiety or even embarrassment (Beebe & Masterson, 1986). Viewed in this economic way, individuals will seek to establish relationships that accrue a net positive analysis. In addition, individuals will enact behaviors to continue those relationships with a positive value.

In 1943, Abraham Maslow presented a first, rough draft of his Need Hierarchy Theory. Subsequently, he and his fellow researchers tested and adapted the theory for organizational settings. Essentially, the theory proposes that human beings have a set of "staircased" needs that interact and "combine with [other] biological, cultural and situational factors to determine behavior" (Miner, 1980). Of interest to us in this discussion is the need in which Maslow includes the desire for a sense of affiliation and general belongingness – broadly termed the "love needs" (Miner, 1980). Along these same lines, Aldefer (1972) included these needs in his "three-staired" Existence-Relatedness-Growth (ERG) Theory as relatedness needs. Both theories propose that when these needs are not satisfied (and the needs below this level are), the behavior of an individual will try to satisfy these needs. For example, until the lower-level "security needs" are satisfied for an individual, that individual will act to satisfy these lower-level needs before acting to satisfy needs on a "higher" stair. The research results showed much more complexity than just discussed, but, in general, the conjectures from the theories have held.

One of the more practical areas that use this need hierarchy model is the job enrichment program. The "need for affiliation" has been found to be a key ingredient in helping with achievement motivation (McClelland, 1961; Shipley & Veroff, 1952) and has been related to job satisfaction (Miner, 1980). Complementing this idea is that of a reference group whereby individuals "express" their "need for affiliation." Kelley (1951) identifies two such groups: comparative group, in which the individual compares and contrasts his or her stature — peer group — and reference group, to which the individual identifies with the general feelings. Students comparing their SAT test scores to others in the class represents a comparative group, while promoting the Sierra Club with a bumper sticker would constitute a reference group.

Technology Interaction Theories

One of the key areas that deals with technology and its impact on manual human-based processes is in the realm of group support systems (GSSs). Group Support Systems add a technology component to how groups work together (DeSanctis & Gallupe, 1985), much like distance education is adding a technology component to learning. GSS research has been a major contributor to the body of knowledge concerning group interactions and learning. In GSSs, manual methods for meetings and group work (Delbecq & Van de Ven, 1971; Linstone & Turoff, 1975; Saaty, 1980; Osborn, 1953) have been automated and the interaction of technology with people studied (Briggs et al., 1998; Fjermestad & Hiltz, 1999). As the researchers studied the impact of automating these processes, theories evolved. Essentially, face-to-face meeting environments are said to have many media to communicate information; these include verbal (e.g., tone of voice, volume) and nonverbal (e.g., body language, facial expressions). As technology is added to the process, it produces a lens that impacts the media by either a) restricting the flow of information, or b) missing some of the information completely. Tu (2000) refers to this as the "technological social presence." Figure 1 provides a simple diagram for further discussion.

Social Information Processing Theory (SIP) (Chidambaram, 1996; Walther, 1992) and Adaptive Structuration Theory (AST) (Poole & DeSanctis, 1990), suggest that the technology – the lens – is a limiting factor or constraint for communication. Each theory, in its own way, discusses how the senders of the cues adapt to the lens. SIP suggests that, over time, the sender will be able to get all the cues through; it simply takes more time. The senders choose to use their limited channel to process the task-oriented communications first, and then, if time permits, the theory predicts that the more social communi-

Figure 1: Technology Lens

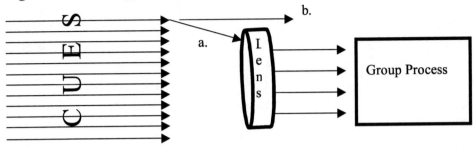

cations would follow. AST proposes a different tactic with the same end; that the senders figure out alternative ways to send the cues based upon what is "allowed" through the lens. The term used for this action is "appropriation" and "refers to the manner in which structures are adapted by a group for its own use ..." (Gopal et al., 1993). A good example here is how a sender of email may use emoticons (e.g., **:)** – sarcastic smile, **;)** – wink, **:o** – exclamation of surprise) to communicate more emotion about the subject to receiver. These theories, SIP and AST, tend to predict that the channel works over a period of time.

Media Richness Theory (Daft & Lengel, 1986) suggests that the inherent characteristics of the technology filter out cues and ultimately these cues do not make it through the lens to provide information to the receiver; in the case of group support systems, to the group process. The richness of the media—the size of the lens—directly impacts the effectiveness of the technology in the situation. The capacity of the channel to provide communication defines the richness of the channel. A face-to-face meeting offers a "richer media" than does a posted letter. Social Presence Theory (Short et al., 1976) argues that since the lens limits the amount of cues that may make it through, most cues will be action or task-oriented. In other words, the lens hampers the cues that provide for the receivers to "observe" any social cues. This means that the ability to observe or understand the other person in the communication is minimized.

Leidner and Jarvenpaa (1995) identify several learning models and propose how the current practices of using information technology works with each. One of the drivers for their work is a concern that information technology may be speeding up ineffective methods of teaching. In their analysis, they create a matrix showing the different technologies being used and to which learning model, each technology fits best. For Leidner and Jarvenpaa (1995), distance learning fit best with the "Objectivist" learning model. They defined this model with the basic premise of "learning is the uncritical absorption of objective knowledge," and the goals of "transfer of knowledge" and "recall of knowledge." The model that has the goal of "promoting socialization," including "group skills [such as] communication, listening, and participation" is termed "Collaborativism." The best technology fit for this learning model was "asynchronous communication across distances" such as email or asynchronous groupware. In essence, they are proposing that different modes of information technology represent different lenses.

CURRENT RESEARCH AND CONJECTURES

The debate still rages as to the effectiveness of distance education. The complex environment contains issues around how students learn, what motivates students to learn, how to make the learning environment better, how to make the environment worthwhile for all the stakeholders and how technology impacts the learning environment. Several researchers and educators are studying how distance education classes create a sense of community (Haythornthwaite et al., 2000; Dede, 1996). The study of these complex issues and interactions falls into the broad field of Social Informatics (Kling, 2000), which is defined as the study of the interaction of information technologies with an institutional and cultural perspective.

Studies are forthcoming. A review of over 400 studies compared distance to traditional classroom instruction with complex and conflicting results (Russell, 2001). On the positive side, faculty at eCollege.com reported that their students learned equally effectively online as they did on campus (TeleEducation NB, 2001). GSS studies are identifying and reconfirming the important characteristics in developing a sense of community, such as satisfaction (Chidambaram & Bostrom, 1997); trust (Aranda et al., 1998); cohesiveness (Chidambaram, 1996); and participation (Nunamaker et al., 1991). However, distance learning environments may be creating some additional concerns such as higher rates of student anxiety and frustration (Hora & Kling, forthcoming) and these environments may inherit the GSS characteristic of less consensus in decision making (Daft & Lengel, 1986; Briggs et al., 1998).

From these perspectives, distance learning must address both the technical content and the social aspects of the individuals. Even if the class is started and taught as an "objectivist" view, students will ultimately include the social aspects of the "collaborativism" view. This seems to be the case in a study wherein distance students performed better than their on-campus counterparts (Black, 1997). The researcher conducting the study attributed the findings to the online students compensating for not having time in class to talk.

Going even further, one can view the "need for affiliation" as a social need that helps with learning. This proposal is best aligned with the Social Information Processing Theory where Chidambaram (1996) describes one underlying premise of the theory this way: "Implicit in the SIP perspective is the idea that users of computer media are driven by these needs [affiliation motive – the need to like and to be liked by others] just as much as those in non-computer settings."

With Figure 1 in mind again, one would assume that the group process created by the technology lens in a distance class would be less "media rich" than that created by the traditional classroom. In addition, the "need for affiliation" between the individuals in two classes should be the same. Combining these two assumptions, one would expect to see more behavior geared to creating or attaining social cues in the distance learning class than in the face-to-face class.

This chapter describes one study performed to look at the above issue in more detail. The study used an MBA-level, introductory Information Systems course to compare traditional on-campus students with students taking the same class in a distance learning environment. The initial hypotheses centered on the need for affiliation; the prediction was that students in distance classes (DIST) would show more "need for affiliation" than students in on-campus classes (ONC). The following outcomes were expected:

H1: DIST will have higher levels of satisfaction with groups and group work than ONC

H2: DIST will have higher levels of group cohesiveness than ONC

H3: DIST will have more participation in groups than ONC.

THE RESEARCH STUDY

A questionnaire with 42 items was given to both groups. The questions asked about demographics, perception of technology and perception of group work. Short answer and seven-point Likert questions were used (1 = Strongly Agree ... 7 = Strongly Disagree). An example of the questionnaire is provided in Appendix A. The questionnaire was provided to both MBA classes. As previously mentioned one class was conducted totally by distance (DIST) while, the other was on-campus (ONC). A total of 42 students responded: 25 from the on-campus class and 17 from the distance class.

The analysis of the data is exploratory in nature and as such is subject to several limitations. First, the questionnaire was developed to measure a broad set of characteristics that interact in many ways. A factor analysis will help decompose these characteristics for revising the questionnaire. Second, the two classes were separated in time; they were taught in subsequent semesters and while the learning goals were the same, the exposure to topics varied. Finally, the low number of responses demands a more conservative statistical analysis that may not find subtle differences. The items with statistically significant results are provided in Table 2 below.

As discussed, the results of the prior research in this area are mixed. H1 and H2 were not supported, and H3 was only partially supported. The ONC group reported meeting more times per week than the DIST group (Q12), and more of the ONC time in meetings was spent on socialization than task (Q13). This is contrary to the expectations in terms of the need for affiliation.

However, the DIST group reported spending more time in meetings (Q11) and a greater percentage of that time on task than ONC group (Q14). So while DIST group held fewer meetings than the ONC group, they spent more time in each meeting than the ONC group. In addition, they spent more time on task than the ONC group. It is interesting to note that the DIST groups strongly disagreed that there was too much socialization in the group (Q24).

It was anticipated that the technology would play a part in how much time was spent in meetings and how much of the meeting time was spent on socialization (Figure 1). It is possible that the technology was inhibiting the number of meetings for the DIST group. The DIST group reported using

Table 2: Distance vs. on-campus characteristics

Item Description (referenced by question number)	On-campus Average	Distance Average	Sig(1)
6. How many hours do you spend each week on your MBA work?	10.10	14.25	**.005**
8. What is your current GPA?	3.54	3.72	**.000**
11. On average, how many hours did you spend with your group each week?	1.82	3.05	**.008**
12. On average, how many meetings did your group hold each week?	1.35	0.75	**.026**
13. On average, what percentage of your meetings was spent on socializing?	20.60	4.61	**.001**
14. On average, what percentage of your meetings was spent on the project task?	79.00	84.00	**.028**
24. There was too much socialization in my group	5.92	6.61	**.005**
27. I was satisfied with this course	2.72	3.56	**.074**
29. I was disappointed in how the course worked out	5.44	4.61	**.094**
31. Everyone in my group did their fair share of work	2.50	3.66	**.061**
Not Statistically Significant			
30.The level of interaction in my group was low	4.72	4.83	.699
32.I participated in this group more than I usually do in other groups	4.56	4.39	.639
41.I felt that I was really part of my group	2.00	2.61	.406
42.I would be willing to work in the same group again	2.60	3.0	.422
(1)- Results of Mann-Whitney test (p. <.100)			

email, phones, and an asynchronous forum for communication. These technologies are not very rich in nature. So it may not be so surprising that the DIST group met less often ("..we've got the technology working, let's keep going while we can…") and had less socializing ("…who knows how much longer the technology will last – better not waste time socializing…"). The DIST group may have used email (at other times) to do their socializing. Examples of this might be sending short emails inquiring about weather or sporting events, inquiring about personal issues, or exchanging jokes. The DIST group may not have considered these emails to be part of a meeting. This scenario is diagrammed below (Figure 2).

The DIST students may have satisfied the need to socialize in other ways, and therefore did not need to do so while in their meetings. This would make sense if the technology they were using for their meetings was not very rich.

Very few satisfaction characteristics were significant. The ONC group disagreed more strongly that it was disappointed with how the course worked out (4.61 for DIST vs. 5.44 for ONC (Q29). At the same time, the DIST students (3.66 for DIST vs. 2.50 for ONC) did not agree as strongly as the ONC students that everyone in the group did their fair share (Q31). With regard to the technology measures, there was no significant difference between the two groups; however, the DIST students did feel that the technology helped them get their work done (2.11). It should be noted that the questionnaire did not explicitly ask them if the technology helped them socialize, or if it inhibited their efforts to socialize.

Figure 2: Social-Task activity overlap

SUMMARY

In summary, as technology moves quickly to enable distance education and learning environments, one concern that has to be dealt with is how students best interact with the technology. In understanding this, one must first understand the process of learning and then the process by which people interact with technology. This paper has provided a brief review of some of the theories in these areas. Socialization and its impact on learning were prevalent themes throughout the reviews. This ultimately led to the proposal to study differences in socialization between an on-campus and distance education class.

The amount of socialization between distance and on-campus respondents showed significance in two areas. First, the on-campus respondents reported more socialization in their group meetings than did the distance education respondents. Second, the distance education respondents strongly disagreed that there was too much socialization, indicating a willingness for more socialization. While both groups were on the 'agree' side of the scale when asked if everyone in their group contributed equally, it needs to be noted that the DIST group agreed significantly less. However, more direct measures for differences in participation did not prove significant.

This study provides the basis for future research in several ways. First, there is some support from this preliminary data that socialization differences do exist between students in on-campus and distance education classes. Second, based on this research, the questionnaire can be refined so that it can better detect the differences. A factor analysis of this questionnaire identifies six factors within the data. In four of these factors, one of the statistically significant characteristics identified in this study provides the anchor. Finally, the identification and corresponding understanding of the socialization needs associated with learning will help distance education better achieve its goal of providing a better learning environment.

REFERENCES

Alderfer, C. P. (1972). *Existence, Relatedness and Growth: Human Needs in Organizational Settings*. New York: Free Press.

Aranda, E. K., Aranda L.H. and Conlon, K. (1998). *Teams: Structure, process, culture and politics*, Englewood Cliffs, NJ: Prentice-Hall.

Bandura, A. (1977). *Social Learning Theory*. Englewood Cliffs, NJ: Prentice-Hall.

Beebe, S. A. and Masterson, J. T. (1986). *Communicating in Small Groups: Principals and Practices, 2ⁿᵈ ed.* Glenview, Illinois: Scott, Foresman and Company.

Bilimoria, D. and Wheeler, J. V. (1995). Learning-centered education: A guide to resources and implementation. *Journal of Management Education*, 19(3), 326-341.

Black, J. (1997). Available on the World Wide Web at: http://www.news.com/News/Item/0,4,7147,00.html. Accessed January 12, 2000.

Briggs, R.O., Nunamaker, J. F., Jr. and Sprague, R. H., Jr. (1998). 1001 unanswered research questions in GSS. *Journal of Management Information Systems*, Winter, 14(3), 3-21.

Carr, H. A. (1931). The laws of association. *Psychological Review*, 38, 212-228.

Chaplin. J. P. and T. S. Krawiec. (1960). *Systems and Theories in Psychology.* New York: Holt, Rinehart and Winston.

Chidambaram, L. (1996). Relational development in computer-supported groups. *MIS Quarterly*, June.

Daft, R. L. and R. H. Lengel. (1986). Organizational information requirements, media richness and structural design. *Management Science*, May, 32(5), 554-571.

Dede, C. (1996). The evolution of distance education: Emerging technologies and distributed learning. *American Journal of Distance Education*, 10(2), 4-36.

DelBecq, A. L. and Van de Ven, A. (1971). A group process model for problem identification and program planning. *The Journal of Applied Behavioral Science*, 7(4), 466-492.

DeSanctis, G. and Gallupe, B. (1985). Group decision support systems: A new frontier. *Data Base*, Winter, 16(1), 3-10.

Ebbinhaus, H. (1913). *Memory, A Contribution to Experimental Psychology*, Translated by Ruger and Bussenius.

Fjermestad, J. and Hiltz, S. R. (1999). An assessment of group support systems experimental research: Methodology and results. *Journal of Management Information Systems*, Winter, 15(3), 7-149.

Gobal, A.G., Bostrom, R. B. and Chin, W. (1993). Applying adaptive structuration theory to investigate the process of group support Systems. *Journal of Management Information Systems*, Winter, 9(3), 45-69.

Gulliksen, H. (1934). A rational equation of the learning curve based upon Thorndike's law of effect. *Journal of General Psychology*, 11, 395-434.

Haythornthwaite, C., Kazmer, M. M., Robins, J. and Showmaker, S. (2000). Community development among distance learners. *Journal of Computer-Mediated Communication*, September, 6(1).

Hearn, G. and Scott, D. (1998). Students staying home. *Futures*, September, 30(7), 731-737.

Hills, H. and Francis, P. (1999). Interaction learning. *People Management*, 5(14), 48-49.

Hogan, D. and Kwiatkowksi, R. (1998). Emotional aspects of large group teaching. *Human Relations*, November, 51(11), 1403-1417.

Hora, N. and Kling, R. (At Press, 2001). *Information, Communications and Society*. Available on the World Wide Web at: http://www.slis.indiana.edu/CSI/wp00-01.html. Accessed January 12, 2001.

Hull, C. (1943). *Principles of Behavior.* New York: Appleton-Century-Crofts.

Kelley, H. H. (1951). Communication in experimentally created hierarchies. *Human Relations*, 4, 39-56.

Kling, R. (2000). Learning about information technologies and social change: The contribution of social informatics. *Information Society*, 16(3), 217-232.

Leidner, D. E. and Jarvenpaa, S. L. (1995). The use of information technology to enhance management school education: A theoretical view. *MIS Quarterly*, September, 265- 291.

Lewin, K. (1951). *Field Theory in Social Science: Selected Theoretical Papers*. Cartwright, D. (Ed.), New York: Harper and Row.

Linstone, H. A. and Turoff, M. (1975). *The Delphi Method: Techniques and Applications* Reading, MA: Addison-Wesley.

Martz, Jr., W. B. and Landof, G. (2000). Information systems careers: A comparison of expectations. *Journal of Computer Information Systems*, Winter, 40(2), 41-46.

McClelland, D. (1961). *The Achieving Society.* New York: Van Nostrand Reinhold.

Miner, J. B. (1980). *Theories of Organizational Behavior*. Hinsdale, IL: Dryden Press, 18.

Nunamaker, Jr., J. F., Dennis, A. R., Valacich, J. S., Vogel, D. R. and George, J. F. (1991). Electronic meeting systems to support group work. *Communications of the ACM*, 34, 42-58.

Osborn, A. F. (1953). *Applied Imagination.* New York: Charles Scribner's and Sons.

Papert, S. (1980). *Mindstorms.* New York: Basic Books.

Poole, M. S. and DeSanctis, G. (1990). Understanding the use of group decision support systems: The theory of adaptive structuration. In Fulk, J. and Steinfeld, C. (Eds.), *Organizations and Communication Technology*. New Bury Park, CA: Sage Publications, 173-193.

Russell, T. (2001). Available on the World Wide Web at: http://nova.teleeducation.nb.ca/nosignificantdifference/. Accessed January 12, 2001.

Saaty, T. L. (1980). *The Analytical Hierarchy Approach*. New York: McGraw-Hill.

Short, J., Williams, E. and Christie, B. (1976). *The Social Psychology of Telecommunications*. New York: John Wiley.

Shipley, T. E. and Veroff, J. (1952). A projective measure of need affiliation. *Journal of Experimental Psychology*, 43, 349-356.

TeleEducation, NB. (2001). Available on the World Wide Web at: http://teleeducation.nb.ca/anygood/. Accessed January 12, 2001.

Tu, C-H. (2000). Online learning migration: From social learning theory to social presence theory in the CMC environment. *Journal of Network and Computer Applications*, 23, 27-37.

Walther, J.B. (1992). "Interpersonal Effects in Computer-Mediated Interaction: A Relational Perspective," *Communications Research*, February, 19(1), 52-90.

APPENDIX: RESEARCH QUESTIONNAIRE

We are looking at ways to improve the MBA program and this survey will help us do that. Please take a few minutes and answer this survey as it pertains to IS619. Some of the questions may seem redundant. The reason for this is to ensure the accuracy of your answers and to make sure this is a valid survey. As such, please read each question carefully and pay particular attention to the scale you are using to answer the question. All data will be kept confidential.

Demographics:
1. What is your gender? (circle one)   male   female
2. In which age group do you fall? (circle one)   21-25   26-30   31-35   36-40   41-45   46-50   50+
3. How many semesters (including this one) have you been in the UCCS MBA program? _____
4. How many MBA courses have you taken (including this semester)? _____ courses
5. If you have a job, how many hours do you work each week? _____ hours/week
6. How many hours do you spend each week on your MBA work? _____ hours/week
7. If you have one, what is your area of emphasis? _____
8. What is your current GPA? _____
9. Some classes require a major group project. How many of these major group project teams have you been on (all MBA classes, including this semester)? _____ teams

You may have had a group project in IS619. If so please answer questions 10 – 14 relating to your experience with your group. If you did not have a required group project, please continue with question 16.

10. Did the instructor assign groups or did the students pick their own group?
     (circle one) <u>instructor assigned</u>   <u>student assigned</u>
11. On average, how many hours did you spend with your group each week? _____ hours/week
12. On average, how many meetings did your group hold each week? _____ meetings/week

For the purpose of this survey, we break down the time spent in meetings as time spent on socializing, and time spent working on the assigned task. For questions 13 and 14 please indicate the percentage of time spent on socializing and the time spent on task. The two percentages should total 100%.

13. On average, what percentage of your meetings was spent on socializing? _____ %
14. On average, what percentage of your meetings was spent on the project task? _____ %
                                                                      Total   100%

15. Not including the groups that were assigned to complete the group project requirements, did you form any group(s) with other students in the class? (indicate by placing an X in the appropriate line)
_____ Yes, it had _____ members
_____ No, I did not form any other groups

It can sometimes take some time before a student feels comfortable with the complexity encountered in a particular class. The following are some of the things included in our definition of feeling comfortable: believing you can meet the expectations outlined for the course; feeling you can ask a fellow student or the instructor for help; following the lectures and participating in the discussions.

16. At what point during the course did you feel comfortable? (please circle one)

<u>first day</u>   <u>¼ of the way through</u>   <u>½ way through</u>   <u>¾ of the way through</u>   <u>never felt comfortable</u>

17. At what point during the course did you first ask non-trivial questions of fellow students or the instructor (e.g. clarification or administrative questions about the syllabus would be considered trivial whereas content-oriented questions for fellow students or the instructor would be considered non-trivial)?

<u>first day</u>   <u>¼ of the way through</u>   <u>½ way through</u>   <u>¾ of the way through</u>   <u>never asked questions</u>

You can accomplish group work in a same-place environment (face-to-face) or at a distance (group members do not meet face-to-face). Questions 17 – 21 refer to the technology (i.e. email, telephone) you used to do group work at a distance. Referring to the scale (1 = strongly agree, 4 = neutral, 7 = strongly disagree), circle the appropriate response. If you always met face-to-face please skip ahead to question 22.

		Strongly Agree 1	2	3	Neutral 4	5	Strongly Disagree 6	7
18.	The technology we used for our group work was easy to use.	1	2	3	4	5	6	7
19.	The technology we used for our group work helped us get our work done.	1	2	3	4	5	6	7
20.	It did not take a lot of extra work to install the technology we used for our group work.	1	2	3	4	5	6	7
21.	I will use this technology again for my next group project.	1	2	3	4	5	6	7

22. What was the name of the technology(ies) that you used? (please list all technologies)

_____

_____

Using your group experience in this course, please indicate your level of agreement with questions 22 – 39 below. Please refer to the scale (1 = strongly agree, 4 = neutral, 7 = strongly disagree) and circle the appropriate response.

		Strongly Agree 1	2	3	Neutral 4	5	Strongly Disagree 6	7
23.	I do not think my work group experience was valuable for my education	1	2	3	4	5	6	7
24.	There was too much socialization in my group	1	2	3	4	5	6	7
25.	The grading of the group project was fair	1	2	3	4	5	6	7
26.	The technology used in the class to support groups was too complex	1	2	3	4	5	6	7
27.	I was satisfied with this course	1	2	3	4	5	6	7
28.	I think this course served my needs	1	2	3	4	5	6	7
29.	I was disappointed in how the course worked out	1	2	3	4	5	6	7
30.	The level of interaction in my group was low	1	2	3	4	5	6	7
31.	Everyone in my group did their fair share of work	1	2	3	4	5	6	7
32.	I participated in this group more than I usually do in my other groups	1	2	3	4	5	6	7
33.	Group work is just busy work in classes	1	2	3	4	5	6	7
34.	Groups do not stay on task and waste time	1	2	3	4	5	6	7
35.	Group work is not important to my career	1	2	3	4	5	6	7
36.	I like working in groups in this program	1	2	3	4	5	6	7
37.	The basic idea of working in groups is good	1	2	3	4	5	6	7
38.	The importance of group work is overemphasized	1	2	3	4	5	6	7
39.	The use of group work in the program is an advantage	1	2	3	4	5	6	7
40.	Technology was helpful for our group work	1	2	3	4	5	6	7
41.	I felt that I was really part of my group	1	2	3	4	5	6	7
42.	I would be willing to work in the same group again	1	2	3	4	5	6	7

Chapter VIII

Online Courses: Strategies for Success

Linda Cooper
Macon State College, USA

A number of post-secondary institutions are looking more seriously at offering online courses to meet the educational needs of a fast-paced, computer-literate society.

In 1998, Macon State College (MSC) began offering an online Business Computer Applications course, and since its inception, approximately 250 students have enrolled in the 16-week (one-semester) course. Business Computer Applications provides instruction in basic computer concepts and terminology as well as instruction using the software program, Microsoft Office. It is one of the core courses required of all business majors; however, many other students also enroll in the class.

This chapter provides instructors who are interested in offering online classes with various strategies used and found successful in the instruction of an online Business Computer Applications course. Topics such as the importance of an initial class meeting, providing diverse instructional materials, the value of student course evaluations, and the dilemma of student assessment procedures will be addressed.

Although a course management system (CMS) is used to manage the online Business Computer Applications course discussed in this chapter, many of the procedures incorporated can be effective in the facilitation of any online course. The advantages of using a CMS to implement and manage online courses will also be discussed later in this chapter.

INTRODUCTION

With working adults becoming an increasingly large percentage of the college population and with greater numbers of students having computer and Internet experience prior to entering college, a number of post-secondary institutions are looking more seriously at offering online instruction to meet students' educational needs.

In fact, according to International Data, "the e-learning market, which includes Internet and Intranet courses, will grow from $4 billion to $15 billion worldwide in the four years ending in 2002" (Jones, 2000); and Market Data Retrieval recently reported that 72% of colleges responding to its Higher Ed Technology Survey offer distance-learning programs that involve online resources of some kind (Technology News, 2001).

This chapter provides instructors who are interested in offering online classes with various strategies used and found successful in the instruction of an online Business Computer Applications course. Topics such as the importance of an initial class meeting, providing diverse instructional materials, the value of student course evaluations, and the dilemma of student assessment procedures will be addressed.

Although a course management system (CMS) is used to manage the online Business Computer Applications course discussed in this chapter, many of the procedures incorporated can be effective in the facilitation of any online course. The advantages of using a CMS to implement and manage online courses will also be discussed later in this chapter.

PLANNING THE ONLINE COURSE

Online instruction can be offered in a variety of formats, and the process selected by instructors will depend on such factors as whether they are encouraged and supported by the administration, have the technological infrastructure available at their school to support online instruction, have access to technical support, or have technical knowledge and expertise themselves.

Once a decision is made regarding the technological format that will be used, the instructor can begin with the course design and planning and developing the course. During the planning stage, it is important that the instructor define course goals and objectives, identify interaction procedures to be used in the class, decide on instructional materials or course content, and determine how the course content will be organized and made available to students online (Cooper, 1999).

Implementation considerations by the instructor include such decisions as how to introduce students to the logistics of online learning, how to evaluate students on their understanding of course content and achievement of course objectives, how students will evaluate the effectiveness of online instruction, and how to continually improve the online course and the online learning process (Cooper, 1999).

Business Computer Applications Background

In 1998, Macon State College (MSC) began offering an online Business Computer Applications course, and since its inception, about 250 students have enrolled in the 16-week (one-semester) course. Approximately 20-25 students enroll in each of the online sections of the course. By limiting the number of students in the course, the instructor is better able to interact with all class members and will minimize the need for logistical support.

Business Computer Applications provides instruction in basic computer concepts and terminology as well as instruction using the software program, Microsoft Office. It is one of the core courses required of all business majors; however, many other students also enroll in the class.

In the past, the course has been taught only in the traditional format. Class activities included instructor lecture, student discussion, instructor demonstration, hands-on computer activities, etc., and although numerous sections of the class are still taught in this traditional format, online sections are offered as well. The online classes provide those students who may already be familiar with the course material, who find it difficult to attend classes on campus because of work or home scheduling conflicts, or who are motivated and able to manage their time effectively the opportunity to complete the class somewhat independently.

Enrollment in the online Business Computer Applications course requires that students have a 2.5 grade point average, Internet access, and access to a computer equipped with Microsoft Office software. Online students attend an initial class meeting or orientation session, during which they meet the instructor and each other and have the opportunity to ask questions.

Because the course provides instruction in theory (computer theory and concepts) and computer software applications (Microsoft Office), two textbooks are used. The theory book contains eight chapters and covers topics such as the history of computing; the design, function, and relationships between internal components of a computer; how data is processed and stored internally and externally; the effect of computers on society; and how to purchase computer hardware and software. Students are responsible for approximately one chapter per week and are tested after every two chapters. These exams are generally objective in nature, administered online, and graded automatically. Students take them on an assigned day but at a time convenient to them. When finished with the exams, students can see the correct answer to each of the questions, as well as their test grade. Students also take a comprehensive final exam over the theory textbook.

The Microsoft Office textbook is divided into six sections. Students learn how to work and manage files in the Windows environment (one-two weeks); how to use the Internet for communicating and research (one week); and how to use the software applications, Microsoft Word, Microsoft Excel, Microsoft Access (three weeks each), and Microsoft PowerPoint (one week). To help them with learning each of the applications, they have a CD-ROM tutorial and access to online videos in addition to step-by-step instructions provided in the textbook.

Students report to campus three times during the semester to take tests over the software applications. They are also required to research a business technology topic using the Internet and then write a research paper and create a PowerPoint presentation on that topic.

Student Profile

During the 1999-2000 academic year, the average student enrolled in the online Business Computer Applications course was 27 years in age, female (61%), and employed. In fact, of the online students, 56% were employed full-time, 28% were employed part-time, and 16% were unemployed. In most cases, the unemployed student was a stay-at-home mother with children.

In comparison, the average student enrolled in the traditional class during the 1999-2000 academic year was 23 years of age, also female (64%), and employed part-time. Of traditional students, 66% were employed part-time, 33% were employed full-time, and 7% were unemployed. Thus, the biggest difference between students enrolled in the online class and the traditional class was employment status (Cooper, 2001).

Initial Class Meeting

Because online learning is a new experience for most students, an initial class meeting is beneficial. It provides an excellent opportunity for students to meet the instructor and each other, ask questions, and become acquainted with course logistics (Cooper, 1999). Students also need to be aware of the hardware and software that they will need as well as the level of computing proficiency required (Hanna et al., 2000).

During the class meeting, it is helpful to go over information typically covered the first day of a regular class such as syllabus, textbook, instructor office hours, testing procedures, etc. In addition to the syllabus, one of the most beneficial handouts to both students and the instructor is the semester calendar (also available online), which includes a timeline or schedule of activities, assignments, and test dates for each week of the semester. Not only does the schedule provide students with a weekly "to do" list, but it also reminds students of their learning objectives and keeps both the students and the instructor on task.

The initial meeting also furnishes students with an explanation of what an online course is, the role of the instructor in the online classroom, student expectations, and the mechanics of how "everything works." Because the instructor has access to the student roster prior to this meeting, it is advantageous to enter all user names into the system beforehand. Doing so allows students during this class session to log on with their assigned user name and password and actually navigate the course website and become familiar with the content and the various online features.

The opportunity for students to actually log onto the course website and become familiar with it helps answer any questions they might have and alleviates any anxieties that they might be experiencing. An introduction to the online course content can also prevent students when later working on their own from wasting time and becoming "frustrated with the system to the point where they abandon it and any subsequent attempts to master its content" (Bayram, 1999).

Given that the majority of problems students encounter are computer-related, it is also helpful to spend time during the initial class meeting demonstrating proper installation of the tutorial CD-ROM, downloading and installing video player software, running a PowerPoint presentation on the Internet, and sending and receiving attachments.

Since students tend to forget some of the information presented during the session, a "FAQ" or "frequently asked questions" link is added to the course homepage. This page provides answers to such questions as "How do I send an attachment?" "How do I install course software?" and "How do I get started in the course?" Should they need additional assistance with any of these operations, students are encouraged to visit the campus lab or contact the instructor.

It is also helpful during the initial class session to have students complete a survey or profile sheet. The information provided by them can be helpful in determining their learning needs and for providing them with diverse instructional materials. It can also help students assess their readiness for online learning (Hanna et al., 2000).

In addition, because students who miss the orientation session are more likely to drop the course, the entire session is videotaped and made available to them—both in the library and online.

When it is not possible to provide an initial class meeting for an online class, other strategies can be utilized. Prior to the beginning of class, the instructor can send students a letter or email introducing him/herself, welcoming students to the class, furnishing them the URL or online course website address, providing instructions for accessing the online learning materials, and highlighting specific online features or Web pages. Although the syllabus and course schedule are both provided online, it is helpful to also include them with the letter.

In this first written communication, it is also helpful if students are asked to communicate with the instructor during the first week of class either through email or telephone to ensure that they understand the content organization and their expectations as online students.

Online Communication

An important and necessary component to successful web-based instruction is ongoing communication. The instructor must be able to communicate with the students throughout the semester, and students must be able to communicate with the instructor and receive prompt assistance when they encounter problems or have questions. Students also need to be able to interact with one another.

Instructor-Student Communication

To maintain regular instructor-student communication, it is beneficial to send students a class announcement every week that provides an overview of the upcoming week's activities, provides any additional information or explanations about course content or assignments, reminds them of test dates, and addresses any student concerns expressed to the instructor during the previous week.

To encourage discussion of course content and interaction of ideas in the Business Computer Applications course, the instructor posts content-related topics regularly. Discussion questions should require thought, problem solving, and/or research but should be brief, as students are more likely to participate if the topic is concise and does not require lengthy responses. Participation is a part of the students' final grades, and although they are graded on the frequency of their participation, they are also graded on the quality of their input. Extra credit points are given to students who take the initiative to begin their own discussion of ideas and/or opinions.

Student-Instructor Communication

Because the students do not see the instructor on a daily basis, the instructor should check email and telephone messages frequently and on weekends if possible, so that students are able to get prompt responses when they do have questions or require assistance. In addition, by keeping specific office hours, the instructor assures students that he/she is available at specific times. To maintain continued student-instructor communication and to prevent students from simply "drifting off" during the semester, students are asked to email the instructor every couple of weeks to keep him/her informed of their progress.

Student-Student Communication

To encourage communication among students and to prevent them from feeling isolated in the class, students are required to participate regularly in class discussion. It is helpful at the beginning of class to have them share with the class some biographical information about themselves. Not only does it help them to get to know each other but to better "understand each other's perspectives" (Hanna et al., 2000).

Using the CMS threaded discussion feature or a listserve, students can respond to topics presented by the instructor, ask questions, or read and respond to other class members' comments or questions. Participation in discussion is very helpful as it enables them to assist each other in their understanding of course material and with assignments. All students in the class are able to read other students' postings in the discussion mode. As mentioned previously, as an incentive to encourage students to initiate their own discussions with other class members, they are given extra credit points for doing so.

Although real-time or chat sessions can prove helpful for test review sessions and during scheduled instructor office hours, most students do not prefer this type of session for discussing course content in large groups. One reason is that when a large number of students are logged on at one time, it takes a considerable amount of time for the instructor and students to discuss a limited amount of course content. Inability to type or a lack of proficiency at using the keyboard also makes it difficult for students to respond quickly to a discussion question. Additionally, real-time chat sessions require that "all participants be online at the same time to communicate" and, therefore, often result in "conversation creep," with the fastest computers getting the most "talk time" (Ciabattari, 1997).

An alternative to large group chat sessions is to assign groups of five or fewer students to a discussion group. In smaller groups, students will have a greater opportunity to participate and to improve the quality of discussion. Additionally, in smaller groups, students are more likely to discuss topics more freely, share their own experiences, and feel more a part of the class.

Students explain in their end-of-semester class evaluations that they generally prefer threaded discussions because they give them time to think about their responses first. Threaded discussions also enable them to participate at a more comfortable pace and at times more convenient to their schedules. In addition, by having access to their weekly assignments and related learning materials beforehand, as they do in the online Business Computer Applications course, they are able to progress through the course with fewer questions and without a great deal of instructor supervision or student assistance.

However, in online classes where instructors use chat sessions to present course assignments, announce test dates, and/or discuss course content, the chat sessions are basically a class meeting and the only source of receiving information for students; therefore, when students miss a session, they get behind in their work.

Regardless of whether the online class uses synchronous or asynchronous communication or both, as in any class some students participate much more readily in class discussion than others. By scheduling discussion sessions in both formats during the term, however, the instructor provides students with the opportunity to engage in the discussion format most convenient to them and with which they are most comfortable.

Diverse Instructional Materials

Since all students have different learning styles and respond differently to various learning activities, it is important to offer them instructional materials in a variety of formats. In addition to providing online learning materials for each module or chapter such as clearly stated learning objectives, lecture notes, and assignments, automatically graded self-tests that evaluate students on achievement of the stated objectives can be included. Answers to chapter questions, PowerPoint presentations that summarize the main points of each chapter or topic, online videos of class lectures, and links to textbook interactive websites can also be included.

The theory segment of the Business Computer Applications class is structured by textbook chapter. When students access the course homepage, one of the options or icons with which they are presented is the title and/or picture of the textbook. When students select this textbook icon, they view a list of chapters. When they select a particular chapter, they are presented with links to Web pages such as chapter objectives, lecture notes or study guides, assignments, readings, answers to end-of-the-chapter questions, practice tests, and the textbook website.

The Microsoft Office segment of the course is structured by software application. When students access the course homepage, they are presented with a link to the online learning resources of the Microsoft Office textbook. When students select this link, they view a list of the various software application modules: Windows Environment, Microsoft Word, Microsoft Excel, Microsoft Access, Microsoft PowerPoint, and the Internet. For each application module, there are links to module objectives, textbook readings, assignments, answers to end-of-the-chapter questions and select exercises, videos, assigned CD-ROM modules, practice tests, and textbook website.

Because students often feel that they are faced with a vast amount of information to read and do not have the advantage of hearing class lectures, it is helpful to provide test study guides and to schedule optional test review sessions either online or on-campus to help them prepare for exams.

In addition, because students in online classes often do not have access to fast Internet connections, it is advantageous to provide as many instructional materials as possible in CD-ROM format. In the Business Computer Applications course, students have a CD-ROM that provides an interactive tutorial to the computer applications. The tutorial is a simulation that sets objectives, asks students to complete specific tasks on the computer, shows them how to complete the task if they don't know, and provides them with feedback after the completion of each task. By using the CD-ROM, students are able to work offline and actually receive individualized instruction in those areas with which they need assistance. CD-ROMs that include videos, interactive exercises, and glossaries today accompany a number of textbooks.

Many textbook vendors have also created their own websites for students to access, and many of these websites will send results of student exercises or practice tests to the instructor. By providing links to these sites, students are encouraged to access them.

Although students may choose not to access all of the online learning resources available to them, by presenting a variety of resources, the instructor increases the chances of reaching each of them at some level; therefore, the chances for learning are also increased.

Student Testing

A continuous dilemma for instructors of online classes is whether to utilize online testing or require students to come to campus to take exams. Objective style online tests can be automatically graded, and can provide immediate feedback to the students, and also eliminate instructor grading. In addition, if a CMS is utilized for online class management, the instructor is able to set up tests in advance.

The consequence of online testing though is that the instructor can never be sure if the student enrolled in the class actually took the test. In the Business Computer Applications course, this dilemma is resolved by requiring students to come to campus for a comprehensive final exam and counting it a substantial percentage of their final grade.

On the other hand, when students are required to come to campus for testing, it often presents a scheduling problem for them. However, on-campus testing does eliminate the need for a comprehensive exam counting such a large percentage of the grade.

For the Business Computer Applications course, both testing formats are utilized. For the hands-on computer exams, students come to campus. To prepare for the applications exams, students can take online practice tests and submit them to the instructor for checking.

For the theory segment of the course, students take online, automatically graded objective tests, and although they are required to take them on specific dates, they can take them at any time on those dates. The final exam then covers only the theory content and is administered on-campus. Thus far, this strategy seems to satisfy most of the students and eliminates the need to count the final exam such a large percentage.

ONLINE COURSE EVALUATIONS

In an effort to continually improve online instruction, frequent evaluations throughout the term are extremely useful. Aspacher (1997) suggests three separate evaluations during the course.

- The first survey asking students to evaluate the orientation session can be distributed during the first week; the results are helpful in planning future orientation sessions. At the midpoint of the course a, telephone survey might be used to ask students about their satisfaction with how the class is progressing. At the end of the term, a more comprehensive written survey can be administered.

- In the Business Computer Applications course, one of the options available to the students is an online "One-Minute Survey." When students access this option, they are asked two simple questions: "What in this course helped your learning?" and "What in this course hindered your learning?" Although the instructor periodically prompts students to complete the survey, they may complete it at any time during the semester.

- At the conclusion of the course, a more formal Online Course Evaluation form is sent to students as an attachment. They are asked to complete it, print it out, and bring it to class on final exam day. On the evaluation form they are asked to evaluate the course, its contents, availability of the instructor, learning resources, testing methods, and interaction procedures, as well as their understanding of the class organization and grading process. Students are also asked what features they liked best and least about the course and are encouraged to make practical suggestions to improve the course.

Student evaluations help determine the effectiveness of the various components of an online course and address areas that may need revision; they also communicate to students that their input is valuable.

Other Tips

Be Knowledgeable of Online Course Technology

By being familiar with the software and hardware used in the class and working through all online class components beforehand, the instructor will be able to answer students' questions—both content-related and technical—promptly and with expertise. He or she will also be able to anticipate student needs and questions before the class begins, which can prevent student problems and frustration later.

Respond to Student Questions and Problems Quickly

By regularly checking email and telephone messages and promptly responding to students' questions and concerns, the instructor lets the students know that he/she is readily available and interested in helping them. Prompt responses also keep students from feeling isolated in the class.

Student Withdrawals

A major obstacle facing online courses is the large number of student withdrawals. Students who enroll in an online course often do not understand the requirements necessary for succeeding. Consequently, they drop the course when they realize they need a more structured environment. Thus, providing information to both faculty and students prior to advisement and registration concerning content organization, student expectations, required hardware and software, and required computer proficiency is a necessary and important factor in student success.

Another step that might be taken to minimize the number of student withdrawals in online classes is to invite online class members to attend the regular class if they feel they need additional assistance. If both the online class and the regular or traditional class follow the same weekly schedule, it is easy for them to determine the classes they would like to attend.

Student Scheduling

Another approach to meet the needs and schedules of students interested in enrolling in an online course is to offer at least two sessions of the class—during the day and during the evening. Because students in the Business Computer Applications course are required to attend class for the orientation session and on selected exam dates, it is important that these sessions be offered at times conducive to their schedules.

Include Fun Activities

Including games or fun activities into the course can add variety to the course as well as make learning more fun for the students. "The World Wide Web provides a wonderful playground to explore and gain new ideas and insights into almost every conceivable topic" (Hanna et al., 2000).

Advantages of Using a Course Management System (CMS)

If teachers have access to a server but possess limited time or technical expertise, they might consider using a commercially developed course management system (CMS) to set up and manage the online class. With a CMS, instructors must still develop their own course content or individual files in HTML format (an easy process when using one of the HTML conversion programs), but the CMS software takes care of linking the documents for student navigation. Examples of such systems include Topclass, Web Course in a Box, and Web CT. The systems generally provide their own tools for communication such as email, threaded discussion, and teacher announcements. Additionally, these systems grade online student tests automatically and allow instructors to track student progress.

WebCT is the CMS used in the management of the Business Computer Applications course discussed in this chapter. The system is purchased by the school, housed on a school server, and administered by the Information Technology Department. Thus, it is available for use by any instructor in the school and alleviates faculty members from system administration responsibilities. The use of a CMS or course management system program offers many advantages.

First, all course content, links to websites, online tests, etc., can be set up prior to the beginning of class. Instructors do not need to be well-versed in programming or be computer experts; if they can create in HTML format the various documents that they want to make available to students (objectives, lecture notes, study guides), uploading them into the CMS is a very simple procedure. In addition, a CMS can make the course more visually appealing and more professional looking with little designer expertise on the part of the instructor.

"In-house" Communication

With a CMS, there is no need to establish separate listservs or keep track of student email addresses, as these functions are built-in components. Using the "email" feature, the instructor or students can send private or personal messages to each other, and email addresses of anyone enrolled in the course are accessible to all other class members.

Instructor announcements and topics for class discussions are sent to the entire class using the "discussion" mode. Real-time discussions are conducted through the "chat" mode.

Using a CMS, users are immediately notified when they log on if they have an email message or if a new discussion item has been posted, a feature that keeps them from having to navigate through the various links in order to read any new messages. Additionally when they log on, students receive pop-up reminders about tests that are scheduled on that day or within the next few days.

Ease of Use by Students

Because the course layout and content organization does not change during the semester, students become familiar with the location of all online components. In addition, they can continue working through class materials where they left off the last time they logged on.

Online Testing

By using a CMS, instructors can set up tests in advance. They can import test questions from test banks, assign points to each test question and set up date and time restrictions. Upon completion of the tests, students can see the correct answer to each question, read background information about each question and answer, and see their grades immediately. In addition, their grades are posted online so both they and the instructor can view them at any time during the semester.

Monitoring Student Activity

Using a CMS allows the instructor the capability to track student activity throughout the term. At any time during the semester, the instructor can check to see which modules students have accessed and the dates on which they accessed them. The instructor can also see which modules were accessed or completed more than once. Being able to do this gives the instructor the capability of observing which students are on task, which ones might need some personal assistance or encouragement, and which modules are giving students difficulty.

Integration of CMS and School Database

Lastly, by using a CMS such as WebCT, the school's database can be used as a source for inputting students into the online class roster. For example, all instructors using the WebCT system follow a specific format when entering enrolled students; by doing so, they only have to enter students' user names. They do not need to input student passwords, as their Social Security number is the automatically assigned password—although students can easily change it once they are enrolled into the online course. Additionally, when students log on, they are logged on to all WebCT online classes in which they are enrolled; and they have to remember only one user name and one password.

CONCLUSION

Online instruction can offer new challenges and opportunities to both students and teachers. They can provide an alternative to regularly scheduled classes and can deliver the same services as a regular classroom environment. Developing an online course consists of: (1) determining the most appropriate technological means for course facilitation and class interaction; (2) planning and developing diverse course materials; (3) deciding the most appropriate means for student assessment; and (4) determining an effective approach for online course evaluation.

A key to involving students in online learning is to provide them with an understanding of how the online class functions and what is expected of them as students. Such information can be provided in an orientation session or a package of introductory information mailed to the students prior to the beginning of class.

Implementation of an online class is an ongoing process. As students evaluate the various components of the course and its overall effectiveness, the instructor is able to make necessary revisions as well as plan and improve future online courses. Instructional materials, testing procedures, or scheduled meeting times may change as a result of both positive and negative class experiences or as students express their opinions of what helped or hindered their learning in the class. There are a number of instructional components and strategies to be considered by instructors or designers when creating and implementing an online course. Table 1 presents a checklist of those presented in this chapter.

If the course is carefully planned and implemented and the instructor is open to student feedback and continuous improvement, online instruction can provide an effective educational environment and offer a viable alternative to traditional classroom instruction.

Additional research is needed, however, to assess the effectiveness of online instruction in this and other classes.

REFERENCES

Anspacher. (1997). Designing a curriculum to meet the needs of online

Table 1: A short survey

Have you....	Yes	No
Included for each unit, chapter or module		
List of objectives		
Required readings		
Vocabulary or list of important terms		
Lecture notes and/or Study Guide		
Assignments		
Answers to Selected questions and/or exercises		
Practice Exams		
Powerpoint presentations		
Online videos		
Links to Web sites		
Decided on Class Communication Procedures		
Threaded discussion		
Chat or Real-time discussion		
Both		
Determined Testing Format and Procedures		
Online exams		
On-campus exams		
Both		
Included the following in the introductory session or letter		
Explanation of online instruction/learning		
Instructor's role		
Student expectations		
Textbook organization		
Syllabus		
Course schedule or weekly calendar of activities, modules, and/or assignments		
Exam dates and testing procedures		
Course URL or Web site address		
Instructions for logging on and maneuvering online course content		
Answers to frequently asked questions		

faculty and students. *The College Board: Delivering Online Courses.* Washington, DC, November.

Bayram, S. (1999). Internet learning initiatives: How well do Turkish virtual classrooms work? *T.H.E. Journal*, May, 65-68.

Ciabattari, M. (1997). Effective delivery systems for online programs. *The College Board: Delivering Online Courses.* Washington, DC, November.

Cooper, L. (2001). A comparison of online and traditional computer applications classes. *T.H.E. Journal*, March, 28(8), 52-58.

Cooper, L. (1999). Anatomy of an online course. *T.H.E. Journal*, February, 26(7), 45-51.

Cooper, L. (1999). Planning an online course. *Business Education Forum*, October, 54(1), 45-46.

Denigris, J. and Witchel, A. (2000). *Teaching the Learning Organization With Tomorrow's Tools Today.* Boston, MA: Pearson Custom Publishing.

Graziadei, W. D., Gallagher, S., Brown, R. and Sasiadek, J. (2001). *Building Asynchronous and Synchronous Teaching-Learning Environments: Exploring a Course/Classroom Management System Solution.* Available on the World Wide Web at: http://horizon.unc.edu/projects/..

Hanna, D. E., Glowacki-Dudka, M. and Conceicao-Runlee, S. (2000). *147 Practical Tips for Teaching Online Groups*: *Essentials of Web-Based Education.* Madison, WI: Atwood Publishing.

James, M. and Voigt, M. (2001). Tips from the trenches: Delivering online courses effectively. *Business Education Forum*, February, 56-60.

Jones, D. (2000). Will business schools go out of business? E-learning, corporate academies change the rules. *USA Today*, May 23.

Kauffman, R. (1996). Assessing the virtual university. *Adult Assessment Forum*, Summer, 13-16.

Palloff, R. M. and Pratt, K. (1999). *Building Learning Communities in Cyberspace: Effective Strategies for the Online Classroom.* San Francisco: Jossey-Bass Publishers.

Serwatka. (1999). Internet distance learning: How do I put my course on the Web? *T.H.E. Journal*, May, 71-74.

Technology News and Notes: Courses With No Class. (2001). *Smart Computing*, January, 12(1), 7.

Terry, N. (2000). MBA student perceptions about the effectiveness of Internet instruction. *Business Education Forum*, April, 42-44.

Chapter IX

Institutional and Library Services for Distance Education Courses and Programs[1]

Elizabeth Buchanan
University of Wisconsin-Milwaukee, USA

Institutions are quickly embracing distance education in the forms of online or web-based courses and programs at phenomenal rates. Often, however, significant institutional structures, including such areas as registration, advising, library, and technical support are overlooked until too late. Institutions must have clear, well-planned strategies in place in order to maximize their students' learning experiences and overall satisfaction with distance education programs to avoid attrition and maximize retention. This chapter provides many useful and easy to implement strategies for institutions considering distance education, as well as for those already engaged in serving students online.

INTRODUCTION

With the emergence of distance education in the form of web-based or online education, new challenges materialize for students, faculty, and institutions. These challenges range widely from adequate library support to student mentoring and advising to institutional coherence and transparency in serving their distant students. This chapter provides an overview of best practices—potential solutions to these many challenges.

This work has grown out of the author's experience as a Distance Education Coordinator and later as a faculty member teaching distance courses. Distance education has reached yet another new phase, a phase in which a systemic change in perspective must occur. Instead of maintaining that it is the student who is remote or distant, institutions, including faculty, staff, and particularly librarians and information specialists, must see it is indeed *they* who are remote. These entities can begin to address the many challenges surrounding efficacious distance education programs by adopting a student-centered perspective in the institutional approach to meeting distance education students' needs. This chapter must be considered a work in progress, as best practices for intuitions must be revisited and continually revised as distance education continues to mature and change. It is an attempt to raise awareness of services and support that contribute to the most rewarding experiences for distance education students. This chapter concentrates primarily on institutional and library services, as best practices and guidelines for online faculty and instructors can be easily identified in the literature.

Recent data from the National Center for Education Statistics (1997) reveals great increases in the number of institutions offering distance education programs or coursework. An analogous rise in formal, well-planned institutional support policies appears to be missing, as many institutions concentrate first and foremost on converting curriculum to an online format and secondly on the delivery and technological infrastructure. However, distance students need *and deserve* accommodations above and beyond their on-campus counterparts; while many of these recommendations will apply to and will assist all students, institutions must be cognizant of the extenuating circumstances that contribute to a distant student's frustrations, and in many cases, attrition. The recommendations here are predicated on some institutional monetary commitment as well, though many can be accomplished with small budget lines. It is the hope of the author that institutions and programs of all sizes can adapt the recommendations on a scale appropriate to them while avoiding budgetary crises.

By initiating, maintaining, and guaranteeing a sound policy for services and support of distance education students, an institution will promote the most efficacious and enjoyable learning experience for every student—near and far.

FIRST STEPS

Planning

Institutions cannot jump into distance education without forethought and careful preparation. Institutions must develop solid and strategic plans for meeting the needs of distance students—including resources and services, not only course delivery. To assess those needs, individual programs and the institution as a whole should develop and administer student needs-surveys on an annual or semiannual basis. To assist in the development of the needs assessment, a distance education student advisory board comprised of four to five students at various stages in the program or institution should be established. The board should meet regularly through virtual means with key players in the institution. The student advisory board serves as a liaison between the students and the institution.

Communication is key, and all students need to know they have a voice and a role in their educational process. Recall that typical characteristics of distance students include being an adult in some form of employment and moreover, they are characterized by autonomy, persistence, maturity and independence, self-direction and motivation, and experience; as Schrum and Luetkehans (1997) suggest, "The great majority of adults learning at a distance were reported to be in the 20-40 age range and studying on a part-time basis from their homes while maintaining full-time jobs" (p. 13). Institutions should capitalize on this knowledge and experience of their distance students in order to create an optimal learning environment; the student advisory board contributes greatly to this environment.

Institutional goals and objectives must be clearly defined and how these will be met according to an institutional timeline must be established. Again, the distance student advisory board contributes to the formation and ongoing assessment of the goals and objectives. The institution's right hand must know every move the left hand is making, to avoid problems such as incorrect billing for out-of-state fees, requiring identification cards when a student may never be on campus to acquire one, inconvenient course scheduling, sudden technological changes in course delivery, among others. Student complaints often revolve around a serious lack of institutional coherence and efficiency, noting that calls (often long distance if a toll free number has not been implemented) must be made to numerous offices in attempts to find the "right person" for their particular questions. An institution must maintain a clear line of contact for questions related specifically to distance education. In the planning stages, institutions would be wise to identify the staff contacts for particular issues and make this listing extremely easy to find and use; such a listing should be maintained on the institution's distance education Web page and it should be mailed to every student with each semester's registration materials. Include such contacts as:

1. Registration Questions
2. Billing Questions
3. Financial Aid Questions
4. Course Access/Technical Questions
5. Library Services
6. Student Services (Advising, Book Store)

Ideally, an "800" number will allow students to be transferred to the appropriate contact at no additional cost to the student. Since 24/7 human contact is most likely impossible, a voice recording of frequently asked questions (FAQs) and answers should be available. A separate "Network Operations" phone line should exist and alert students to scheduled down-times or unexpected network crashes. If students are unable to access their online course, they should know why and for approximately how long. If institutions do consider *themselves* as remote, time zones should be irrelevant and complete access should be readily available for anyone at any time. This is a service model towards which institutions are moving.

In addition, institutions should have mandatory staff briefings on their distance education programs, so any individual is competent in answering questions or referring students to the appropriate person. Staff should be aware of distance offerings at the program, course, and non-degree levels; residency, differences in tuition or billing, technology requirements, computer/information literacy requirements must be understood. By allowing the distance student advisory board to assist in the staff briefings through video streams or net conferencing, staff will become immersed in the student-centered perspective and realize that there are many questions students consider that the institution never has. Even if an individual is far-removed from the operations of the distance program, she or he should be aware of the institutional commitment to and investment in distance education. This is the systemic change towards which institutions committed to distance education will move.

Moreover, ongoing needs assessment, virtual focus groups, and pre- and post-course surveys should be administered regularly so institutions remain informed and able to meet the shifting needs of distance students. In particular, the surveys should be available on the distance education Web page and should ask for questions, concerns, or needs of students ahead of time. Returning students could offer suggestions based on previous experience. Anticipation of problems is key in the distance environment: time is of the essence. As many involved in distance education know, if a problem causes a student to fall behind in course work, it becomes very difficult to catch up in the fast-paced DE environment. The post-course survey would offer an opportunity for students to evaluate the course, the professor, and the institution, and encourage students' suggestions for improvement. Of note, since many faculty are learning how to teach online as they do it, student recommendations for faculty provide significant information.

The maintenance of a distinct distance education Web page proves critical. These Web pages should follow the guidelines of the Center for Applied Special Technology for Accessibility (1997). Students should have multiple means of access, including text-only versions of Web pages, voice recordings, and easy access from the lowest modem rate connections and computers that are not only state of the art. As the Web Accessibility Initiative points out, "The power of the Web is in its universality. Access by everyone regardless of disability is an essential aspect" (http://www.w3.org/WAI/). While many online course programs, including Blackboard, WebCT, and Top Class currently fail to comply with the accessibility guidelines, institutions should be demanding accessible software from vendors and requesting significant improvements in this area. The main distance education information pages are distinct from the Student Services Web page described below, though both sites should be consistent in content, layout, form, and function. Institutions may also wish to implement a standard template for course design, based on the look and feel of the public Web pages, while still allowing faculty artistic and intellectual individuality. Students will appreciate some conformity and standards among course logins and modules.

Finally, institutions must ensure that students have immediate access to all pertinent institutional information, including student handbooks (a separate distance student handbook is encouraged), policy guidelines, support services, contact information, and any other formal materials. While these should be posted online, a paper copy must be sent to all distance students immediately after the student contacts the institution for information.

Understand Distance Education and Its Specificity

As noted above, institutions must identify their key players in the distance programs early on and staff briefings on the state of distance education should be offered regularly. In order for distance students' needs to be served in the best possible way, faculty, librarians, and other key players at the host institution need to *understand and embrace* distance education and its particularities. Individuals responsible for working with the distance programs must be introduced to its pedagogical specificity, characteristics of students, technological mechanisms used in the course offerings, and the distance program in general.

Understanding and staying informed are critical. Institutions and individuals responsible for administering distance programs must become advocates for distance education at the host institution and work to promote quality and best practices throughout all aspects of the program. Anyone involved must believe in what they are doing. Students quickly recognize when an instructor or institution as a whole is disengaged from the philosophy of distance education. All key players must receive appropriate training and institutions should be prepared to hire more staff to meet the labor intensity of distance education programming. Depending on the size of the institution, number of students enrolled in the distance programs, number of courses available, and support structures within individual programs, institutions can formulate an appropriate ratio of support staff.

Likewise, students embarking on distance education should be aware of the pedagogical specificity of this form of education. Buchanan (2000) has suggested that students and faculty engage in pre-assessment tests to determine their suitability in a web-based environment. Institutions may want to be less formal and instead have a question on application materials that simply asks, "Why is distance education right for you?"[2]. This will encourage distance students to consider their commitment to distance education in a nonthreatening manner. Guest access to online courses, with prospective students encouraged to examine a course prior to enrollment is recommended in order to allow students to make informed decisions concerning the appropriateness of distance education for them.

IMPLEMENTATION
Efficient and Effective Communication and Support

Distance students rely on efficient communication in the forms of email, chat rooms, toll-free phone lines, faxes, or other electronic means as their academic lifelines. Lack of clear communication feeds into student dissatisfaction and ultimately, attrition. As more institutions and for-profit ventures offer distance education, students do not have to settle for inadequate services—they have choices and will explore them if an institution cannot or will not meet their needs.

A 24/7 service should be offered. Institutions should advise students to leave their time zone when making requests or inquiries so proper response times can be established. As part of staff development, individuals should learn the basics of computer-mediated communication. For instance, in the library setting, librarians should be trained on virtual bibliographic instruction, including virtual reference interviews. Individuals working with distance students must learn more effective interviewing techniques in the absence of voice intonation or facial and body expression.

Academic advisors working with distance students must learn the emerging legal issues surrounding student records privacy. Advisors should exercise caution when sending personal information to a distance student who uses a family email account, for instance. Headers indicating "This message is intended for—and may contain confidential information for that individual only" should be used. All correspondence should be thoroughly documented, and upon completion of telephone discussions with distance students, advisors or other individuals should write a report of the conversation, send it to the student for confirmation, and place it in the student file.

Importantly too, advisors must explore creative ways of advising students at a distance, many of whom are changing careers. Institutions must consider video streams and/or archived video files of student services such as resume writing, job hunting, and the like.

To assist with student advising and peer networking, institutions should develop a voluntary peer mentor system. This is simple and extremely cost-effective: The institutional distance education coordinator maintains a database of students and their status in the program (how many courses taken) and he/she will coordinate pairs of mentor/mentees. When a new student enrolls, he/she should be paired with a veteran DE student who has agreed to serve as a mentor. Emails and phone numbers should be exchanged. The mentor can share process advice, technological advice, and student support. Remember that attrition rates remain high in distance education programs (See for instance, Terry, 2001; Carr, 2000; Morgan & Tam, 1999); this peer relationship may help curb this by providing an informal networking and peer support system within a program. The mentee can feel comfortable asking a peer for advice on the ins and outs of the DE program, securing materials, course participation, and maneuvering through the institutional channels.

Finally, distance students need syllabi, reading lists, other resources lists, and course access available at least three weeks prior to the inception of a class. Faculty teaching distance education must be alerted to this, and they must be able to comply; teaching online requires great planning, organization, and forethought. Faculty cannot expect to "wing it" online, and an institutional commitment to a rigorous timeline for distance programs may alleviate many common complaints of online faculty and coursework. While faculty may complain about this additional burden, preparedness is a major key in successful distance education.

This enables students to prepare, gather materials through whatever means necessary, work out technical glitches in access and course participation, and be ready to engage in the actual learning process when the course begins. Since many distance students need to acquire course materials through interlibrary loan, purchase through an online or campus bookstore, or download materials from online resources, three weeks provides ample time. If faculty recognize that they have large files to download, a CD-ROM or other format option should be available.

Student-to-Student Services

In addition to student mentoring, the host institution should establish a course module for Student-to-Student Services for use *only* by students. This is a place where students can sell or trade course texts with each other, share group information; it serves as a virtual lounge. The Student Services site is both formal and informal, serving to unite distance students in a friendly way, as well as serving as a formal point of information dissemination.

FAQs (in nontechnical language) can be posted within the module; course schedules, syllabi and readings lists, and other institutional information can be disseminated easily. Anonymous postings on a bulletin board should be allowed, however, guidelines for responsible and appropriate use of the forums must be established. Distance students should have the same safe place to talk about instructors, courses, or other issues as on-site students who whisper to each other before or after classes in the hallways. The distance education coordinator should monitor the module and update it regularly, however, the coordinator must respect the rights and privacy of distance students' and their communications.

To keep this student site most effective, define the goals and objectives of the site, and remain focused on that audience and those objectives as the site materializes. The distance student advisory board will be active in the creation and ongoing revisions of the site. All distance students should be polled on what kinds of information they would find useful and valuable on the site, and key players from the institution should be polled on the types of questions to which they frequently respond.

The site must comply with accessibility guidelines, and it must be designed based on feedback from distance students and graduates. Keep the perspective entirely student-centered. Do a rough web-ready version of the general structure and post it to the Web and ask your student advisory board to provide feedback. Revise as needed. The site should be readily available to students, and it should be a "one-stop shop." Ongoing maintenance is requisite, and in the institutional goals and objectives, a revision schedule for the student services website must be established and adhered to. Continue to be mindful of the initial objectives and audience so that the site does not gradually stray from its intended purpose.[3]

LIBRARY AND INFORMATION RESOURCES

Finally, library services and support for distance education must be considered. The Association of College and Research Libraries' guidelines (1998) define distance education library services as "those library services in support of college, university, or other post-secondary courses and programs offered away from a main campus, or in the absence of a traditional campus, and regardless of where credit is given...The phrase is inclusive of courses in all post-secondary programs designated as: extension, extended, off-campus, extended campus, distance, distributed, open, flexible, franchising, virtual, synchronous or asynchronous." The ACRL's guidelines are a major step in the appropriate provision of services for distance students. They address eight main areas:

1. Management
2. Finances
3. Personnel
4. Facilities
5. Resources
6. Services
7. Documentation
8. Library Education

Ultimately, the guidelines call for libraries and information centers to assume a new-found and prominent role in light of distance education. Libraries are integral to the institution as a whole and should work in close collaboration with their parent institutions in the development and delivery of distance education. Just as libraries must engage in collection development for any institutional programs, the library must be active in determining how it will meet the needs of off-campus students through collection development. As distance education continues to lack credence in some circles, a proactive library and library staff can contribute to a sound pedagogical experience for students by ensuring high-quality, scholarly materials in a number of formats. It cannot be assumed that distance students can acquire scholarly materials easily through their local libraries or "online." Mechanisms must be established to ensure quality resources for all students.

Partnerships and Relationships with Multiple Libraries

While politics and the mighty dollar still prohibit true resource sharing across states and even within states, advances are being made through different means such as the Z39.50 information retrieval protocol, interlibrary loans, and commercial enterprises. The impetus falls on the delivering institution, however, to contact local libraries where their distance students live, and to provide information on the types of resources that would be needed locally for the student. Depending on the size of the distance education program, this may prove impossible, but institutions must recognize that they need to support the student. If the institutional library does not make resources available electronically or through delivery mechanisms, some formal channels of communication should occur to provide a solid library and information resource base. For instance, the Open University partners with the Indiana University library system, and other consortial agreements are emerging as beneficial for meeting distance education students' information needs.

Electronic Resources Available Easily and Efficiently

More specifically, libraries can engage in best practices that will provide efficient and effective use by their distance students. A reliable electronic reserve system should be established with respect to the emerging copyright laws (see the Digital Millennium Copyright Act for details). The e-reserve system must be kept updated, with each semester's materials available well ahead of the course inception (three weeks). The system's downtime, if any, must be minimal, with advance notice to students of the scheduled downtime. Information concerning the library's network should be updated on the "Network Operations" line mentioned earlier.

Documents available for electronic reserve must be of superior quality; the scans should be done at the highest possible resolution, with large documents separated into parts, with file size indicated. Articles' "black space," the result of poor photocopying, should be trimmed to save students' printer ink. Provide a chart of download times for different access rates. If a student cannot obtain the electronic reserve materials, mechanisms for sending a paper copy or CD-ROM must be in place.

Students must have 24/7 access to online indexes and databases, preferably full text if possible. Importantly, the library must know what programs and courses are available throughout the institution so that temporary license agreements can be established if students will need particular resources. Verification of students can be ensured through proxy servers or other secure logins. Automation systems that allow browsing of "shelves" and in particular, tables of contents are desirable. Catalogers are now regularly using a variable length contents field (the 505 field) for MARC records that enables tables of contents to be included in records. This is particularly valuable for distance students who may need to request a book, only to receive it two weeks later to find it is inappropriate. Libraries may also want to explore links to book reviews and other authoritative sources within their circulation systems.

The library should follow the guidelines established by the institution closely, adhering to accessible Web pages, a toll-free line for reference requests, appropriate mechanisms for borrowing privileges (which should be longer for distance students than on-site students)—and clear points of contact and information. Libraries would be wise to employ a full-time distance education librarian[4] who serves actively throughout the institution on committees and curriculum groups. The distance education librarian must be able to coordinate resources, services, and materials, as well as serve a liaison between students and computer resources. He or she will be conversant with the "techies" but also able to articulate clearly to students who may need assistance with the technological aspects of library use. The distance education librarian should hold virtual bibliographic instruction sessions at the inception of each semester. These sessions should be videotaped or digitally recorded so students are comfortably literate with the library and its online resources; these should be available for circulation, ensuring multiple copies are available, or download. Finally, libraries must be committed to implementing a synchronous chat room and email line for ready reference and other "quick" questions. Services for database searching should be available at a cost not prohibitive to students.

With the rapid changes impacting libraries, these strategies may become quickly obsolete. Librarians are encouraged to keep up with revisions and announcements from the ACRL, attend distance education conferences, and remain committed to proactive communication, visibility on campus, and to serving distance education students with library and information resources in the best possible ways.

SUGGESTED TIMELINE FOR INSTITUTIONAL PLANNING

In the best scenario, an institution will have close to a year of preparation time before the inception of courses. This preparation time will allow staff to be trained and/or hired, marketing and recruitment efforts implemented, and departments, library and computer services revised and reorganized. Many institutions of higher education will also need to work with curriculum committees, accreditation bodies, and graduate schools for online course approval. This will vary by institution.

Unfortunately, most institutions will not have a year of planning and preparation. A strategic plan of action is recommended, in which priorities are established and implementation plans arranged. The strategic plan, which will impact all layers of the institution and must be coordinated.

Table 1: The five steps

Step One	Faculty and staff training and awareness of distance education pedagogy and specificity. This is truly a top level priority, as lack of commitment and embrace of distance education shows to students. A superficial attempt at launching a distance program is worse than no attempt at all.
Step Two	Establish advisory boards and conduct focus groups to develop institutional policies. Include major stakeholders from various facets of the institution. Develop a mission, strategic plan, institutional objectives and goals, and a timeline for meeting these.
Stage Three	Prepare the library and computing services for the new programs. The question is not will additional resources and personnel be required, but how much and of what type? Institutions may implement an additional fee structure for distance tuition to offset some of the additional personnel lines and resources.
Stage Four	Design, develop, and go public with distance student services web pages and be sure to include the requisite information, including course schedules projected to at least one year out. Be certain the web pages are updated frequently and reflect an accessible, student-centered perspective.
Stage Five	Ongoing needs assessment, revision, review of institutional goals and objectives and their completion, new programs and courses brought online, ongoing marketing and recruitment—all done in close consultation with Student Advisory Board and focus groups. A sample checklist is included in Appendix A.

CONCLUSIONS

This chapter has offered various strategies for best serving distance education students. They are certain to change as distance education itself evolves, but it provides a strategic starting point for planning and implementation of distance education. With the library as an integral component in student success, various library strategies were described. Each institution would be wise to consider these strategies, assemble your student advisory group, and embark on a needs assessment. This will be an ongoing process—your institutional work will not end once your programs or courses are online. Consider and maintain the student perspective, for it is the students who will make or break your distance education initiatives; be ready to embrace change, and most importantly, embrace the philosophy of distance education. The challenges will not stop, but you will be armed with solutions and strategies for efficacious distance education.

ENDNOTES

1 I am particularly grateful to the graduate students in the School of Information Studies course, "Library and Information Services and Resources for Distance Education," (Winter 2001) for their insights and keen articulation of a student-centered perspective on serving distance students.

2 Thanks to David Jordan for this succinct question.

3 Thanks to Lori Pesik for her suggestions here.

4 Librarians are encouraged to take courses such as "Library and Information Resources and Services for Distance Education" to learn strategies, procedures, resources, and instructional techniques for serving distance students. Traditional library and information science coursework does not address distance services directly, thus, elective courses are advised.

REFERENCES

Association of College and Research Libraries. (1998). *ACRL Guidelines for Distance Learning Library Services*. Chicago: ALA.

Buchanan, E. (2000). Assessment measures: Pretests for successful distance teaching and learning? *Journal of Distance Learning Administration*, 2(4). Available on the World Wide Web at: http://www.westga.edu/~distance/buchanan24.html.

Carr, S. (2000). As distance education comes of age, the challenge is keeping the students. *Chronicle of Higher Education*, 46(23), A39-A41.

Center for Applied Special Technology. (1997). *Web Content Accessibility Guidelines*. Available on the World Wide Web at: http://www.w3.org/WAI/.

Morgan, C. and Tam, M. (1999). Unraveling the complexities of distance education student attrition. *Distance Education-An International Journal*, 20(1), 96-108.

National Center for Education Statistics. (1997). *Distance Education in Higher Education Institutions*. Available on the World Wide Web at: http://nces.ed.gov/pubs98/distance/.

Schrum, L. and Luetkehans, L. (1997). *A Primer on Distance Education: Considerations for Decision Makers*. Washington, DC: AECT.

Terry, N. (2001). Assessing enrollment and attrition rates for the online MBA. *T.H.E. Journal*, 28(7), 64-69.

APPENDIX A: SAMPLE INSTITUTIONAL CHECKLIST

Goal/Objective/Action	Stakeholders Involved	Budget Allocation	Date Completed	Next Steps
Faculty and staff have received appropriate training.				
Institutional Distance Education Committee and Student Advisory Board established.				
Institutional goals, objectives, and plans established with reasonable timeline for completion.				
Departments and programs oriented to distance education services and provisions.				
Marketing plans implemented.				
Student services, materials and web pages created and made available.				
Schedule for ongoing assessment and review established and supported throughout the institution.				

Chapter X

Quality Assurance of Online Courses

Richard Ryan
University of Oklahoma, USA

THE CONCERN ABOUT QUALITY ASSURANCE

The Potential to Compromise Quality

Today, many university programs are integrating online classes into their curriculums. According to Stephen Ehrmann, reasons for online course offerings typically fall into two categories.

> *One type wanted to use distance learning technology to increase enrollments, often by reaching out to certain types of people who would not otherwise get an education. Some reviewers charge that these proposals were cheating students of most of the support needed for excellence: laboratories, rich libraries, interactive seminars, and informal interaction on campus.*
>
> *The other type of proposal used computer technology to change what students learned or how they learned. Some reviewers accused such proposals of being tiny bastions of expensive exclusivity, hoarding rich resources for the lucky or the strong, excluding the vast majority of learners who were most in need of excellent teaching.*
>
> *In other words, most technology proposals were designed either to enlarge the number of learners or to improve what some learners could learn, but not both. (Ehrmann, 1999)*

Both objectives, improving access and improving quality, offer incentive for creation of online classes and degree programs. The benefits of using the economical Internet for distance learning are just beginning to be explored and documented. It is almost assured that, as more classes are offered online and become interchangeable at different universities, the proliferation of use by students will increase because of the "any-where, anytime nature" of the Internet.

Based upon the author's experience, the convenience of Internet delivery and anytime online class availability are often the primary reasons students enroll in online courses. The quality of the online educational experience is often a secondary consideration to the student. Many times these students are willing to miss the in-class experience and interaction in order to receive credit for online coverage of certain required subject matter. Because of this attitude, there is also the potential for students and potential employers to perceive an online class or degree program as an "alternative" or the "next best thing" to attending traditional lecture classes. This attitude needs to be minimized if students are to utilize online and traditional classes equivalently in their degrees. The same level of quality for the class experience and content should be expected if online and traditional lecture classes are to be considered equivalent. Making an online class as engaging as a lecture class using the Internet is a worthy goal. "Jumping in with both feet is not for timid souls. Internet offerings require large amounts of time in the preparation of course materials. Everything must be viewed in a global sense for an entire semester at the offset." (Kubala, 1998).

Assuring that the quality of the online class experience is equivalent to the traditional lecture class experience, using a medium that embodies working independently at one's own pace, and communicating anonymously is a challenge. In fact, at this current stage of development, it is unproven as to whether this objective can be achieved. Class administrators and students must ask themselves, "Is there a trade-off of class quality for the convenience of the delivery method?" Motivations for offering and taking online classes should be fully explored. Class quality should not be compromised for the sake of posting a class online for business reasons, because others are doing it or for the convenience using the Internet brings. Motivations for offering online classes should be based in both improving access and quality. Achieving this level of quality will greatly influence online class acceptability across curriculums and universities, hopefully resulting in better use of classes and Instructor expertise.

At this stage of online education development, there is great potential for the traditional university experience to be reshaped using the Internet.

Strategies for quality assurance of online offerings must be defined and implemented if this is to happen. Optimizing use of the Internet to remove the physical limitations of the traditional university is just beginning. The quality of online classes will improve as Internet technology advances. As with any emerging endeavor, programs that implement quality assurance plans for online class offerings will probably have greater success in this effort.

Equal Quality Expectation for Traditional and Online Construction Classes

At the April 1999 National Construction Industry Education Forum (NCIEF) in Las Vegas, Nevada, discussion focused on quality assurance of online construction courses. During this discussion between construction academicians and construction industry representatives, it was agreed that online construction classes should meet the same quality expectations as traditional lecture classes. It was further recognized that these expectations should be evaluated the same way for both types of classes. It was hoped that all classes in a construction program, regardless of the delivery method, would be held to the same level of quality expectation. It was further hoped that by maintaining the same level of quality expectation issues of curriculum suitability, faculty receiving workload credit and acceptance of class credits at other universities would be minimized. This would also assure potential employers in the construction industry that the current education experience would not be compromised.

Comparisons of online classes to traditional lecture classes are just being documented to support this NCIEF discussion. Schulman and Sims (1999) found that "the learning of the online students is equal to the learning of in-class students," comparing pre- and post-tests of knowledge for both groups of participants. This quantitative comparison addresses one of the components of quality assessment—comparison of outcomes or grades. Their evidence shows that the online learning environment can be as effective as the traditional lecture environment. Regarding student performance, Dominguez and Ridley (1999) found that "distance education supporters recognize the value and necessity of employing the same yardstick to establish the legitimacy of their programs. Institutions that offer distance education programs to adult learners in any form —from correspondence to web-based courses— have been honor bound to establish that such courses provide student learning and content equivalent to that found with campus-based instruction."

Evaluating students' qualitative perceptions of the learning experience is the other component that must be evaluated for quality assurance of a class. Further discussion about the cns4913online Construction Equipment and

Methods classes shows that the online learning environment can be as effective as the traditional lecture environment. Recognizing that the traditional lecture and online delivery methods can and should be evaluated the same is a necessary step toward establishing quality expectations for online construction classes. For online classes to be equivalent to traditional lecture classes, there must be a quality equivalency of student performance and the class experience as well.

Online Class Quality Assessment Using In-Place Criteria

A convenient, efficient and equivalent means of gathering online class quality assessment is to use criteria already in place for traditional lecture classes. Most universities have a quality assurance strategy in place for current course offerings. Along with outcomes assessment, the online students' perception of the class experience is measured and used for quality assurance of the class. This qualitative perception typically influences the students' level of interaction, attitude and ultimate feeling about the class experience. These considerations subsequently affect the students' outcome assessments.

Part of class quality assurance for University of Oklahoma College of Architecture classes is a subjective student survey taken at the end of each class offering. Student reaction to the instructor, class content and content delivery are rated. The results of the survey are to be used by the instructor to refine and improve the class. Student perceptions of the class are also used as criteria for the instructor's yearly faculty evaluation.

Part of the previously mentioned NCIEF quality assurance discussion focused on the cns4913online Construction Equipment and Methods classes offered Spring 1998 and Spring 1999 by the University of Oklahoma (OU) Construction Science Division (CNS). The classes were the first complete semester length, online construction classes to be offered to Associated Schools of Construction member programs. Twenty-five students from nine geographically separate accredited university construction programs successfully completed the online classes. As part of the lecture and online class evaluations, the instructor used the OU College of Architecture (CoA) Non-Studio Course Evaluation to gather student ratings concerning the course instructor, course content and student performance. As with traditional classes, the online students' perception of the class experience was measured and used for assessment and improvement of the class. Success of the online classes was evaluated by comparing traditional lecture and online class assessments using the Non-Studio Course Evaluation instrument, class exercise, and exam grades.

THE CONSTRUCTION EQUIPMENT AND METHODS CLASSES

Class Criteria

The objective of the CNS 4913, Construction Equipment and Methods class was to provide an overview of different types of construction equipment and methods. Students investigated different types of equipment, performance criteria, the selection process, the economics of ownership, and inclusion of equipment costs in the project estimate. American Council of Construction Education accredited (ACCE) construction programs are encouraged to include this content in their curriculums, though not necessarily in a dedicated class. This class is not part of the OU CNS "core" of classes, but all CNS students are required to successfully complete it. Assignments and exams were medium level difficulty. Correct answers to exercises were determined using algorithmic formula, visual association or procedural understanding. Learning the formula or process was typically the objective of the exercises and the correct answer was a product of this understanding. In other problem-solving exercises, assessment was based on the approach to the problem and the steps of the solution, not just the correct answer. The typical lecture class atmosphere was open, using student inquiries to drive the lecture when appropriate. Students typically enjoyed the class because of the visual-based learning, the overall level of class difficulty, and the classroom atmosphere.

The 1998 Class

During the Spring 1998 semester, a web-based online Construction Equipment and Methods class was taught in conjunction with a 26 student lecture class meeting twice a week at OU. The online class was administered from a custom-built website designed, implemented and maintained to replace the traditional lecture delivery. The online teaching model required the online class student to check the website regularly, as the traditional teaching model required the traditional class student to attend lectures regularly. The website was formatted like a "book" of organized information to be used as a class information resource. Students were required to use Windows 95 and Office 97 for assignments. Email, the telephone, the Chat feature and limited desktop video conferencing were used for communication between students and the instructor.

The interactive online course was started and completed by 11 students from five accredited construction programs across the United States. Each student enrolled in an elective or directed reading class with an assigned faculty sponsor at their university. Invited faculty sponsors were initially responsible for finding students in their programs interested in taking the class. This method of recruitment was used due to the new and unproven delivery method. Student reasons for taking the online class included interest in taking an online course for the first time, using the class to conveniently help fulfill their degree requirements or the content was not offered in their program. The cns4913online class was the first comprehensive, semester-length construction course to be offered by an Associated Schools of Construction (ASC) program to other ASC programs using the Internet. Participating construction programs included Oklahoma State, Texas A&M, Auburn, East Carolina and Cincinnati Universities.

Students in the 1998 OU CNS 4913 lecture class did not have access to the class website. Course content was delivered in lecture format requiring note taking, but allowing for questions and observations. The delivery sequence was the same for both classes. Students in both classes were given the same homework assignments and exams at approximately the same times during the semester. Class assessment for both groups was mostly closed-book and required a faculty proctor for all examinations. Online students were given the same amount of time to complete their exams as the lecture class students. Sponsor professors served in this capacity for their respective students. The primary purpose of the parallel classes was for direct performance and administration comparison between the two delivery strategies.

An interesting observation was made as the semester progressed. Lectures typically contained and followed information in the website. Traditional students took notes during these lectures to be used for homework and exams. The online students did not attend lectures, but actually obtained a better hard-copy set of notes than the students attending the traditional lectures by printing the website pages for reference. This was not what the author envisioned at the beginning of the class. The trade-off, obviously, is that the online students missed the lecture class interaction reinforcing which information was the most important. This class interaction was also a more convenient format in which to answer questions.

The 1999 Class

Based upon this experience, in addition to the results of the CoA Course Evaluations and subjective assessment gathered from students at the end of the class, the website and class were upgraded. Prior to the start of the Spring semester, the class was advertised to all ASC faculty using an email listserv provided by the ASC. A promotional website was created and posted so that interested students could preview the website operation, class structure, content and how the class worked. During Spring 1999, 14 students from Oklahoma State, Texas A&M, Texas Tech, Auburn, University of Wisconsin-Stout and Cal Poly-San Luis Obispo participated in the online class along with 26 OU students in the lecture group. During these classes all students used the website for information, communication and to obtain homework exercises. The instructor decided to fully optimize the opportunity students had to work independently by making examinations open book with no outside faculty intervention required for online students or lecture students. Exams were similar to those given in the 1998 classes, but used more problem-solving and discussion questions. Students confirmed an ethics statement on each exam, stating that they worked individually.

Because it was the second time the online class was offered, the author took special note of the reasons that students requested enrollment. Students' reasons for taking the class were very similar to the 1998 class. Most students viewed the class as a convenient means to fill a curriculum gap with minimal effort required of on-site faculty. For many the class was considered acceptable as an elective, a replacement for a missed class or as makeup work. Several students were aware of the class because of affiliation with an online class member or a faculty sponsor from the 1998 class. Several students took the class because the content was not addressed in their curriculums and they wanted to go into equipment intensive construction.

QUALITY COMPARISON OF THE LECTURE AND ONLINE CLASSES

Comparison Methodology

Paralleling the CNS 4913 class deliveries provided a unique opportunity for comparison of students' quality perceptions of traditional lecture and online strategies. The author believed that if the online students' quality perceptions and the outcome assessment grades were similar to those of the lecture class, then it could be assumed that the online class was as effective as the lecture class and the quality of the classes was equivalent.

With the help of Ken Williamson, Ph.D., Texas A&M University, the 1998 lecture and web student groups were compared to determine whether the participants were similar in background, knowledge and attitude. The Test of Logical Thinking (TOLT) was administered between groups to compare basic reasoning ability. The test was given once as a pretest. The Test of Construction Attitude (TOCA) was used to investigate empowerment, attitude and motivation toward professional construction management. It was also used to evaluate student attitudes and motivation toward learning and instruction within and between groups. The TOCA was administered pre- and post-course.

The OU CoA Non-Studio Course Evaluation was used for the 1998 and 1999 classes to gather students' perceptions of instructor performance, course content and self-evaluation at the end of each semester. Additional information was also collected from the online classes using a participant survey at the conclusion of the course offerings, instructor observations and online participant communications.

Comparison Results

Results of the TOLT instrument indicated that the difference between the two groups was not significant. Results of the TOCA indicated that the online students considered themselves to be more professional than the lecture class. These instruments were not used in the Spring 1999 class.

Results of the OU CoA Non-Studio Course Evaluation for the CNS 4913 lecture and online classes are shown below. The questions are listed in order as they appear on the evaluation form. The mean evaluation ratings for the class for each question are noted in the responses columns on the right. Columns list the mean evaluations by delivery method (lect = lecture or ol = online) and the semester of the class (98 or 99). It should be noted that responses in the web classes have greater percentage influence on the overall average ratings for the questions than in the larger lecture classes

The course evaluation instrument is divided into four categories. Questions 1-7 rate qualities of the instructor and administration of the class. A rating scale of 1 = definitely yes, and 5 = definitely no was used. Questions 8-10 rate prerequisite knowledge required for the class and class assignments. A rating scale of 1 = far too much, and 5 = far too little was used. Question 11 rates the number of exams. A rating scale of 1 = far too many, and 5 = far too few was used. The last category, questions 12-15 compare the Instructor to other Instructors and the students' perception of themselves. A rating scale of 1 = excellent, and 5 = poor was used.

Upon initial review, it appears that several of the evaluation questions are not applicable because of the online delivery of the class. For instance, questions dealing with instructor communication (Questions 2 and 4) and comparison of the instructor to other faculty members (Question 12) do not seem applicable because of the anonymity of the class delivery. These

Table 1: Student evaluation results

Questions	Responses			
	lect 98	ol 98	lect 99	ol 99
1. Adequate preparation for class by Instructor	1.30	1.61	1.56	1.18
2. Expressing clearly and concisely by Instructor	1.50	1.96	1.76	1.91
3. Clarifying material in reading assignments by Instructor	2.09	2.00	1.88	1.75
4. Availability and helpfulness outside of class by instructor	2.09	1.69	1.48	1.54
5. Well thought out assignments	2.00	1.80	1.80	1.91
6. Reasonable coverage of materials by exams and quizzes	1.91	1.69	1.80	1.91
7. Adequate measuring of knowledge by exams and quizzes	2.00	2.07	1.80	1.91
8. Knowledge about the prerequisite subjects	2.18	3.00	3.00	3.00
9. Time required for homework assignments	3.00	2.88	2.88	3.08
10. Credit given for homework assignments	3.10	3.00	3.00	3.00
11. Number of exams	3.18	2.92	3.00	3.00
12. Rating Instructor compared to other faculty members	1.75	1.61	1.24	1.91
13. Rating the course with the course content only	2.09	1.61	1.68	1.58
14. Rating the course with the gaining of knowledge	2.63	1.61	1.64	2.08
15. Rating oneself as a student in the course	2.63	1.80	1.56	2.00

questions are still applicable used in the context of online class delivery. Effective communication and availability of the instructor are still an integral part of a successful class experience regardless of the delivery method. "No reply" to an email or missing a Chat session parallels missing an "office hour." Effective communication demands fulfilling defined obligations to students, such as office hours or online Chat sessions. The instructor's performance can be compared to other construction faculty at the participants' programs. Though the online relationship is mostly anonymous and using email, the instructor's personality and attitudes are still very evident in correspondence and grading. The instructor's effort to be personable in email and telephone conversations and to share observations and interests can greatly influence students' perception of the instructor, just as in face-to-face communication.

Eleven assignments, three exams and a comprehensive final exam were completed during both class offerings. There was no notable difference in any homework or exam grades. The average final grades for the 1998 lecture and online classes were 86.38 and 81.64 respectively. The average final grades for the 1999 lecture and online classes were 85.58 and 87.28 respectively.

Observations Based on Comparison

The actual numerical ratings for each question are not the focus of this comparison. It is very important, however, that ratings for both methods of class delivery were consistent for both semesters the classes were offered. There are no trends or evidence of different quality perception between the classes based upon answers in the survey. The final grades for online and lecture participants were not significantly different for either course offering. To the author, these comparisons demonstrate that the teaching techniques and styles are suitable for both delivery methods. Based upon this comparison of the Construction Equipment and Methods classes, the author also concludes that students can evaluate online and lecture classes using the same quality criteria. It should be noted, however, that meeting and exceeding the quality expectation of any class, regardless of the delivery method, is strongly influenced by the motivation of the instructor and students.

The web classes ratings of Question 2 (Expressing clearly and concisely by instructor) and Question 4 (Availability and helpfulness outside of class by instructor) are very close for both semesters. These ratings are consistent with the lecture classes' ratings. It should be noted that of the 26 online students completing the Non-Studio Class Evaluation during the two class offerings, three participants marked "not applicable" on the assessment form for these questions.

Though still in the excellent (rating = 1) to good (rating = 2) range like the Spring 98 classes, the rating of Question 12 (Rating instructor compared to other faculty members) for Spring 99 was 1.24 for the lecture class and 1.91 for the online class. A possible reason for this difference is that the online students that semester did not interact with the instructor enough to form a more favorable opinion.

Interaction using email, the telephone or Chat demands greater communication efficiency than oral discussion in a classroom setting. This is perhaps the greatest limitation of the online delivery method. Based upon the subjective survey at the end of the classes, almost all online students felt this was the greatest weakness of the class. Several suggested that mandatory times for interaction be included in the class format. Contradictory to this suggestion, it should be noted that when the instructor was available in Chat at announced specified times, participation by online students was limited. This perhaps can be attributed to the great effort expended by the instructor to communicate in a timely, understandable and comprehensive manner concerning content questions and feedback about students' performance. Based upon the subjective survey at the end of the classes, the availability of the class on the Internet all the time was the greatest strength. Many students also commented about the effectiveness of the class website.

Performance levels of several individuals in both groups decreased at the end of the semester. This is a trend typically occurring in most classes. It was typical for students to collaborate on homework with other class members at their universities. Rarely did they collaborate with someone from another university, unless required for a specific exercise.

DIRECTIONS AND FUTURE CHALLENGES

Meeting the Quality Challenges

To meet the challenges of assuring online and traditional class quality equivalence, several items must be considered when developing and administering online classes. Based upon the author's experience, the following items should be part of the quality assurance strategy for online class development and administration. These items should be considered regardless of the delivery method, but deserve special consideration due to the nature of online classes.

Match Content to Required Assessment

Testing required for evaluation of a student's understanding and use of presented information is the primary content suitability consideration for online delivery. Rigor of exercises and tests must be equally demanding for online and lecture classes to be considered equivalent.

If group or essay-based exercises and exams are used, the class is a strong candidate for online delivery. Authentic performance exercises assess the student's ability to apply knowledge to solve real-life problems. Exercises can require planning and application of knowledge in new and different ways. The abundant and convenient resources available online can add great depth to these types of problem-solving exercises. Classes incorporating a large visual component, such as the construction equipment class, are very good examples of this suitability. Manufacturers' websites providing information about equipment, specifications and services are ideal for many technology subjects. One of the greatest advantages of the Internet as a medium for delivering a class is the ability to greatly enhance and increase the information that can be included in class content. With minimal instructor effort, exploration of information contained in linked websites was incorporated into equipment selection and management learning exercises. Developing a custom website is an excellent opportunity for the instructor to offer self-collected resources and to express observations and suggestions about specific topics not covered in traditional class materials. Much of the content of the cns4913online website addressed topics that the instructor felt were inadequately addressed in the textbook and other course resources.

Classes requiring outside supervision for exercises and exams are not the best candidates for online delivery. The assessment method requires greater effort to assure the demonstrated learning. If this cannot be done efficiently and economically, than perhaps the content is not as suitable for online delivery at this time. "Developing effective and reliable assessment methods for online class participants perhaps will demand the greatest effort for innovation and departure from traditional practices." (Ryan, 1999).

"Open book" testing is the easiest assessment method for online classes, because it requires the least amount of faculty intervention. However the rigor of "open book" assessment is suspect when using automatically graded true/false, yes/no, numerical, fill-in-the-blank, specific phrase or multiple-choice answers. Many times the right answer is easily found in the content if the student takes the time to search. Unless time limits are imposed for completion of questions or activities, developed competency is not truly demonstrated. It should be noted, however, that this form of combining assessment and content review is an effective means of teaching online. Questions can be used to prompt the student to review certain content or complete an activity. Exercises or assessment can be crafted so that questions are sequenced and must be answered correctly before proceeding to new information. This is an effective means of focusing students' efforts on required knowledge and regulating their progression through the class.

As assessment becomes more interactive and automated greater responsibility will be placed on the student to work independently and follow specified guidelines. Efficient verification of students' identities is a limitation for online delivery today. Eventually, technology will overcome this issue, but for now it strongly influences the assessment technique that is used. Computerized adaptive testing has great potential for minimizing this concern. Using this method, the difficulty of the next question is determined or adjusted based on the previous responses. Selection of questions is database driven and the assessment fashions itself individually for each student as answers are provided. This is an excellent format for totally automated, individualized online assessment.

Determine Required Collaboration and Communication

Two of the primary benefits of using the Internet are the opportunity to work independently at one's own pace and to communicate anonymously and economically from a remote site. The instructor must decide how strongly these benefits are to be embraced in the online administration strategy. Required collaboration demands much greater communication effort and efficiency. Success of exercises requiring collaboration will greatly depend on students' characteristics, backgrounds and motivations. Group interaction is an effective teaching technique, but must be used appropriately. Communicating face-to-face is much easier than current email, Chat or desktop-to-desktop audio/video communication. It should be noted that communication using the Internet will continue to become more efficient as real-time audio and video are more effectively combined and delivered. This future interface will minimize many of the current communication limitations.

Communications required for an instructor-paced online class are similar to communications required for traditional lecture classes. The instructor sequences content coverage, exercise durations and assessment. Communication by announcement on the website or email from the instructor is typically required for class activities to be initiated and completed. Classes incorporating extensive group collaboration, group interaction and a feedback loop require greater communication effort by the instructor and students. The instructor should anticipate spending extra time communicating with students and motivating these students to communicate with each other. As observed by the instructor, during collaborative online class activities, effective and timely communication between group members has the potential to be as challenging as the actual completion of the exercise objectives.

An automated or self-paced class format requires the least instructor interaction for class administration. This format truly embraces the benefits of the Internet. However, creating and implementing an automated online format requires much greater initial effort than an instructor-paced class. The entire content and delivery strategy must be determined before implementing the class. Automatic mechanisms must be built into the class to pace student content review and assessment. Much greater effort must be expended to make content presentation organized, comprehensive and interesting. Interactive features, video and animation can be used to support learning and make the experience more enjoyable for the student.

Optimize Internet Capabilities

Internet presentation and communication technologies are becoming increasingly "user friendly," incorporating more efficient and interactive features. Having an understanding of both content and these technological capabilities will greatly enrich the style and delivery format that can be incorporated into an online class. Online classes fully optimizing these capabilities to deliver content, exercises and assessment have the potential to be better than traditional lecture classes. Meeting this challenge demands the greatest instructor organization and coordination effort.

Internet capabilities are often incorporated into online classes by someone other than the instructor of the class or by placing packaged information into courseware shells to create class websites. The drawback to these methods of online class creation is that the Instructor may not understand the capabilities of Internet for making content delivery interactive and more engrossing to the student. The use of posted PowerPoint slides or videos of recorded lectures is a rather non-creative approach to content delivery using the Internet. This is basically using the Internet for traditional teaching. If information delivery without regard for the quality of the experience is the objective, then this format is suitable. Ultimately these classes will be perceived as "correspondence courses," using the Internet for information transfer and communication.

The Online Class Quality Challenge

One of the primary reasons that teaching takes place in a classroom is that it is the easiest medium for content delivery and learning assessment. It is the path of least resistance for teaching and learning. The lack of face-to-face interaction makes the online experience much more demanding. Today, the online experience requires more motivation for successful teaching and learning than the traditional method. The instructor's motivation and enthusiasm to create and administer an effective class and the students' willingness to accept a greater responsibility for communicating are two of the primary influences on class success. A necessary step for any class quality assurance is determining how quality is to be evaluated by students. Comparison of assessment results and class evaluations for the Construction Equipment and Methods classes supports the NCIEF recognition that online construction courses can and should be evaluated the same as traditional lecture classes. Quality expectations for online and lecture classes should be the same for the classes to be considered equal. Otherwise, online classes will continue to be considered an "alternative" or the "next best thing" to attending traditional lecture classes. As part of a quality assurance plan, online instructors should seek to expand teaching methods and approaches using the Internet. There is great potential for using automated online content delivery for self-paced interactive learning exercises taking advantage of animation, video and audio. Content can be crafted to take advantage of the growing pool of resources available on the Internet.

How these capabilities are embraced should be part of an online class quality assurance strategy. Offering resource rich online classes using the Internet is a cost efficient opportunity for industry and academia to partner. There is great potential for exceptional classes to be industry-sponsored productions, combining emerging capabilities of the Internet, the best Instructors and the latest industry driven content.

REFERENCES

Dominguez, P. S. and Ridley, D. (1999). Reassessing the Assessment of Distance Education Courses. Available on the World Wide Web at: http://www.thejournal.com/magazine/vault/A2223.cfm.

Ehrmann, S. C. (1999). Access and/or Quality? Redefining Choices in the Third Revolution. Available on the World Wide Web at: http://www.tltgroup.org/resources/or%20quality.htm.

Kubala, T. (1998). Addressing Student Needs: Teaching on the Internet. Available on the World Wide Web at: http://www.thejournal.com/magazine/vault/A2026.cfm.

The Quality Assurance Agency for Higher Education. (2001). Distance Learning Guidelines. Available on the World Wide Web at: http://www.qaa.ac.uk/public/dlg/guidelin.htm.

Ryan, R. (1999). Best practice suggestions for custom building a technology class website and administering the class. *Journal of Construction Education.* Available on the World Wide Web at: http://www.ascweb.org/jce/, 4(1), 4-17.

Ryan, R. C. (2000). Student assessment comparison of lecture and online construction equipment and methods classes. *T. H. E. Journal*, 27(6), 78-83.

Schulman, A. H. and Sims, R. L. (1999). Learning in an online format versus an in-class format: An experimental study. *T. H. E. Journal*, 26(11), 54-56.

Suen, H. K. and Parkes, J. (2001). Challenges and Opportunities in Distance Education Evaluation. Available on the World Wide Web at: http://www.music.ecu.edu/DistEd/EVALUATION.html.

Section III

Implementing Distance Education: Programs, Designs and Experiences

Chapter XI

Distance Education Quality: Success Factors for Resources, Practices and Results

Cathy Cavanaugh
University of North Florida, USA

INTRODUCTION

The current growth in distance education is a result of a convergence of factors. The delivery technology has become more affordable, available, familiar and interactive. With improvements in the technology, distance courses are now more realistic, engaging, inexpensive, and varied. The audience of learners is more experienced and capable with the technology, due to the increased availability of distance education, and they welcome distance learning into their busy lives. Technology-mediated distance education research has matured enough to produce an extensive body of evidence that distance education can be at least as effective as classroom instruction.

The exciting convergence that brought about the growth in distance education also presented distance learners with a challenge: how to choose the best distance learning opportunities from the vast catalog of options. Distance learners can easily compare the costs, technical needs, cognitive requirements, and time demands of distance learning courses. Learners are less well equipped to distinguish high quality courses from the offerings. Distance education programs have the responsibility of communicating to students the quality assurance measures they employ, whether the measures consist of in-house practices or accreditation by outside bodies.

This chapter describes trends that have led to the growth of distance education from elementary school through higher education and professional development. The following sections present critical success factors that institutions, course developers, instructors, and students have found through practice to lead to high quality distance education experiences. These guidelines are presented as they inform the three stages of the distance education development cycle: resources, practices, and results. In addition, two distance education programs are described as case illustrations that exemplify the successful application of success factors.

TRENDS CONTRIBUTING TO THE GROWTH OF DISTANCE EDUCATION

Distance education, as experienced via the Internet, is a result of the convergence of several recent trends. Access to the Internet is now available in some form to most Americans, and distance education is increasingly seen as a practical and effective pathway to learning. A growing concern among distance learners is determining the level of quality of distance education programs. This section examines the trends leading to the growth of distance education and the need for distance education quality assurance.

Interest in Distance Education

Interest in distance learning is on the rise among high school students, college students and professionals. A recent survey found that the majority of parents polled obtained Internet access for their children's education (Grunwald Associates, 2000), and as of the year 2000, a full 15% of U.S. high schools offered access to online classes (Market Data Retrieval, 2000). By the year 2002, over 2 million distance learning students are expected in higher education (Web-Based Education Commission, 2000). In a survey of working adults the majority stated that they believe college courses offered via the Internet are the future of higher education, with 32% expressing a preference for online courses over classroom learning, given equal quality of education (CyberAtlas, 2000). A survey of business managers who have used Internet-based training found that nearly 100% of respondents would recommend it, mainly because of "anytime, anywhere" access (CyberAtlas, 2000). While the expense of developing high-quality distance education materials can be high, return on investment analyses are beginning to show that training efficiency and resulting productivity gains make distance education worthwhile.

Effectiveness of Distance Education

Traditional reviews of distance education literature conducted in the 1980s indicated that adult learners achieve as well in distance education programs as they do in classroom settings (Moore, 1989). A quantitative review of the achievement of over 900 students in K-12 distance education programs found no significant differences in student achievement between distance learners and classroom learners (Cavanaugh, 1999). Other studies described by Moore and Thompson (1990) indicate that the instructional format itself has little effect on student achievement as long as the delivery technology is appropriate for the content and timely teacher-to-student feedback is included. Good distance teaching practices have been found to be fundamentally identical to good classroom teaching practices, with quality factors being universal across environments and populations (Wilkes & Burnham, 1991).

Assurance of Quality in Distance Education

With obstacles such as access and convenience largely overcome, students and workers are embracing distance education as a solution to the educational problems of course variety, time flexibility, and transportation limitations. As consumers of distance learning become more experienced and as distance education offerings become more varied, demand for high quality in distance education grows. Distance education providers vary widely in the methods they use to establish quality criteria, ensure that they meet the criteria, and communicate their quality assurance procedures to students. Instructors have concerns regarding the identity and honesty of the students doing the work in distance education courses. Administrators at many traditional institutions fear that public perception about the meaning of a college degree will erode if distance learning courses are added to the curriculum (Office of Educational Research and Improvement, 2000). In response, online and traditional institutions of higher education have implemented standards for accreditation. This chapter offers an examination of success factors for quality distance education, with exemplary cases included to illustrate best practices.

Defining Quality

In its December 2000 report to Congress, the Web-Based Education Commission made high-quality online educational content one of its seven critical issues. In order for a student or institution to determine whether quality has been achieved, quality must be defined. A primary goal of educators is developing independent learners who can capably apply their knowledge to new situations. To ensure that distance education offerings meet this goal, providers must identify desired learning outcomes and instructional methods. Quality indicates that instruction is effective and appropriate. The definition of quality may include quantitative elements such as completion rates, student performance, and student evaluations of the learning experience. Qualitative dimensions may include ratings of teaching-learning events, materials, learning process, pace, activities, content and options offered to students. Effective and appropriate outcomes and methods for distance education are adopted from educational practice, business systems, and learning research. The following sections apply specific approaches from education, business and research to achieve quality distance education experiences.

THE QUALITY DISTANCE EDUCATION CYCLE

The process of developing and implementing effective distance education happens in an iterative cycle. Broadly considered, the three stages in the cycle are (1) procurement and preparation of the resources necessary to meet the distance education goals, (2) delivery of instruction using the best practices from education, business and research, and (3) analysis of the results of distance education to gauge achievement of the goals. Each stage of the Resources-Practices-Results (RPR) cycle continually revisits lessons learned in the other stages and builds upon the successes realized in the other stages. Each stage requires participation of all stakeholders, including students, instructors, support and design professionals, administrators, and the community. The critical success factors discussed in each stage are based on decades of research and experience with learners from professions, higher education and K-12 education (Barker, 1999; Bruce, Fallon & Horton, 2000; Cavanaugh, 1999; Educational Development Associates, 1998; Fredericksen, Peltz, & Swan, 2000; Institute for Higher Education Policy, 2000; Mantyla, 1999).

The Resources Phase of the RPR Cycle

The resources required to sustain a quality distance education program exist to support students, faculty, and the program or institution toward achieving the goal of effective and appropriate learning. Responsive and flexible human resources, knowledge, skills, policies, procedures and technical infrastructure enable quality practices and contribute to quality results. Procurement, development and adaptation of resources are ongoing processes. The discussion of the critical resources for quality distance education

Figure 1: The phases of the RPR Cycle

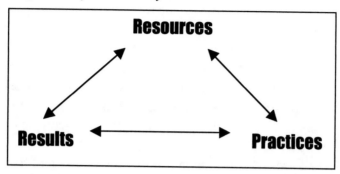

begins at the institutional level, and continues with faculty, students, and technology. A case description illustrates an institution where a significant and ongoing commitment of resources has resulted in a high-quality distance education program.

Institutional and Program Resources

To provide a vigorous quality distance education program, an institution begins with policy that values distance education as an endeavor that integrates seamlessly with the institution's mission and goals. With such a policy in place, understood by administration and staff, the institution is positioned to create a strategic plan for delivering distance education to students. In planning, distance education administrators and instructors engage in continuous dialogue with a broad range of stakeholders in specifying quality benchmarks (Vaughan, 2000). Providers forge consensus with past, present and potential future students about the perceived effectiveness of courses, and they communicate with employers to determine the match between the skills and knowledge required on the job and those developed in the course (Kearsley, 2000).

The strategic plan is a financial and philosophical commitment that gives the direction to personnel who make specific decisions regarding program implementation. It is a commitment to team support for distance educators and students, technology led by the program's current and future goals, and development of program standards. Course developers and instructors need target standards to guide course design and delivery. As a partner to the standards, program review procedures must be developed, implemented, and revised frequently to ensure that all components of the program meet standards and to ensure that the standards contribute to program goals. For example, academic accrediting bodies may limit the amount or type of learning that may occur via distance education, or faculty may decide that certain courses such as laboratory courses are inappropriate for distance education. Standards and results of reviews are used to drive future decision-making, including selection of qualified experienced instructors and levels of support needed throughout the program.

Administration of a quality distance education program depends on clear and accurate communication to students. Students need access to information about admission, tuition, materials, technical requirements, learning expectations and support available to them. For students to be successful, the program must advise entering students, including screening for students who display success indicators for the program, and consideration of prior learning experiences. Registered students need orientation and counseling so they will be properly placed in the program. Students need assurance that their rights are protected and their records will be confidentially maintained as well as available to other institutions. Student privacy and security in online activities must also be ensured.

All education programs are built essentially on their people. For facility-free distance education programs, this fact is critical, making human resources a vital responsibility of the institution. Qualified instructors and support staff must be recruited, they must be provided with development opportunities related to instruction, content knowledge and technical skill, and they must receive feedback on their teaching. Because students often learn to fulfill a career goal, the program benefits when employers and other community members understand, support and contribute to the program's goals, policies, and outcomes.

Community members, who may be thought of as consumers of the program's products, are valuable sources for program evaluation data. Qualitative input about student performance, satisfaction, and success is at least as important as quantitative data such as enrollment, costs, utilization of technology, and hiring rates. The elements of the comprehensive program evaluation process should be communicated to all stakeholders in advance, and the results should be reported completely and efficiently.

Faculty and Course Support Resources

Qualified and experienced distance education instructors are likely to have the desired attitudes and understanding of the distance education teaching and learning process. For faculty members to succeed in distance education, they need to be supported with accurate and complete information and training in order to develop their skills and understanding. Successful distance educators understand the distance learning environment and the options that exist for instruction. They recognize the time and effort necessary for producing and teaching an effective course, and are provided with release time in advance for course preparation. They have experience using the tools of distance education, and receive opportunities to learn and practice with new tools. Ideally, instructors are involved in the evaluation and selection of technology resources and in the development of policy for their programs. In addition to their distance education competencies, faculty in high-quality programs excel in their academic field, have earned credentials in the profession, and contribute to scholarship in their subject.

In support of the design and delivery of quality courses, institutions are responsible for providing training and resources for instructors. All distance education faculty members require training aligned with their needs in pedagogical and technical skills, including distance learning course organization, planning, teaching and assessment strategies. This training is most effective when it is followed up with ongoing course design assistance and peer mentoring throughout course delivery. The training should cover pacing and sequencing of activities, broadcast or online communication skills, and methods of interaction with students that develop critical thinking and problem-solving skills.

Instructors need continual access to the physical resources and human support that will enable development of high-quality teaching materials. Materials used by students must be appropriate for the content area, using the media and delivery technology that suits the content. Most distance learning courses are highly visual, but many arts, communication, science and other courses depend on high-quality audio and motion capabilities. Materials should be presented in an organized, functional and easily navigated structure. The materials used in successful distance learning courses are comfortable and affordable for students to use, accessible to all learners, in accordance with copyright restrictions, and free of errors and bias. The materials result in quality learning when they are interesting and attractive, varied to support different learning styles, and used in meaningful work. The best distance learning courses use complete and up-to-date materials to increase the information literacy of students, while allowing opportunities for creative expression and mastery of concepts.

Student Support Resources

The focus of distance education is the students, whose work is made better when they receive well-designed instruction in a well-planned program. For students to maximize the time and effort they spend on their learning, they must minimize the time and effort they spend on solving nonacademic problems and seeking answers. Many questions are answered in comprehensive orientation opportunities that cover "the what" and "the how" of distance learning, the processes of the institution, and the requirements of the program. Orientation is accomplished with synchronous online or face-to-face sessions and with asynchronous print or web-based guides. Some students need hands-on technical training using the tools employed in courses and in using general learning tools such as libraries and information archives. Information literacy training should include guidance in the legal and ethical uses of electronic information. As students begin the work of learning, they need continual access to instructors, libraries and other student resources. They also need a streamlined technical support system accessible through several channels, such as toll-free phone, fax, email, web, and help desk.

As an example, the Southern Regional Electronic Campus (SREB), a distance learning clearinghouse for higher education institutions, publishes a guide called Principles of Good Practice (2000). Institutions following the principles assure students of the quality of the courses listed and endorsed by the SREB. The principles require an online course or program to provide students with "clear, complete and timely information" on requirements, interaction, prerequisite skills, equipment requirements, support services, financial resources, and costs. Students must have adequate access to resources appropriate to support their learning. The institution must assess the student's ability to succeed in online learning.

Technical Resources

Even given the best plan, program, instructors, materials and students, distance learning does not occur without the technology for delivery. Technology selection decisions involve all stakeholders. A technology plan guides decision-makers in considering student outcomes, program goals, and technical feasibility. Technology selection must consider tools used by professionals, the skills and budget of students, and the institution's ability to provide support. The technology and infrastructure contribute to quality learning when they are reliable, secure and fully supported. Support extends to all users of the technology for all facets of the learning process. Users require assistance with hardware and software uses. Students require assistance with access of electronic resources. Instructors require assistance with lesson development and delivery, including editing, graphic design, research, and communication with students.

The eight education accrediting commissions acted together in 2000 to draft the Guidelines for the Evaluation of Electronically Offered Degree and

Certification Programs (Council of Regional Accrediting Commissions). In the area of technical resources, the guidelines specify that institutions must "strive to assure a consistent and coherent technical framework for students and faculty." The technology must be selected based on appropriateness for students and curriculum, reasonable cost for students, maximum reliability, and a plan to keep the technology updated. In support of the technical framework, institutions must provide technical support for each hardware, software and delivery system required in a program. Support mechanisms recommended in the guidelines were a help desk with person-to-person contact and a well-designed FAQ.

Exemplary Case: University of Central Florida

In the days before electronic distance education, the University of Central Florida was called Florida Technological University. While the university's focus has expanded, it has not lost touch with its technological roots. In 2000, UCF received the United States Distance Learning Association's award for Excellence in Distance Learning Programming for Higher Education. The award and the success of the university's distance education programs are a direct result of an institutional commitment of significant resources to distance education. Located in Orlando, Florida, the university serves a large geographic area in the state's high-tech corridor. The university's strategic plan embraces distance education as a way to facilitate the learning of a growing clientele. Beginning with senior administrators, UCF's organizational structure supports its "Virtual Campus." The Center for Distributed Learning and the Course Development and Web Services Department both fall under the auspices of two Vice-Provosts.

The university's budget reflects the importance of distance learning programs in meeting institutional goals. The university funds the technical infrastructure, faculty development, learner support, research and development in distance learning, and impact evaluation. The technical infrastructure consists of wired and wireless network connections to every building, access to Internet2, dedicated servers for online courses, and always-on access to information and services for all students and staff. Faculty development services are especially noteworthy. All distance teaching faculty take a faculty development course, for which they receive a stipend or a laptop computer. Faculty members are given release time and stipends for course development and are assisted in all phases of course design and delivery by trained Tech Rangers. Course instructors are required to file an RFP for a planned distance learning course to ensure that it meets the needs of programs and students. A university evaluation unit collects data on courses and students for use in future planning.

To support learners, UCF enables students to apply for admission and register for courses online. Course schedules, technical guides, distance education orientation courses, financial aid information, library access, and textbook purchasing are all accomplished on the Web. Technical support is always available by phone or Web, and a group of CyberKnights acts as student computer consultants (so named for the university's mascot, the knight). A CD-ROM contains Internet software, a browser test, tutorials, and automatic configuration for network dial-up access. The university's research and development projects investigate technical solutions for distance education and they study the effectiveness of various approaches to teaching distance courses.

Impact evaluation at UCF concentrates on student and faculty issues related to successful distance education. Student issues include success rates, withdrawal rates, learning styles, attitudes and demographics. Faculty issues include instructional tools, data warehousing, action research, and program accreditation. For more details, see UCF's Virtual Campus website at http://distrib.ucf.edu.

The Practices Phase of the RPR Cycle

With the right resources in place, the stage is set for dramatic distance learning performance. At this point the spotlight shifts from the institution to the instructor. Quality distance teaching begins with the careful design of courses, materials and learning activities. Next, the instructional practices employed during instruction will aim at developing independent learners with the ability to transfer their learning to novel situations. Throughout the course, effective communication and community building are essential foundations for all events. This section details critical success practices in course design, instruction and communication.

Course Design Practices

Course design is a series of decisions regarding objectives and the most effective methods of ensuring that students accomplish the objectives. Distance course design requires the methods to be effective in a technology-mediated environment. The requirements of the curriculum and the needs of the students lead the technological decisions in a well-designed course. The skills and knowledge included in the most effective courses are relevant to students, either in their current lives or in their future roles. The skills and knowledge also represent the most desirable learning in the current state of the field of study. The information presented is credible, respectable, balanced and accurate, offered in rigorous and appropriate depth. The instructor is responsible for structuring the information in an organized way and presenting it in a context that is motivating to students.

Regardless of the content, students learn best when they are comfortable, have some control over their learning, and are sufficiently challenged. A balance of comfort, control and challenge can be difficult for distant instructors to achieve, and depends on psychosocial rather than academic strategies. Instructors contribute to the comfort of students by providing fast accurate answers to questions. Many instructors strive for a 24-hour turnaround time in sending students feedback on assignments, and they answer questions from students immediately. Students are comfortable with a familiar visual design in course materials. Written and electronic material should be consistent with few distractions, divided into short chunks. Students are more confident in the importance of their work when course criteria are stated clearly and are viewed as realistic. To give students a sense of control, instructors offer choices of activities and topics or they allow students to negotiate options. Control in distance learning often involves flexibility in scheduling activities and deadlines, although students need structure and prompting to keep up a reasonable pace of work. Students are challenged when there are high expectations for them to succeed at new tasks that they view as beneficial to them. An important aspect of student comfort and challenge is complete understanding of student evaluation techniques, which will be discussed in more detail in a later section.

Drawing from a business model of education in which students are consumers of services, many instructors and institutions have adopted quality educational service practices such as Total Quality Management. Quality service centers on providing learners with excellent support integrated into the course and systems for communication within the course (Vaughan, 2000). The focus is on the needs of learners and the learning process, rather than content. The quality service approach emphasizes the course structure and interactions in order to supply flexible scaffolding to learners as needed.

Communication Practices

Because learning is an interactive activity and constructed socially, a key to success lies in communication between students and others. A quality benchmark is to involve students in communication during 50% of the time they spend on the course. Frequent and active communication with the instructor, fellow students, or experts in the subject is essential in making students feel that they are part of the community of learners. Connection is vastly more motivating than isolation. Students need to know that others care about them and that they are contributing to an educational endeavor larger than themselves. Instructors should strive to know students on a personal level, and maintain a conversational tone in all communications during the course.

Interaction in a distance learning course is most effective when it occurs through a variety of media, when it occurs with a variety of sources, and when it is integrated into the overall course design. The course should offer students opportunities to interact through more than one media channel, and the student should become proficient at choosing the most appropriate channel for specific needs. Media channels for course interaction include email, chat, discussion forum, listserv, phone, audio-video conference, fax and face-to face meetings. Most institutions offer a range of media services and many are now available on the web for free. Students should be encouraged to interact with sources including classmates, professionals, experts, and nonhuman sources of information such as databases, print material and audio/video media. Students access such media remotely online and locally in their communities. Very effective learning in an online course may occur offline, in labs, businesses, and other settings. Interactions are most effective when experienced within the context of other course activities.

Communication in a course has the greatest value for students when it authentically approaches the kinds of communication students will experience beyond the course. Students should work in cooperative teams to solve realistic problems. The instructor's role is to set up situations that approximate the professional world and require high levels of interdependence for success. The instructor must also model and require respect for student diversity and various learning styles.

Instructional Practices

Successful distance educators understand that motivation is among the most important factors in promoting student learning. Distance learners function very independently and are generally intrinsically motivated, but they often require extrinsic motivation to keep up their pace in a course. Instructors provide extrinsic motivation through course structure, communication and activities. At the outset, instructors must clearly state the benefits of learning the course content to the student. The course activities should foster both knowledge construction and content understanding through active learning. To succeed in the course and later endeavors, students in the distance education environment need education in the subject blended with information literacy and applied technical skills. The education in the subject should focus on higher-level cognitive skills such as analysis, synthesis and evaluation. The information literacy skills should include information retrieval, evaluating resources and communicating a viewpoint. The technical skills relate to the hardware, software and online applications used in the field of study.

The Results Phase of the RPR Cycle

The only way to know whether a distance education program has achieved quality is to compare the program results to established quality benchmarks. Measures of quality are tied to institutional goals, and account for the specific context of the program. To maintain success, a distance education program evaluation must account for institutional and instructional factors as well as student factors. Evaluation of course and program results is a continual process that involves all stakeholders and requires a wide range of tools. This section presents evaluation strategies used for ensuring quality distance education programs. The strategies evaluate success through assessment of student learning, program review, and program accreditation.

Assessing Learning

When experiencing quality learning, students shift roles from audience to actors as they acquire skills and display their abilities. The display of student abilities is the most important result of distance education. In the course of developing their abilities, successful students manage their learning by engaging in frequent self-assessment. Because self-assessment does not come naturally to all students, it is helpful when instructors guide and encourage students to assess themselves. Instruments such as rubrics, checklists, and journals are effective tools for helping students become independent and responsible learners. Such assessments provide information to students about their strengths and about the gaps in their knowledge.

Students receive the greatest long-term benefit when they have extensive opportunities during a course to develop their skills in a realistic context, and assessment of skills should occur within that context. As professionals or lifelong learners, students need experience using peer review as a way of assessing their competencies. During the distance learning course, students may be grouped with others in the class or they may be directed to practicing professionals for feedback on their work. A peer review process known as 360-Degree Feedback calls for reflection on student self-perception along with anonymous feedback from superiors, subordinates and peers (Palloff & Pratt, 1999). Another approach that incorporates a professional context is the use of portfolios of student work. Construction of a portfolio is an engaging endeavor that requires the habits of mind in the field of study. Portfolios are commonly developed using the framework of the field of study, but they allow a degree of freedom and flexibility as students showcase the range of their accomplishments.

Using varied assessment methods is a key to student assessment that gives an accurate picture of student abilities. In addition to authentic assessments that show student application of knowledge, tests may be needed to show student acquisition of knowledge. Constructing valid and reliable tests for distance education is no different from a traditional environment. The special challenge of giving tests and accepting other work at a distance is maintaining academic integrity. In a student-centered course where assignments are open-ended and require critical thinking, little cheating occurs (Palloff & Pratt, 1999). Instructors use multiple sources including the record of student dialogue throughout the course when evaluating assignments. Tests in a distance course may be delivered electronically via the Web or computer disk, or at a proctored site. Online tests can be made available during a specific time frame, during which all students take the test simultaneously, or may be monitored using videoconferencing cameras (Kearsley, 2000).

Program Review

Evaluation of course effectiveness by students is most useful when it is an ongoing feature of the course. At intervals during the course, students should be asked to explain their satisfaction with their experience, including likes and dislikes. When the course climate is open and supportive, students generally offer honest and constructive feedback that can be used toward continuous improvement of the course (Palloff & Pratt, 1999).

Participation of students, instructors and the institution is needed to determine the quality of the distance education program. Students should have the opportunity to offer feedback regarding their access to learning activities, course delivery, and technical support. Scope and sequence of courses are important factors for students, too. Student feedback is collected using printed or electronic surveys, narrative messages, and interviews. Program faculty should be asked about their experiences with course access, delivery and support. More importantly, faculty members need to express whether they have adequate access to training and development resources.

The intended program outcomes must undergo review at the institutional level to ensure their clarity and their appropriateness to students who move into work or higher learning roles. Learning outcomes for distance education programs should be clear to instructors and students. Achievement of outcomes in specific courses should be observable and measurable against a known scale or set of criteria. The methods and materials used in attaining program outcomes must also be included in the review. Comprehensive program review considers the quality of the course materials, instructional design of courses, and instruction and technical support provided to students. Qualitative assessments of program components, accounting for the learning context, can reveal patterns of student performance in relation to different course features. Quantitative data on student achievement and satisfaction are important parameters that contribute to future program success. Students and faculty need alternatives if they discover that a distance learning course is not appropriate for a student. Proper placement of students contributes to program success, reflecting positively on the institution.

Accreditation

Accreditation gives an institution a seal of quality because educational standards have been met. A student who expects a distance education course to transfer to another school must be sure that a regionally accredited institution offers the course. Institutions with distance education programs approach accreditation in several ways. The accreditation process varies according to whether a distance education program is offered by a high school, a traditional institute of higher education, or dedicated distance education provider.

Traditional institutions such as high schools, colleges and universities offer distance education programs to meet the needs of students and to accomplish institutional goals. Regional accrediting commissions generally accredit programs at these institutions. To maintain accreditation currently, distance education programs must meet the same criteria as on-campus programs. Most public online high schools are not currently accredited as independent institutions because they offer courses a la carte to students attending a local accredited school. The local school districts and the online high school reach agreement about course standards and funding. Examples are: Florida Online High School (http://fhs.com), Kentucky Virtual High School (http://www.kvhs.org), and the Concord Consortium Virtual High School (http://vhs.concord.org). Private online high schools seek accreditation through regional independent school accrediting agencies. A private online high school, Class.com is accredited through the North Central Association of Colleges and Schools, and the Commission on International Transregional Accreditation accredits Apex Learning.

The eight bodies that accredit colleges and universities in the US have released a draft of Guidelines for the Evaluation of Electronically Offered Degree and Certification Programs. The guidelines address institutional activity in the areas of institutional context and commitment, curriculum and instruction, faculty support, student support, and evaluation and assessment.

The regional commissions will implement the guidelines in a manner compatible with their policies and procedures (Council of Regional Accrediting Commissions, 2000).

An accrediting group specifically focused on distance education is the Distance Education and Training Council (DETC). Since the 1950s, the DETC has accredited correspondence schools and nontraditional online programs. DETC accreditation means that quality standards have been met, and that students may be eligible for federal financial aid. DETC accreditation is not a guarantee that credit will be granted in a degree program (DETC, 2000). New organizations are appearing that claim to accredit online programs, however, many of them are not recognized by the US Secretary of Education or the Council for Higher Education Accreditation (Johnstone, 2001).

The Web-Based Education Commission has called for enhancement of the accreditation process in which institutions and programs participate voluntarily. The Commission's goal is to provide more clarity for students regarding online options. The Commission recommends common standards and requirements for online programs comparable to standards for on-campus programs (2000). Disreputable accrediting bodies exist, enforcing virtually no educational standards. The public needs information to help them distinguish among the accrediting bodies and the quality control they provide.

Exemplary Case: Virtual High School

Virtual High School (VHS), operated by the Concord Consortium, MA, began offering online courses to high school students in 1996. Initially funded by a US Department of Education grant, VHS is a consortium of high schools that offer web-based courses for students in participating schools. This not-for-profit organization does not provide a comprehensive accredited high school diploma, but provides courses taught by certified teachers as part of a student's local public or private high school education. As of the 2000-2001 school year, VHS serves 4,000 students taking 150 courses in 30 states. The core program goal of VHS is to expand the offerings available to high school students through a wide range of quality, innovative online courses. The process used to evaluate the results of the program stems directly from the core goal.

During its four-year history, VHS has conducted reviews of its programs with the help of research firm SRI International. Program reviews provided information about program results that was critical in improving the program's resources and practices. Evaluations have judged the qualifications of VHS teachers, the usability of the infrastructure, and student/teacher satisfaction.

The results of instructor reviews led to the implementation of a graduate level professional development course in online pedagogy for teachers. A panel of experts reviewed the quality of courses in the areas of content, pedagogy, design, and assessment. A Course Evaluation Board sets standards for course design and delivery.

The most recent review targeted the advantages of VHS relative to classroom courses. Quantitative and qualitative factors were included in a case study of four VHS courses also offered face-to-face. Comparison of factors such as dropout rate, content, goals, assignments, use of technology tools, interest in the course, assessment of course quality, and student scores revealed no significant differences. These findings are supported by the results of an analysis of 16 programs comparing face-to-face with distance learning at the K-12 level (Cavanaugh, 1999). However, the VHS case study indicated that differences exist in student interaction and community building. The students and teachers in the online courses reported less satisfaction in these areas than did participants in classroom courses. The program is addressing the need for increased interaction and sense of community through teacher training and improved technology infrastructure. For details on the Virtual High School evaluation process, see http://vhs.concord.org.

CONCLUSION

With the worldwide number of Internet users expected to reach 600 million by 2002 (Computer Industry Almanac, 2000), and the increasingly frequent need for employees to update their knowledge and skills to adapt to the rapidly changing workplace, interest in distance education will continue to grow. In response, distance education offerings will grow, and competition for students will grow. Students online have access to any online course, and the tools of the Web allow students to quickly compare courses. A strength of distance education is its potential to focus the learning process on the student. Courses and programs that emphasize their focus on the student's strengths and needs will succeed in attracting students. In order to build their reputations and keep students, courses and programs must reach quality goals.

High-quality distance education achievement is the outcome of the dedication of all constituents in the continual quest for the best possible resources, practices and results. With increased need for new career skills and improvement in delivery technology, distance education students will demand evidence of quality and authenticity in distance courses. It is imperative that distance education providers implement and review quality benchmarks regarding Resources-Practices-Results in response to the needs of students, employers and the community. Educational institutions must take the lead in developing and maintaining standards, and they must clearly communicate those standards to the public. When students benefit from an education program that meets their needs, the community benefits as well.

ACKNOWLEDGMENTS

Many thanks to my colleagues at the University of North Florida for sharing their expertise, ideas, and support with me during the development of this chapter, especially Zella Boulware, Terry Cavanaugh, David Jaffe, and Phil Riner.

REFERENCES

Barker, K. (1999). Quality guidelines for technology-assisted distance education. Washington, DC: U.S. Department of Education Office of Learning Technologies.

Bruce, B., Fallon, C. and Horton, W. (2000). Getting started with online learning. *Macromedia, Inc.* Available on the World Wide Web at: http://www.macromedia.com/learning/online_learning_guide.pdf [Accessed 10/15/2000].

Cavanaugh, C. (1999). The effectiveness of interactive distance education technologies in K-12 learning: A meta-analysis. *Proceedings of American Education Research Association Annual Meeting*, Montreal, Canada.

Computer Industry Almanac, Inc. (2000). *Fifteen Leading Countries in Internet Users Per Capita.* Arlington Heights, IL. Available on the World Wide Web at: http://www.c-i-a.com [Accessed 11/22/2000].

Council of Regional Accrediting Commissions. (2000). Statement of the regional accrediting commissions on the evaluation of electronically offered degree and certificate programs and guidelines for the evaluation of electronically offered degree and certificate programs. Available on the World Wide Web at: http://www.ncacihe.org/resources/draftdistanceguide/ [Accessed 9/9/2000].

CyberAtlas. (2000). *Demographics.* Available on the World Wide Web at: http://cyberatlas.internet.com/big_picture/demographics/ [Accessed 11/22/2000].

Distance Education and Training Council. (2000). *Accreditation Standards.* Available on the World Wide Web at: http://www.detc.org/content/accredStandards.html [Accessed 11/22/2000]

Educational Development Associates. (1998). *What Quality Distance Learning Courses for an Institution?* Las Cruces, NM.

Fredericksen, E., Peltz, W. and Swan, K. (2000). Student satisfaction and perceived learning with online courses: Principles and examples from the SUNY learning network. *Journal of Asynchronous Learning Networks*, 4(2).

Grunwald Associates. (2000). *Children, Families and the Internet.* Burlingame, CA: Author.

Institute for Higher Education Policy. (2000). *Quality on the Line: Benchmarks for Success in Internet-Based Distance Education.* Washington, DC.

Johnstone, S. (2001). Does accreditation really mean accredited? *Syllabus,* 14(6), 22.

Kearsley, G. (2000). *Online Education.* Belmont, CA: Wadsworth/Thomson Learning.

Mantyla, K. (1999). *Interactive Distance Learning Exercises that Really Work.* Alexandria, VA: American Society for Training and Development.

Market Data Retrieval. (2000). *Technology in Education 2000.* Shelton, CT.

Moore, M. and Thompson, M. (with Quigley, A., Clark, G. and Goff, G.). (1990). The effects of distance learning: A summary of the literature. *Research Monograph No. 2* University Park, PA: The Pennsylvania State University, American Center for the Study of Distance Education.

Moore, M. (1989). Effects of distance learning: A summary of the literature. Washington, DC: Office of Technical Assessment.

Palloff, R. and Pratt, K. (1999). *Building Learning Communities in Cyberspace.* San Francisco: Jossey-Bass Publishers.

Southern Regional Electronic Campus. (2000). *Principles of Good Practice.* Available on the World Wide Web at: http://www.srec.sreb.org/student/srecinfo/principles/principles.html [Accessed 9/20/2000]

U.S. Department of Commerce. (2000). *Falling Through the Net: Toward Digital Inclusion.* Washington, DC.

Vaughan, M. (2000). Summary of quality issues in distance education. *Center for Excellence in Distance Learning.* Available on the World Wide Web at: http://www.lucent.com/cedl/sumqual.html [Accessed 10/15/2000].

Web-Based Education Commission. (2000). *The Power of the Internet for Learning.* Washington, DC: U.S. Department of Education.

Wilkes, C. and Burnham, B. (1991). Adult learner motivations and electronics distance education. *The American Journal of Distance Education,* 5(1), 43-50.

Chapter XII

Establishing Successful Online Distance Learning Environments: Distinguishing Factors that Contribute to Online Courses and Programs

Lynne Schrum and Angela Benson
University of Georgia, USA

This chapter looks at factors that promote development and implementation of successful online distance learning environments from the perspectives of educators and learners. It provides an overview of current tensions between the requirements of the faculty, the needs of the students, and the forces driving the development of online programs. The work is based on the authors' current research as well as past experiences in the design, development, and delivery of online distance learning environments.

INTRODUCTION

Today's learners are demanding "anytime and anywhere education," and institutions are responding by committing substantial resources to providing online distance learning through courses and full degree programs at the post-secondary and high school levels. Such courses and programs may include some face-to-face interaction, but the teacher and student are separated for the majority of activities. One or more forms of technology are used to mediate the teaching, and several forms of technology may be used for communication.

Distance education has long been viewed as a way in which to offer lifelong learning to those who are geographically separated from traditional institutions, have obligations that limit their ability to attend regular courses, or prefer to learn in new ways. One challenge has been to balance the need for intense and personal interaction with the reality of limited financial and other resources. Organizations and universities have turned to technology that has evolved to the point where it can provide the needed experiences through electronic networks and groupware (Gerencher, 1998; Mangan, 1999; Schrum, 1998). This chapter presents a review of the trend towards online distance learning environments by identifying challenges to faculty, students, and program planners.

BACKGROUND EXPERIENCES

Several previous studies were analyzed and amalgamated in this chapter. Schrum and Benson (2000a; 2000b; 2000c) investigated the first two years of a collaborative effort between a large financial corporation and a large southeastern university College of Business's MBA program to provide expanded learning opportunities for the corporation's professional workers who wished to further their education while maintaining full-time employment. In a qualitative case study of a distance learning consortium launched by the university system of a southeastern state, Benson (2001) described and analyzed the planning and implementation of the consortium's first online degree programs from the perspectives of the primary stakeholders: the consortium planning committee, the administrators at the universities providing the courses, the instructors developing and delivering the courses, the students enrolled in the courses, the university system administration, and the business community with workforce needs. Schrum (1998; 2000) identified characteristics of successful online learners, based on literature and interviews. In a qualitative case study of students enrolled in two online school library media courses at a large southeastern university, Benson et al. (in press) and Tallman and Benson (2000) investigated the effectiveness of online course delivery for the university's school library media program. From these four studies and the relevant literature, the authors have identified factors that influence educators' success in teaching in this context, specific dimensions that appear to influence student success, and factors that contribute to the overall success in creating online programs.

CONSIDERATIONS OF DISTANCE LEARNING FOR EDUCATORS

Teaching in Online Distance Learning Environments

Educators face specific challenges in moving from their comfort zone in traditional classrooms to teaching in online distance environments. Faculty members have had an especially difficult time changing the ways in which they teach, regardless of their own personal use of electronic media (Candiotti & Clarke, 1998). In an online environment, the role of faculty changes in many ways. Specifically, the traditional hierarchy is flattened, and the power and control are redistributed. Faculty are forced to develop and design their activities and interactions in new ways, and they may be frustrated without the ability to recognize students' furrowed brows (Schrum & Berge, 1998).

Faculty members, with little knowledge or experience of teaching online, also have voiced uncertainty about their abilities to provide appropriate educational experiences and opportunities, design meaningful interaction, and meet the needs of all their students. They worry about the extra time demands necessary to teach successfully in this manner, and specifically if meeting those time demands would be counted toward the yardstick of promotion and tenure. Further, librarians voiced concerns that some students who have few skills in evaluation of Web information, bibliographic searching or retrieval strategies may take online classes. Their worry is that this lack of knowledge would negatively impact students' success and learning.

Kember (1995) urged instructors to work toward deep learning, which requires moving away from excessive assignments, shallow assessments, and lack of freedom in activities. Heeren and Lewis (1997) suggested matching the media with the task, keeping media lean for tasks that do not require much interaction such as electronic mail, and reserving rich media for things that require more interaction and a broader spectrum of activity. These challenges go far beyond the instructor's need to be comfortable with the reliance on technology to support their courses (Schrum, 1998).

Course Design in Online Distance Learning Environments

Wiesenberg and Hutton (1996) identified three major challenges for the online course designer to consider: accommodating the increased time for delivery of the course (they estimate two or three times what is necessary for a traditional course), the creation of a community online, and encouraging students to become independent learners. Before any decisions can be made about delivery or models, however, each instructor must make pedagogical decisions about the fundamental goals of a course. The salient questions when creating an educational experience have always been, "What are the instructional and personal goals of this course for all students?" and "What is the purpose of this course?" These are questions that all educators must ask themselves when designing courses, and in general, they have become comfortable and adept at doing this.

The structure of the course, the planning for educational and personal needs, and the teacher's role must all be reconceptualized. It is clear that active and independent learning must take place. The designer will have to determine what actions will promote this type of learning. Further, from adult learning theory, it is clear that authentic learning, relevant materials, and negotiated assignments are required to ensure the participation, involvement, and action necessary to meet these goals. This is an ideal opportunity to create a Development Team, composed of a Subject Matter Expert (SME), an instructional designer, and at least one person with experience in distance education.

Evaluation in Online Distance Learning Environments

The nature of online teaching requires the instructor to rethink the evaluation process as well. The evaluation component must be ongoing and continual; just leaving everything to one midterm and a final paper would put everyone at a disadvantage. The instructor must become familiar with each student's work, and the only way to accomplish that is through many instructional activities. One possibility is to have weekly questions for students to answer individually, even if the students are working on group projects. They may have to answer a content question, or explain something in the readings. They may also be asked to explain what they have done in the various parts of the course.

A feedback loop is also essential, so perhaps it is wise to include specific times during the term when students fill out an anonymous questionnaire regarding the progress and process of the course. Some faculty members have included one question each week that requires students to consider various aspects of the content, interaction, and affective reaction to the online environment. It is important that the teacher respond to class concerns, when possible, to demonstrate attention to students' needs.

CHALLENGES OF ONLINE DISTANCE LEARNING FOR LEARNERS

Learners face incredible challenges in adapting to online distance learning. Cognitive science and software engineers suggest that individuals must create mental models to be able to understand and internalize what is happening in this new environment (Brandt, 1997). One study suggested that students had to take time to move through the initial efforts of learning the tools before they began constructing new knowledge (Yakimovicz & Murphy, 1995). Another study confirms the necessity for learners to have support to learn and act out their roles in these situations (Olson & Bly, 1991).

One graduate course demonstrated that even in the case of having independent online lessons, it was useful to add a component that required students to interact with their colleagues in some way (Dehler & Poirras-Hernandez, 1998). Eastmond (1995) found that students reported feelings of isolation if they didn't keep up with the interactions, and had to be taught to take personal responsibility for involving themselves. Similarly, it is important to build in practice opportunities for the students to refine their evaluative and analytical skills to be able to successfully use the enormous amount of information on the Internet (King, 1998).

In recent work, Schrum (2001) identified seven dimensions of student success in online distance learning environments. These were the result of investigations of assessment instruments and information gathering from experienced online educators. While these dimensions are presented separately, in reality they do not function independently. Rather, they are similar to an organic system, and work together to support or challenge the online learner.

Access to Tools

The first dimension concerns tools that students must have readily available. Research has demonstrated that easy access to technology, at home or at work, is one of the most significant contributors to success in online learning environments (Benson & Wright, 1999; Bonk & Dennen, 1999; Schrum, 1998). It is worthwhile to create a minimum standard for hardware and software, including peripherals. An institution can provide a convenient and effective way of ensuring that student equipment meets the standards by offering a free mini-course to experiment with the components and also to demonstrate exactly what an online learning experience might be like.

Technology Experience

While having convenient access to the tools is the first step, experience using the tools for personal or work-related activities is also important. More than one study has suggested that students who have little technological experience delay learning new content while they learn the tools (Schrum, 1998; Yakimovicz & Murphy, 1995). Important experiences for new online learners include writing documents using a word processor, printing, sending email on a regular basis, sending and receiving files via email, conducting searches through the World Wide Web, and accessing online information.

Students who are comfortable and adept at these tools will be able to solve small technical problems, such as rebooting their machine, installing software, changing printer cartridges, and answering simple configuration questions. They will also be able to distinguish between the problems related to their individual hardware and software that they can solve and those problems that are better referred to the system administrator or institution for assistance.

Learning Preferences

Students may be concerned that they might miss traditional face-to-face instruction. It is true that each person learns in a unique way—in general, people know the ways in which they are best able to remember a phone number or address. Some people will write it down, others will say it several times, and still others will make a rhyme out of it. Each is appropriate for the individual who uses it. It is important to recognize that when students learn off-campus, individual strengths and weaknesses may be amplified (Bonk & Dennen, 1999). Online instructors must have strategies that accommodate these learning preferences.

Study Habits and Skills

One of the greatest benefits of learning in online distance environments is also one of its greatest challenges. Learners appear to appreciate the greater control over their learning, yet with that control comes substantial responsibility for completing assignments and being prepared (Schrum & Benson, 2000c). Learners must be able to turn off the television and concentrate on their work in a timely fashion, in order to stay on track in turning in assignments. It is clear that those students who do not keep up with the class and the coursework are in greater danger of dropping out. A student may need to assess his/her basic academic proficiencies, such as skimming for information, and then reading the important portions more carefully.

Goals and Purpose

Adults have a variety of reasons for seeking educational experiences, and these may include a mandated upgrade of skills, a requirement for additional credits to maintain licensure, a need to change careers, or a simple desire to gain knowledge. Realization of these goals, however, is often subject to the strength of the motivation that drives these desires (Benson, 1998; Schrum & Benson, 2000a). Motivation describes the internal and external conditions that influence behavior and is one of the most significant factors in persistence in online learning (Schrum, 1998). A non-motivated student may experience difficulty in completing an online course.

Lifestyle Factors

Today's population leads extremely busy lives–with many adults having obligations beyond work. These potential learners must determine if they have 10-20 hours a week to devote to studying. They must also ascertain if they have flexibility in their schedules, or if little room exists for rearrangement. It is vital that learners have the full support of their family, friends, and employers. When competing demands put stress on a student, they often feel they must give up or minimize their studying to keep peace in the family (Schrum & Benson, 2000c). It may also be helpful for the student to find someone who has taken distance courses to act as a mentor for support and advice.

Personal Traits and Characteristics

A few of the dimensions have touched on the ways in which individuals study and learn, but this dimension offers a perspective on fundamental ways in which individuals actually handle their daily activities, and patterns of behavior that go far beyond school-related issues. This includes examining the way one completes daily tasks. For example, is the individual always on time for appointments, or do simple tasks get forgotten in the midst of daily activities? Looking at our personal qualities can be somewhat difficult, but it is an important step toward successful online learning. If learners are aware of their deficiencies, they can seek help in overcoming them. For example, Eastmond (1995) found students must be instructed in ways to take personal responsibility for becoming involved in the interactions and with their colleagues.

CHALLENGES OF PROGRAM PLANNING FOR ONLINE DISTANCE LEARNING

Administrators and program planners face many challenges in adapting degree and certificate programs to an online environment. The distance education literature is short on program-level planning models (e.g., Holmberg, 1995; Knott, 1994; Rumble, 1986). For the most part, the literature has focused on individual courses (e.g., Andriole, 1997; Benson, 1998; Benson & Wright, 1999; Bourne et al., 1997; Cooper, 1999; Lauzon, 1992; Mason, 1998; Pincas, 1998). Recent research conducted by the authors suggests that success with online distance learning at the program level require attention to seven key areas: faculty development, technical support, student services, curriculum design, program format, course design, and marketing.

Faculty Development

The strength of the faculty largely determines the success of any program, traditional or online, but in an online distance learning program, faculty development cannot be overemphasized. This development includes technical training, pedagogical training, and administrative support.

First, faculty must have more than a general familiarity with the technology being used. Faculty teaching online for the first time have identified a need for more familiarity with software and hardware (Benson, 2001). Faculty members who are familiar with the technology and comfortable with its use will be more likely to model appropriate use. Providing opportunities for instructors to participate in an online course will give them needed experience and allow them to experience the online environment as their students will. Some organizations conduct a portion of the technology and pedagogical training online to gain this benefit.

Second, faculty need pedagogical training to be successful in this new environment. In many ways the technology training and the pedagogical training go hand-in-hand. Introducing faculty to the interactions model of learning is an effective way to begin the pedagogical training. The interactions model specifies four types of interactions required for an effective learning environment: learner to instructor, learner to content, learner to learner, and learner to technology (Hillman, Willis, & Gunawardena, 1994; Moore, 1989). Once faculty start thinking of their courses in terms of these interactions, they can be introduced to online tools that facilitate the interactions. For example, asynchronous communication over a bulletin board or discussion list can facilitate the learner to learner interaction.

Faculty also must have appropriate administrative support and concomitant rewards if they are to be successful in an online environment. Faculty members require freedom to perform in the online distance learning environment without being forced to adhere unnecessarily to the restraints and constraints of the traditional classroom. For example, the performance review process for faculty teaching online must accommodate the differences between teaching online and teaching in a traditional classroom. Peers of the online instructor may not understand the additional demands on an instructor teaching online and thus, may not account for those differences in their peer reviews. Traditional course evaluations may not address the specifics of the online course, so new course evaluations may need to be introduced into the program structure. These evaluations may need to be delivered in nontraditional ways (Schrum & Benson, 2000c).

Technical Support

Technical support is a mandatory requirement. Technical support goes beyond providing continued technical training and includes the ongoing support that faculty and students need. Faculty and students experiencing online distance learning for the first time will run into problems; however, these problems can be overcome if an adequate support system is provided. Help Desk functions are now commonly associated with online distance learning programs. Many institutions and organizations provide such functions on a 24 hours/7 days a week basis to accommodate the "anytime, anyplace" nature of online learning (Benson, 2001).

Student Services

Student Services are important in online distance learning environments. Online students require all the support functions of traditional students: registration, financial aide, bookstore, library services, counseling, and access to appropriate equipment and technology. Since the online student is learning at a distance, Student Services functions need to be provided online. It is obvious how a school's registration, financial aide, bookstore, and library functions can be put online, but online counseling is a relatively new area (Benson, 2001).

First, online learning students should be assigned a single counselor whom they can contact for all issues related to their experience, and this person should be trained to address a wide variety of student concerns. It would be unfair to force the online student to have eight points of contact. Second, this counselor must be knowledgeable about learning in an online environment so that she or he can provide the specialized support required by these learners.

Curriculum Design

Choosing a curriculum for an online distance learning program is nontrivial. Educational institutions want to assure that their online program meets regional accreditation standards, and fortunately, many accreditation associations have developed criteria. For example, traditional standards require a fixed amount of face-to-face time for each credit hour assigned to a course. Obviously, that requirement can't be met in an online distance learning environment, so a revised requirement is needed. Accrediting agencies are beginning to examine these kinds of differences and to provide alternative standards more suited to the online environment (Benson, 2001).

Another curriculum issue concerns the determination of which courses to offer in the online program. Successful online programs have tended to limit the number of student course options (Schrum & Benson, 2000a). For example, a student in an on-campus MBA program may have seven specialization areas from which to choose, while the online student may only have two. As more students choose online program delivery, increased options may be provided to them.

A final curriculum issue deals with the structure of course offerings. Programs may choose a cohort model, an independent study model, or some variation of both. In the cohort model, students progress lock step through the courses in the program, typically on a traditional school-year schedule. In the independent study model, students are free to enroll in courses at any time, and are given a fixed time to complete each course. Few programs have chosen this latter option. Most choose a pure cohort system, or a modified cohort system. In the modified cohort system, students enroll in a course in the program and move through that course in a lock-step fashion, but they don't necessarily move through all the courses in the program together (Benson, 2001).

Program Technologies

A key to program success in online distance learning environments is the use of multiple technologies. Varying combinations of email, bulletin boards, chat rooms, white boards, audio, and streaming media can provide significant value to an online course. While instructors may be warned to avoid lecturing online, recent research has shown that students have a favorable attitude towards the use of narrated PowerPoint presentations to supplement their coursework (Schrum & Benson, 2000b). Of course, not all students will find all media equally valuable, but using multiple media will give students choices and address a variety of learning style preferences.

Many programs have come to rely almost exclusively on online technologies and ignore the value of using the telephone, fax, and even face-to-face experiences to supplement the online experience. Online students should feel as free to call an instructor during office hours as they do to send him or her an email message, or visit him or her in a chat room. Programs using the cohort model have found success with initial face-to-face sessions where they begin building a sense of community among the enrolled students. For many programs that initial face-to-face session is the only contact the cohort has; other programs have chosen to infuse their design with multiple face-to-face sessions (Schrum & Benson, 2000a). The choice depends on the nature of the program and financial resources of the students who would have to travel to the meeting site.

Course Design

Course design in the online distance learning environment is the focus of much discussion and research. Everyone seems to agree that developing an online course requires more than physically moving the course to the electronic medium; rather, the course and its goals must be reconceptualized for the new medium. Similarly, when moving an entire program, the courses must be reconceptualized as part of the online program. For example, research shows that asynchronous bulletin boards can be used to support the learner-learner interaction as well as higher-order thinking skills (Shapley, 2000); thus, online instructors may want to make use of this tool. In reconceptualizing the courses as part of an online program, faculty members may decide to have a common bulletin board for discussion of topics related to multiple courses. Alternatively, faculty members may choose to redistribute one course's content across multiple courses.

All the courses in a single program may have a consistent look and feel. Unless there is a valid reason dictated by course content and learning goals, students should not be required to learn a new set of tools for each course in the program. A tool set should be established at the program level, and those tools used by all faculty.

Marketing and Pricing

Marketing and pricing the online program should not be ignored. Some institutions have found success by entering into partnerships with corporations to provide online degrees and programs for the corporations' employees (Schrum & Benson, 2000c). These institutions have been able to fully recover their costs, and in many cases, make a profit. Other institutions have targeted a specific student population in a specific subject area, and spent marketing dollars to reach that population. No institution should take the "if we build it, they will come" attitude.

CONCLUSION

This chapter has identified significant issues related to online distance learning for educators, learners, and program planners. It synthesized information from a growing literature base and included the results of several studies that the authors have completed. But this article only reflects the beginning of the trend towards online distance learning. Postsecondary institutions are under pressure to provide greater access to educational opportunities, and they face intense competition from industry and for-profit companies for students' attention. This pressure may cause decisions to be made without full consideration, and the authors suggest that larger ethical, legal, and social questions have yet to be answered. Some of these include:

- What will happen to intellectual property rights of professors who locate their resources online?
- Is it possible that less skilled workers might be hired to deliver these courses (Noble, 1998)?
- Will students become "guinea pigs" in experimental trials of online courses?
- Should students be paid for their participation, or at least be allowed to take the courses for free?
- Is it possible that education will become a compilation of individual courses, rather a broader whole that is greater than the sum of its parts?

The possibilities in the online world are immeasurable. Educators and the public at large have an opportunity to take a proactive stand in the development of courses and programs to insure that they are pedagogically sound, organizationally strong, and programmatically effective. The result will be the best possible online distance learning environments.

REFERENCES

Andriole, S. J. (1997). Requirements-driven ALN course design, development, delivery & evaluation. *Journal of Asynchronous Learning Environments*, 1(2).

Benson, A. D. (1998). Focus: From face-to-face lecture to asynchronous online collaboration. *Open Learning Systems News*, 65, 1-4.

Benson, A. D. (2001). *Planning and Implementing Online Degree Programs: A Case Study of A Statewide University System Distance Learning Consortium*. Manuscript in progress.

Benson, A. and Wright, E. (1999). Pedagogy and policy in the age of the wired professor: A case study of teaching Spanish language online. *T.H.E. Journal*, (27)4, 60-68.

Benson, A., Guy, T. and Tallman, J. (in press). Viewing online learning through the lens of perspective transformation. *International Journal of Educational Telecommunications*.

Bonk, C. J. and Dennen, V. (1999). Learner issues with WWW-based systems. *International Journal of Educational Telecommunications*, 5(4), 401-417.

Bourne, J. R., McMaster, E., Rieger, J. and Campbell, J. O. (1997). Paradigms for on-line learning: A case study in the design and implementation of an Asynchronous Learning Environments (ALN) course. *Journal of Asynchronous Learning Environments*, 1(2).

Brandt, D. S. (1997). Constructivism: Teaching for understanding of the Internet. *Communications of the ACM*, 40(10), 112-117.

Candiotti, A. and Clarke, N. (1998). Combining universal access with faculty development and academic facilities. *Communications of the ACM*, 41(1), 36-41.

Cooper, L. (1999). Anatomy of an online course. *T.H.E. Journal*, 26(7), 49-51.

Dehler, C. and Poirras-Hernandez, L. H. (1998). Using computer-mediated communication (CMC) to promote experiential learning in graduate studies. *Educational Technology*, 38(5), 52-55.

Eastmond, D. V. (1995). *Alone But Together: Adult Distance Study Through Computer Conferencing*. Cresskill, NJ: Hampton Press, Inc.

Gerencher, K. (1998). MBA programs go online. *InfoWorld*, December, 20, 71-72.

Heeren, E. and Lewis, R. (1997). Selecting communication media for distributed communities. *Journal of Computer Assisted Learning*, 13(2), 85-98.

Hillman, C. D., Willis, D. J. and Gunawardena, C. N. (1994). Learner-interface interaction in distance education: an extension of contemporary models and strategies for practitioners. *The American Journal of Distance Education*, 8(2), 30-42.

Holmberg, B. (1995). *Theory and Practice of Distance Education*. (2nd ed.). London: Routledge.

Kember, D. (1995). *Open Learning Courses for Adults: A Model of Student Progress*. Englewood Cliffs, NJ: Educational Technology Publications.

King, K. P. (1998). Course development on the World Wide Web. In Cahoon, B. (Ed.), *Adult Learning and the Internet*, 78, 25-32. San Francisco: Jossey-Bass Publishers.

Knott, T. (1994). *Planning and Evaluating Distance Education: A Guide to Collaboration*. Memphis, TN: Diaphera Publications.

Lauzon, A. C. (1992). Integrating computer-based instruction with computer conferencing: An evaluation of a model for designing online education. *American Journal of Distance Education*, 6(2), 32-46.

Mangan, K. S. (1999). Top business schools seek to ride a bull market in on-line MBA's. *The Chronicle of Higher Education*, 45(19), A27-A28.

Mason, R. (1998). Models of online courses. *ALN Magazine*, October, 2.

Moore, M. G. (1989). Three types of interaction. *The American Journal of Distance Education*, 3(2), 1-7.

Noble, D. (1998). Digital diploma mills: The automation of higher education. *First Monday*, 3(1).

Olson, M. H. and Bly, S. A. (1991). The Portland experience: A report on a distributed research group. In Greenberg, S. (Ed.), *Computer Supported Cooperative Work and Groupware*, 81-98. San Diego, CA: Academic Press Limited.

Pincas, A. (1998). Successful online course design: Virtual frameworks for discourse construction. *Educational Technology & Society*, 1(1).

Radford, A. (1997). The future of multimedia in education. *First Monday*, 2(11). Available on the World Wide Web at: http://131.193.231/issues/issue2_11/radford/index.html.

Rumble, G. (1986). *The Planning and Management of Distance Education*. London: Croom Helm

Schrum, L. (2001). Creating Distance Learning environments: A challenge for educators and learners. *Proceedings of the Conference on the 21st Century University*. Muscat, Oman.

Schrum, L. (2000). Online teaching and learning: Essential conditions for success. In Lau, L. (Ed.), *Distance Learning Technologies: Issues, Trends, and Opportunities*, 91-106. Hershey, PA: Idea Group Publishing.

Schrum, L. (1998). Online education in the information age: A study of emerging pedagogy. In Cahoon, B. (Ed.), *Adult Learning and the Internet*, 53-61. San Francisco: Jossey-Bass Publishers.

Schrum, L. and Benson, A. (2000a). Online professional education: A case study of an MBA program through its transition to an online model. *Journal of Asynchronous Learning Environments*, (4)1. Available on the World Wide Web at: http://www.aln.org/alnweb/journal/Vol4_issue1/schrum.htm.

Schrum, L. and Benson, A. (2000b). Lessons to consider: Online learning from student and faculty perspectives. In Mann, B. L. (Ed.), *Perspectives in Web Course Management*, 225-238. Toronto: Canadian Scholars' Press, Inc.

Schrum, L. and Benson, A. (2000c). A case study of one online MBA program: Lessons from the first iteration of an innovative educational experience. *The Business, Education and Technology Journal*, 2(2), 38-46.

Schrum, L. and Berge, Z. L. (1998). Creating student interaction within the educational experience: A challenge for online teachers. *Canadian Journal of Educational Communication*, 26(3), 133-144.

Shapley, P. (2000). On-line education to develop complex reasoning skills in organic chemistry. *Journal of Asynchronous Learning Environments*, (4)2. Available on the World Wide Web at: http://www.aln.org/alnweb/journal/Vol4_issue2/le/shapley/LE-shapley.htm.

Tallman, J. and Benson, A. (2000). Mental models and web-based learning: Examining the change in personal learning models of graduate students enrolled in an online library media course. *Journal of Education for Library and Information Science*, (41)3, 207-223.

Wiesenberg, F. and Hutton, S. (1996). Teaching a graduate program using computer-mediated conferencing software. *Journal of Distance Education*, 11(1), 83-100.

Yakimovicz, A. D. and Murphy, K. L. (1995). Constructivism and collaboration on the Internet: Case study of a graduate class experience. *Computers and Education*, 24(3), 203-209.

Chapter XIII

A Case Study in Managing a Distance Education Consortium

Vicky A. Seehusen
Colorado Electronic Community College, USA

This chapter describes the unique distance education consortium called CCCOnline developed by the Community Colleges of Colorado System (CC of C). CC of C is comprised of 14 Colorado Community Colleges and delivers courses, certificates and degrees to more than 250,000 students per year. The CCCOnline consortium, managed by the Colorado Electronic Community College (CECC), provides centralized management of faculty and curriculum and the consortial member colleges provide most of the student services to their students enrolled in the program.

This chapter traces the organizational evolution of CCCOnline. CCCOnline was very much a "top-down" creation. It was also built very quickly. The creators of CCCOnline believed that speed was necessary to get educational offerings online and that internal relationships could be dealt with later. Neuhauser, Bender, and Stromberg (2000) echo this belief. They state that adding an e-business to traditional business creates a parallel culture. Furthermore, they believe that, at present, many consumers seem to accept that new products will have a few bugs and that the key is to figure out how to deliver speed and quality over the long run.

At the time CCCOnline was created, there was little information about designing online distance education consortia. Witherspoon (1996) had compiled a planner's casebook that included real world experiences of a number of universities and colleges that had created distance education courses or programs. Dixon (1996) had compiled a guide for students that includes chapters on quality in distance education and what to expect in a virtual classroom. Porter (1997) had endeavored to give practical advice on putting together effective programs and courses, including a checklist for course design and evaluation. All of these books were useful but only barely prepared CECC for issues, challenges, problems and confrontations to come.

In retrospect, CECC's lack of knowledge of the potential difficulties might have been a good thing, because the management team proceeded without fear of the difficulties ahead.

CECC staff didn't plan for every contingency and consequently development was not stalled. The CECC staff plugged along, without complete awareness of the difficulties of trying to merge the instructional and student services policies of 14 colleges. CECC didn't even know how to go about improving its awareness and how to best work with the colleges. Every activity the CECC management team undertook to educate these colleges about the workings of the centralized management team and the program policies and procedures became an activity that educated the management team. CECC soon recognized that each college, while part of the same system, still had individual policies and processes that had to be taken into account.

Over time, intra and intercollegiate teams and committees have been created to facilitate governance and management of the program and to deliver high-quality instructional and student services. These committees and teams allow all the member colleges to have a voice in guiding program management and the future direction. The committees and teams strive to be inclusive and often call upon subject matter experts from other parts of the college(s) to solve problems or create new online educational approaches. These teams and committees act as connecting agents back to their college constituents and improve information flow between the constituents and the management team.

A CASE STUDY IN MANAGING A DISTANCE EDUCATION CONSORTIUM

CCCOnline is a unique consortial approach to distance education created in September 1997 by the Community Colleges of Colorado (hereinafter referred to as "CC of C"). CC of C oversees 13 NCA-accredited Colorado community colleges and one nonaccredited community college called Colorado Electronic Community College (CECC). Together, these colleges serve almost 250,000 Colorado students annually.

In the fall of 1997, the CC of C System president convened a meeting of the 14 community college presidents. He proposed the creation of an online degree and certificate program that would be developed and delivered consortially. The colleges would share the development costs equally but would receive revenue based upon their individual college enrollments. A contract was negotiated with a for-profit vendor to provide the course management software and support on its computer servers. The vendor's initial $100,000 development charge (not including faculty costs) was divided equally among the colleges.

CECC was selected to provide leadership and management support for the new online program. Since 1995, CECC had managed an Associate of Arts telecourse degree program that linked an accredited CC of C college with an outside vendor. The accredited CC of C college provided the financial aid and transcripted the credit, and the vendor provided national marketing, a call center, and bookstore/videotape delivery services. CECC hired faculty, provided the instructional materials, advising and registration services, and managed the relationships with the vendor and the accredited CC of C college. So CECC was a logical choice to lead the new consortium because of its previous experience managing college/for-profit partnerships. Also, because CECC was not accredited and did not enroll students, the member colleges considered it noncompetitive.

The name chosen for the new online consortial model was CCCOnline. The first degree CCCOnline offered was an Associate of Applied Science in Business. Many of CC of C colleges already had their own versions of this degree, and it was a popular degree. So it was a generally held belief that this degree would generate high enrollments. Still in the early days of the development of CCCOnline, two main challenges were identified:

1. Creating a degree with a consistent list of course offerings and requirements on which colleges could mutually agree. All of the colleges offered all of the courses that would be part of the online Associate of Applied Science in Business. However, for some colleges the new online degree required giving up one or two courses from their current business degrees. For other colleges, the new online degree obligated them to accept new courses that were not required in their current business degrees.

2. Creating an equitable financial model. From the beginning, CECC, managing CCCOnline on behalf of the consortium, was intended to be mainly self-supporting. The model had to allow for a management fee to support CECC and create enough new state general fund support and tuition funds for member colleges.

The CECC management team put in long, intense days during the first two months of operation. The management team strived to meet the goals of the program and simultaneously respond to implementation challenges. There were two program goals:

1. To eliminate redundancy of online offerings.
2. To expand educational offerings to rural students.

Many community colleges, especially in the Denver metropolitan area, were already offering online courses. In the year prior to the creation of CCCOnline, these colleges became aware that they could no longer control a service area marked by geographic boundaries. Therefore, these colleges could not depend on students residing in the college service areas to continue to fulfill their educational requirements at the local community college. Also, the colleges duplicated other colleges' online course offerings, and CC of C believed that this duplication was an inefficient use of the hardware, software, personnel, and financial resources of the individual colleges.

Additionally, students in rural Colorado were faced with a limited number of choices when it came to community college courses and programs. Due to demands and economies of scale, many classes that could be offered in heavily populated urban areas could not be offered in the rural areas. Also, it was often difficult in rural areas to find faculty with subject matter expertise needed to teach certain classes.

During the start-up days of CCCOnline, CECC remained the focal point for all communications regarding instructional, administrative, and student services issues. Communications between CECC staff and college staff were extensive. Misunderstandings were abundant, and even when policies and procedures were clarified, it wasn't always clear who should receive the clarifications and whether the information would be widely disseminated. However, the CECC management team remained focused on working with the college partners to provide high-quality instruction and student services, and to eliminate barriers to online teaching and learning. Ad hoc teams of interested individuals were created to deal with immediate and obvious issues. These teams are defined the next section.

AD HOC TEAMS

The College Teams

Despite resistance from many of the local community colleges and limited policies and procedures, the first degree was online within 100 days of the creation of CCCOnline. A number of member colleges provided faculty to develop the initial 20 classes. Colleges that volunteered the initial faculty did so at their own expense, either paying the faculty overload fees or providing paid release time. The college presidents agreed that once the first degree was developed, all the colleges enrolling students in CCCOnline courses would jointly absorb future course development costs. Even those colleges where resistance to the consortial model was the highest were anxious to be contributors for fear that they might be left out of a potentially successful program.

New policies and procedures written in early days were designed to address student services issues. Member college registrars met to discuss student record processes: 1) how the courses would be entered into their databases, 2) how to distinguish these courses from other campus offerings, 3) how and when to create semesters and sessions; and, 4) what semester and session start and stop dates would be.

Other ad hoc student services teams were created as required. These teams met to discuss how to deliver online advising, provide financial aid services online, and develop a common online application form. While CECC gradually realized that long-term committees and new ways of communicating would have to be established after the program was built, its initial, primary goal was to get its CCCOnline up and running.

The Course Management Provider Team

Using an outside vendor with its own hardware, software, and personnel resources allowed the instructors to focus on the development of high-quality course materials. The local vendor, eCollege.com, provided the course management software and was initially chosen because it could provide an application and registration software in addition to the course management software. The existing Student Information System (SIS), registration software used by the community colleges, did not allow for online registration. We strove to create a one-stop online site for students, regardless of the college that would grant the credit. The vendor provided the online application and registration software. Students could visit the central website, choose a "home" college from among the consortial members, apply, and enroll. Once classes began, students could access the same online site to receive their instruction. For these services, the vendor charged a onetime, up-front, development fee for each course created on its system. The vendor also charged a per-student enrollment fee that would be computed and billed the day after the last date to drop in any given session (14 days after the course start date).

The enrollment data collected by the vendor's software was uploaded to the member colleges' computerized SIS every night. It helped that every college in the consortium used the same SIS; only one program had to be written to update the records of the consortial member colleges.

The Centralized Computer Services Team

CC of C centrally maintains the SIS for the member colleges. Staff from the CC of C's Computer Department worked very closely with the vendor's technical staff. Together, they formed a team that wrote the program that would upload and download data between CC of C computers and vendor computers. the CC of C's Computer Department also wrote programs that would search college SIS databases and remove the duplicate records that were sure to be created. Duplication was inevitable because all students, even those currently enrolled in traditional courses at member colleges, were required to reapply the first time they elected to take CCCOnline courses. This was necessary so that the vendor could establish a student database and build course rosters. Additionally, the CC of C's Computer Department met with the registrars and CECC staff and created procedures to assure that online courses were included in each college's database.

In January 1998, CCCOnline began offering the Associate of Applied Science in Business degree. The first semester, slightly less than 300 students enrolled in CCCOnline courses. CECC considered this a great start considering that very little advertising and virtually no up-front marketing had been done. From the onset, it was clear that there was a market for this type of educational offering and that the program was destined to grow.

A SAMPLING OF PROBLEMS ENCOUNTERED

During CCCOnline's first two months of online operation, a majority of the problems related to instructional content. However, towards the last week of the first semester, a host of issues surfaced. Student services, instructional services, and business services departments across the consortium began identifying issues needing resolution. Some of the more gripping issues the consortium faced are described below.

Student Services Issues

During the short time of "program creation to market delivery," little thought was given to the way that student services would be handled at the individual member colleges. Because all of the colleges were part of CC of C, it was generally believed that all colleges operated with similar student services procedures. As CCCOnline moved towards the end of the first semester, there was a gradual realization that individual college student services departments varied widely in their practices. Among other things, the colleges did not use common grading policies or common forms.

For example: some colleges did not use an F as a part of their grading scale; some colleges allowed the student to receive an S for satisfactory work; and other colleges did not allow an S letter grade. The colleges were reluctant to change their traditional grading policies. This meant that the instructor had to read the policies of the home college of each student in his/her class to determine the appropriate grading policy. The grading policy, initially posted on CCCOnline, reflected each college's individual grading policy and was 37 pages long!

Also, each college had its own grade change, withdrawal and incomplete forms, so instructors wishing to use one of these forms on behalf of an individual student had to contact the student's home college and request and submit the proper forms. It wasn't long before faculty began to complain loudly.

Instructional Services Issues

Faculty were dissatisfied with the myriad of forms that they had to use and some were dissatisfied with the faculty pay plan. When CCCOnline was created, a separate faculty pay plan was developed. Under this plan, the colleges who employed the instructors teaching for CCCOnline would prepare "overload contracts" for those instructors. The colleges would then request reimbursement from CECC for these contracts. CECC would reimburse each college the same flat rate, hourly amount regardless of how much the colleges paid their faculty for normal overload contracts. Most colleges paid their CCCOnline instructors the total amount that would be reimbursed by CECC; some colleges paid their CCCOnline instructors *more* than the reimbursement from CECC and absorbed the additional costs internally; and a small minority of colleges paid their CCCOnline instructors *less* than the reimbursement amount from CECC. Faculty who were being paid less demanded that they be paid on par with their contemporaries. The colleges that were paying less stated that they would not compromise existing overload pay plans and that it would be unfair to pay their CCCOnline faculty higher overload rates than the traditional overload rates.

The second concern that surfaced quickly was how to develop new courses and degrees consortially. Within a couple months of placing the associate degree online, CECC began investigating the development of other degrees that would allow students to upgrade their skills for new employment or career advancement. From the beginning, small groups of faculty at different colleges complained that they had no input into the original degree and demanded a more inclusive process for degree development.

Business Services Issues

Almost immediately upon opening the CCCOnline website to enrollments, the business services units of the colleges identified two areas of high concern. Students complained that they could apply and enroll online but they could not pay tuition online. All of the colleges accepted credit card payments in person or over the telephone, but there was no protected, encrypted software program that allowed students to pay online. System business services staff, the CC of C's computer services staff, and the vendor's technical staff held many meetings to iron out the timeline and the roles each unit would play in securing an online payment service for students.

Enrollment reconciliation, however, caused the most angst for the business officers. After the census date, the vendor would submit an invoice based upon the number of credit hours the CCCOnline students were enrolled. Most of the time, the enrollment figures reported by the vendor were higher than the enrollment figures reported by the individual colleges. Generally, this reconciliation problem occurred because students would manually drop their CCCOnline class at the home college and the information did not get uploaded into the vendor's database, or the software designed to update the vendor database failed. Reconciliation took several weeks.

All of the issues served to drive home the need for more and better ways of communicating with our college partners and soliciting feedback.

COMMITTEES FORMED TO DEAL WITH ONGOING ISSUES

As CCCOnline evolved and grew, three major teams or committees were formed. They are the Community College Coordinators (CCC), the Ready Response Team (RRT), and the Online Curriculum Committee (OCC). Each of these committees or teams plays a vital role in the success and future growth of CCCOnline.

Community College Coordinators

The Community College Coordinators (CCC) was the first committee created. The presidents of each of the member colleges designated a person to represent them on this committee. Representation includes instructional and student services administrators, registrars, business officers, instructors, and campus distance education staff. The CCC meets quarterly. They discuss the current status of the program and receive information about how the program is changing or evolving (including new policies and procedures). When the CCC was first formed, its major role was to identify and discuss issues that the colleges uncovered in the ongoing maintenance and implementation of CCCOnline. These frank discussions surfaced problems identified by one college but actually impacting many colleges. These issues were then sent to the Educational Services Council for resolution.

The Educational Services Council is comprised of all the member college vice-presidents for student services, vice-presidents for instruction, and some CC of C support staff. Approximately 40 people from around the state attend the monthly Educational Services Council meetings. The size of the Council quickly became a deterrent to quick resolution of issues. The Council determined that a smaller team was needed to investigate issues and make recommendations to the full group. As a result, the Ready Response Team was created.

Ready Response Team

Initial membership of the Ready Response Team (RRT) was comprised of ten Educational Service Council members (including vice-presidents of student services and vice-presidents of instruction). Over time, some of the vice-presidents sent representatives in their place. Some of these representatives became members of the team, providing different perspectives and useful suggestions. From its inception, the RRT met monthly to discuss and study current issues, and recommend new policies and procedures to deal with these issues. As the issues submitted to the team broadened, the RRT expanded its membership to include business services staff and college distance education directors. At present, there are 14 people on this committee, representing eight urban and rural member colleges and CC of C office.

Participation in the RRT is high and issues or concerns brought to the RRT are discussed in great detail. Timeliness is key, however, and the goal is to create a policy/procedure recommendation within two months after reviewing an issue. Some issues, such as the online grading policy, may take longer than two months to resolve. However, every issue brought before the RRT has resulted in policy or procedure recommendation within five months.

If the RRT determines it doesn't have enough information or subject matter expertise to deal with an issue, the issue is submitted to another CC of C committee for resolution. For example, the RRT requested that the college registrars create draft forms for the approval of the Educational Services Council when it was determined that common grade change and incomplete forms would improve efficiency. When enrollment reconciliation continued to pose problems and delays, the RRT asked the college Business Officers and the CC of C's centralized Computer Department to meet and create a better process. When concerns were expressed about how new degrees would be developed, the RRT created a flow chart of what activities should occur, what college committees needed to be involved/informed, and the order in which activities needed to take place. When CCCOnline faculty requested a common grading policy, the RRT developed a proposal, sent it to the registrars for comment, and then returned the completed proposal to the Educational Services Council for approval.

The RRT was also responsible for the creation of the third major committee, the Online Curriculum Committee (OCC). The RRT spent many months discussing how to enhance communications to faculty groups at the colleges and improve faculty buy-in. The OCC seemed to be the most aggressive way to deal with the faculty concerns about the academic integrity of the curriculum. It was also a response to faculty complaints about lack of inclusion in the course and degree development process.

Online Curriculum Committee

The OCC approves the online program curriculum once Educational Services has approved development of a degree or certificate. This committee has a representative from every college in the consortium. The committee also has one registrar. Once curriculum is approved by the OCC, it can be developed on the CCCOnline site. The OCC does not have authority to approve curriculum that will be used in the traditional classroom. However, any individual college that wishes to use the approved online curriculum in the traditional classroom may do so.

LESSONS LEARNED

I can often be heard saying, "you can't mandate what matters." CCCOnline was created by the combined visions of very small group of people. If the people you need to be successful don't "buy-in" to your vision, then it will be difficult, if not impossible to implement. The argument that "everyone else is doing it" is not likely to make an impression on most of your constituents. As

I worked with the many different constituents and groups in the CC of C, I realized that, in times of plenty or scarcity, each constituent has very different motivators for doing something above and beyond the norm.

The constituents are also loyal to their individual college missions. A program that removes local management and control of any facet of providing education or services to students will be met with dislike, distaste, and distrust. The following practices would serve a management team well:

1) The team must be continually attentive and take the time to get to know the constituents, seek out their hidden motivators and make efforts to integrate these motivators into the program development.

2) The team has to be dependable and follow through on any commitments to research topics and vendors, develop courses, and provide information requested by constituents.

3) The team must provide requested services in a timely fashion.

4) The team must continually move the program forward and simultaneously respect the fact that different constituents will adapt to change at different rates.

5) The team must live service leadership and be genuine when it states, "We are here to serve you and your colleges. Together, we all win."

CONCLUSION

A consortium of the size and scope of CCCOnline continues to face new issues on an almost daily basis. Communications are many and yet never seem to be enough. Sometimes well-intentioned procedures and processes are approved and implemented, and then revised within a few weeks after implementation because new data is received making changes imperative. Additionally, as the state commission on higher education changes its policies, CCCOnline is required to change its policies or procedures to be in compliance.

There is little literature available for personnel involved in the management of an online consortium of the size and scope of CCCOnline. The consortial clients for CCCOnline are colleges that are endeavoring to respond to their individual communities by providing learning and training options for personal and workforce development. Service to local communities is a primary mission. Growth of the consortium will be stymied if the consortium cannot show how serving a more global community will enhance services to the local community. Interacting with members of other colleges will allow the various staff and faculty to get a wider perspective on issues. They get to see beyond their college's back-door.

Building cross-college teams and committees allows for a cross-pollination of ideas and allow consortial members to see where their goals converge and diverge from other members. The staff that manages the consortium has to be vigilant of current events in the online educational marketplace. The staff should present this information to the teams and committees, thereby expanding knowledge and encouraging committee and team members to think about ways to provide new learning and student services to online and traditional students.

Resources used by CECC include League for Innovation publications such as *Teaching at a Distance* (Boaz et al., 1999), and the *Faculty Guide for Moving Teaching and Learning to the Web* (Boettcher & Conrad, 1999). Another resource that was particularly helpful as the consortium began to form teams and define team missions was *New Connections: A Guide to Distance Education* (Gross, Gross, & Pirkl, 1998), a publication of the Instructional Telecommunications Council. All of these were useful resources for educating team and committee members.

The consortium believes that the key to CCCOnline's continued success is the long-term commitment and support of these committees and teams by our member colleges. The development of CCCOnline initially drove large change in CC of C and it continues to drive great change. These days however, the committees and teams that support CCCOnline are used to this change and excited to be a part of the evolution of CCCOnline. Enrollment in CCCOnline programs has increased every semester since inception and there's every reason to believe that this trend will continue. Online learning has become mainstream. Our member colleges know that providing high quality online learning and student services is only possible with continual vigilance and willingness to change. Witherspoon (1997) states, "the Colorado Model is one to watch."

REFERENCES

Boaz, M., Elliott, B., Foshee, D., Hardy, D., Jarmon, C. amd Olcott, D. (1999). *Teaching at A Distance*. Mission Viejo, CA: League for Innovation in the Community College and Archipelago Productions.

Boettcher, J. and Conrad, R. (1999). *Faculty Guide for Moving Teaching and Learning to the Web*. Mission Viejo, CA: League for Innovation in the Community College.

Dixon P. (1996). *Virtual College*. Princeton, NJ: Peterson's.

Gross, R., Gross, D. and Pirkl, R. (1998). *New Connections: A Guide to Distance Education*. Washington DC: Instructional Telecommunications Council.

Neuhauser. P., Bender, R. and Stromberg, K. (2000). *Culture.com: Building Corporate Culture in the Connected Workplace.* New York: John Wiley & Sons.

Porter, L. R. (1997). *Virtual Classroom: Distance Learning With the Internet.* New York: John Wiley & Sons.

Witherspoon, J. (1996). *Distance Education: A Planner's Casebook.* Boulder, CO. Western Interstate Commission for Higher Education.

Chapter XIV

Using Tutored Video Instruction Methodology to Deliver Management Education at a Distance in China

L. William Murray and Alev M. Efendioglu
University of San Francisco, USA

INTRODUCTION

This chapter summarizes a report of a systematic study of distance education programs whose audience was middle- and upper-level managers employed full-time at two Chinese companies. These programs were evaluated in terms of their educational effectiveness; i.e., did these students, and the companies who paid for their education, receive good value for their investment of time and money?

Unfortunately, few studies have attempted to validate benefits or to substantiate the shortcomings of distance education and associated technologies, especially in the area of international management education. The conclusions of two of the earliest systematic studies of distance suggested that using television as a means of delivering instruction to students, regardless of grade levels or subject matter, *could* result in student performance that was equal to that of "live" classes, (Chu & Schramm, 1967; Schramm, 1967).

In the early 1970s, the engineering school of Stanford University was approached by Hewlett-Packard (HP) to assist them in expanding the educational and training opportunities for employees working in company facilities at some distance from Stanford's campus (and HP's corporate headquarters). Based on the early results of Chu and Schramm, Stanford's engineering program pioneered the development of an experimental distance education methodology—Tutored Video Instruction (TVI)—for the purpose of providing graduate engineering education to Hewlett-Packard engineers located in Santa Rosa, California, approximately 100 miles from Stanford's campus. The engineering courses required for Master's degree completion were videotaped and were then sent to HP's plant in Santa Rosa, where the students met as a group to view and discuss the videotapes once per week. No in-person (i.e., "live") contact with the faculty was permitted, and Stanford University or HP did not support electronic messaging between the students and the faculty.

A local tutor was hired and trained to direct the students' learning at the Santa Rosa site. The tutor was charged with three functions: (1) to distribute materials for the instructor and to collect assignments; (2) to answer questions if possible; otherwise, to obtain answers from the instructor; and (3) to encourage discussion. Initially, the tutor was a retired HP engineer.

An evaluation of these initial TVI courses included these observations (Gibbons et al., 1977):

- TVI student grades were statistically higher than those of the on-campus students (whose "live" class had been taped for subsequent viewing off-campus).
- Smaller student groups liked TVI more than larger classes.
- The lower the distance student's undergraduate grade point average (GPA), the more effective was the TVI experience, as measured by each student's grade in the TVI classes.
- Tutors who answered questions directly (i.e., technically proficient) were less effective than those tutors who drew students into discussion (i.e., discussion facilitation).

There have been several studies of the effectiveness of TVI since Stanford's introductory program. For example, Stone (1990) conducted a cross-sectional analysis of TVI distance education offerings in engineering education. The results of this study directly support those of the pioneering Stanford study. Arentz (1995) conducted a study to compare the effectiveness of various distance education methodologies employed in teaching engineering to students in Norway. In direct comparison to other means of learning at a distance, TVI was clearly the preferred method of learning.

During the 1980s, a study comparing the effectiveness of TVI directly to "live" instruction was undertaken (Appleton et al., 1989). A study of 144 Australian undergraduate students concluded that TVI student performance was at least equal to that of on-campus students enrolled in live classes at their main campus. Further, TVI was found to be more effective as a learning technology when compared to the other forms of distance learning being used by the institution at the same time: correspondence education, audiotaped programs, and videotaped courses.

TUTORED VIDEO INSTRUCTION

In 1988, a senior human resources executive from a company in Hong Kong approached the School of Business and Management (SOBAM) at the University of San Francisco and asked that SOBAM faculty be used to offer an MBA program to selected executives of their company. The company was unable to afford to either pay for such a program if it required "live" instruction by transporting MBA faculty to Hong Kong or to send their executives to San Francisco to attend regular MBA classes. Since China had only recently become "open" to the West, many SOBAM faculty were interested in pursuing this opportunity. Thus, it was evident that to respond to this company's request would require the use of some form of distance education methodology.

Program Objectives

At this time, less than one-third of the SOBAM US-born faculty had spent more than three weeks abroad in any foreign country, and only a very few of the entire faculty had ever traveled to Asia for any purpose. None of the faculty had direct experience with distance learning in any form before this experiment.

After some investigation, a faculty committee discovered the aforementioned research on TVI and decided to investigate its use further. Two of the faculty visited Stanford University's television network where they talked with the retired engineering faculty member who led the initial Hewlett-Packard program and some of the technical personnel who responsible for the videotaping of the classes. They also talked with the initial on-site tutor and two of the faculty who had taught live classes in engineering, TVI classes, and on-campus classes that were being taped "live" to be viewed simultaneously by students at distance locations. From a final review of the research on distance education, SOBAM faculty made a direct comparison of the research on various distance learning methodologies (i.e., acquisition; faculty and staff training; equipment; delivery; student performance) with their benefits, and concluded that TVI offered the best alternative.

SOBAM faculty set these goals for this initial TVI program:

- To enhance the "international perspectives" of the faculty;
- To increase the faculty's experience with executive education;
- To learn a distance learning technology;
- To improve the overall "quality" of our graduate students; and
- To gain experience in developing and delivering an in-house program on a cohort basis (i.e., the same group of students take the same courses throughout their educational program).

Initial Program Characteristics

The first TVI program began in 1990 with China Resources Holding Company (CRC), a private company owned by the Ministry of Foreign Affairs of the People's Republic of China and headquartered in Hong Kong. CRC hired a local coordinator who assisted SOBAM faculty in identifying 100 of the CRC mid-career managers who were interested in pursuing a MBA degree, whose English skills were sufficient, who had undergraduate degrees, and whose superiors would support these efforts. Before being admitted into the program, the SOBAM Associate Dean and the Program Coordinator interviewed each applicant. Before admittance, each prospective student was given math and English exams to determine their proficiencies with basic skills. The initial class consisted of thirty-six executives. Each student remained fully employed (i.e., on a full-time basis) during the program.

Two local tutors were hired and trained (by the SOBAM Associate Dean) in discussion-generating techniques. Each was a young executive of the company whose English language skills permitted him or her to lead a discussion in this language. Both tutors had limited management experience and, therefore, would be unable to answer questions on the technical issues included within the specific topical areas covered by the MBA courses.

Accreditation

At this time, the University was conducting its self-study as required for reaccreditation by the Western Association of Schools and Colleges (WASC). Since this program was a substantial deviation from the normal form of educational delivery, the SOBAM dean decided that it would be prudent to file an addendum to the self-study report that focused on the proposed distance education program. Upon consultation, it was decided that:

(1) The CRC MBA program would consist of exactly the same courses and course sequence as that required for on-campus students;

(2) To insure that the CRC students were equally served by the program in Hong Kong, the CRC program coordinator would become a SOBAM faculty member;

(3) SOBAM faculty would be required to use a common final examination in order to evaluate the TVI students directly against those on-campus students whose classes were being videotaped; and

(4) "Live instruction" would be one-third of the total program.

The American Association of Collegiate Schools of Business (AACSB) also accredits the SOBAM. This organization has no specific accreditation issues regarding distance education program. Further, since the average age of the first cohort was 36, it was apparent from the research that the regular MBA admissions "screening" device, the Graduate Management Aptitude Test (GMAT), would have limited value.

Program Delivery

CRC students attended two MBA video viewings and discussions on one night per week and on Saturday during a 10-week academic session in a room specially designed for videotape viewing at the company's training center in Hong Kong. At a typical session, the tutor would start and stop the videotape if questions were raised, and upon completion of that session's videotaped materials would then conduct a discussion formed around questions supplied by the course's instructor. Faculty submitted discussion questions for their tutors and required formal weekly feedback from the tutor via fax. Further, a formal faculty "feedback" mechanism was established in the form of a videotaped interview with each of the faculty who taught in the program (thereby permitting faculty who would be teaching in the TVI program for the first time to "get on the learning curve" quickly).

Each set of TVI faculty was flown to Hong Kong to spend 12 "live" contact hours with the students over a 6-day period. Visiting faculty used the mornings and afternoons for "live classes," and held these classes in the same classrooms regularly used by the students to meet and view the videotapes. Each faculty member was encouraged to personally evaluate the work of the students while he/she was engaged in the "live" portion of the course. These "live" sessions were scheduled at the end of each course to permit the faculty to be onsite for the required final exam. (In the later cohorts these "live" sessions were moved to the middle of each course because the students preferred earlier-in-the-course direct contact with the faculty.) On a routine basis, the tutor collected the course assignments and sent them to the instructor for evaluation. The Program Coordinator administered the quizzes, midterm examinations, and case analysis discussions on-site and sent the materials to the instructor for grading.

The on-campus classes that were videotaped for subsequent viewing in Hong Kong were held in a small, windowless room located in the University's instructional media complex, where no more than 16 MBA students could be wedged into the available space. Two students could use a small video monitor mounted on the table in front of them if they wanted to see what the instructor was writing on a pad (which was being videotaped via on overhead projector). Microphones were placed between each two students so that both the student's questions and the instructor's responses were captured on the videotape.

Subsequent Programs

The first CRC cohort graduated in 1993, the second in 1996, and the third class graduated in 1999. For the second and third CRC cohorts, separate classes, both videotape viewing and "live," were held for executives working in Beijing and Hong Kong. In 1993, the University contracted with a second Hong Kong-based firm, Guangdong Enterprises (GD), to deliver a TVI MBA program to their mid-career executives who were working at three different locations in Guangdong (Canton) Province and in adjacent Hong Kong. The first GD class graduated in 1997, and a second class graduated in 2000. [For purposes of discussion, we have identified these groups as CRC1, CRC2, CRC3, GD1, and GD2.]

An Interim Evaluation

After completing the CRC1 program, an analysis of the student evaluations of the TVI courses was undertaken. Several significant technical problems (e.g., poor quality video; inability to hear student questions or comments) were identified. Further, the Chinese students clearly preferred more "live time" with the faculty. To accommodate these concerns the amount of on-site live instruction time was increased from 12 to 15 hours. New overhead cameras, additional microphones, and more powerful "multi-directional" microphones were installed so that TVI students were better able to see more clearly what the instructor was trying to illustrate and to hear "live" student responses. The videotaping was moved to a much larger classroom. The addition of a third camera permitted coverage of students as they asked questions or responded to the faculty. Faculty were encouraged to post their email addresses on their TVI course syllabi, to supply copies of all materials distributed to the "live" students, to make better use of the tutor, and to prepare separate course schedules to coincide with the videotape viewing schedules of their TVI students.

In 1996, the SOBAM faculty undertook a formal evaluation of the faculty's experiences with the TVI programs (Murray, 1996). By this time, the first CRC1 cohort had completed the MBA program and both CRC2 and GD1 were in progress. SOBAM faculty:

- Felt that the TVI technology and the enhanced email-based feedback loop was not working; i.e., the students were not getting full value from their TVI experiences;
- Desired to have even more "live" time with their TVI students;
- Had not used a common final examination or any other means that would permit a direct comparison of the academic performances of their TVI and "live" students;
- Were not using the tutor for feedback purposes or were not providing directions for the tutor
- Were unhappy with the overall quality of the Hong Kong students efforts, as evidenced by their grades on exams, student projects, papers, case analyses and presentations, and written work in general; e.g., grammar, spelling, and syntax; and
- Felt that despite these problems the overall TVI experience was a rewarding one for themselves and their Hong Kong students.

TVI student evaluations continued to note both continued technical difficulties and renewed requests for more "live" time in place of TVI (Murray & Efendioglu, 1999).

A LONGITUDAL STUDY OF PERFORMANCE AND EFFECTIVENESS

In 1997, a formal survey of current and past CRC and GD students was initiated. Thirteen (36%) of the 36 students enrolled in the CRC1 program, the first TVI MBA cohort, responded to the survey. 13 (39%) of the 33 students enrolled in CRC2, 20 (59%) of the 34 GD1 cohorts, 28 (74%) of the GD2 cohort, and 24 (72%) of the CRC3 cohort, responded to a formal attitudinal survey. By 2000, it was possible to compare the results of the attitudinal surveys, grades, and the means of the student evaluations to see if there were significant differences that were due to the different instructional methodologies across all five TVI cohorts.

Because of the prior research on TVI, we expected these adult learners would perform better when compared to the students taking these same classes on a "live" basis (Moore 1989). Further, we expected that overall the TVI students would judge their educational experiences to be at least comparable to that those who were being educated on a "live" basis (Wilkes and Burnham, 1991). Therefore, we formed the following hypotheses:

H₁: Student performance in TVI courses would be superior to "live" courses

H_1: Student performance in TVI courses would be superior to "live" courses

H_2: Students rate their TVI experiences as at least as effective as "live" instruction

H_3: There would be no differences in TVI effectiveness between subject areas.

Student Performance

As shown in Table 1 below, TVI students received slightly lower average grades, 3.37 vs. 3.43 (calculated on a 4-point scale), as compared to the average grade received by the MBA student that participated in the "live" videotaped class. On the average, both the TVI and corresponding "live" students received the highest grades in the environment/law MBA classes and performed least well in economics courses. In performance, "live" students received significantly higher grades in environment/law, communications, MIS, management and marketing while, TVI students out-performed the corresponding "live" students in accounting classes. It was not possible to obtain the grades for the students whose classes were videotaped for CRC1, so that information is not listed in this table.

Student Course Evaluations

The TVI students were asked to fill out a specially adapted student course evaluation form at the end of each course. The results of these evaluations were then summarized into three categories: course content, technology (tapes and taping process), and the "live" teaching component of the course.

Table 1: Student GPA for all programs and all courses (by program and teaching area)

Program		ACC	COMM	DS	ECON	ENV/LAW	FIN	MGMT	MIS	MKT	Overall
						TEACHING AREA					
CRC2	Average of China GPA	3.34	4.00	3.30	3.13	3.55	3.37	3.28	3.40		3.37
	Average of USF GPA	3.39	3.53	3.35	3.21	3.67	3.42	3.52	3.33		3.44
CRC3	Average of China GPA	3.47	3.39	3.47	3.08	3.52	3.39	3.37	3.00	3.46	3.36
	Average of USF GPA	3.29	3.55	3.57	3.40	3.96	3.45	3.58	3.38	3.85	3.52
GD1	Average of China GPA	3.37	3.27	3.41	3.15		3.33	3.46	3.06	3.36	3.34
	Average of USF GPA	3.21	3.62	3.31	3.20	3.52	3.39	3.51	3.26	3.47	3.39
GD2	Average of China GPA	3.57	3.45	3.45	3.36	3.83	3.33	3.50	3.38	3.29	3.44
	Average of USF GPA	3.48	3.51	3.36	3.08	4.00	3.28	3.47	3.24	3.55	3.43
Total Average of China GPA		3.44	3.47	3.42	3.18	3.61	3.36	3.40	3.21	3.34	3.38
Total Average of USF GPA		3.34	3.56	3.38	3.22	3.76	3.40	3.52	3.30	3.57	3.44

The survey asked the students to use a 5-point Likert scale to indicate their agreement with a set of statements about the course that they had just taken (1 = Strongly Disagree to 5 = Strongly Agree).

Table 2 shows the combined results of these three cohorts. On the average, TVI student responses indicated a general level of satisfaction with these courses. The "live" components of the courses were felt to be of greater value than those received via TVI. In general, the course content issues were more highly ranked than those associated with the technical issues involving the videotaping and viewing. By averaging the scores in each of the three categories by subject area, we were able to identify differences in delivery effectiveness. According to the TVI students, the delivery of their accounting classes were significantly superior while the delivery of the management and MIS courses were thought to be significantly inferior, as compared to the average TVI course. In each of the instructional areas, a direct comparison of the average scores indicated that the students felt that the "live" component of their MBA classes were delivered more effectively than were either the TVI course content or videotape components.

Table 2: Average of response means for all off-site programs

	AREA									
	ACC	COM	DS	ECON	ENV/LAW	FIN	MGMT	MIS	MKT	Overall Avg.
COURSE CONTENT:										
a. Well defined course objectives	4.597	4.123	4.144	4.077	3.876	4.204	4.027	3.697	4.182	4.141
b. Appropriate difficulty level	4.115	3.863	3.922	3.636	3.783	3.771	3.835	3.353	3.942	3.852
c. Helpful assignments	4.360	4.016	4.152	3.847	3.845	3.854	3.815	3.692	4.030	3.995
d. Helpful to my professional activity	4.231	4.211	3.734	3.822	3.798	3.929	3.786	3.599	3.938	3.892
e. Helpful to my professional goals	4.372	4.265	4.021	3.911	3.952	4.112	4.038	3.722	4.112	4.075
f. Reading assignments helpful & easy	4.147	3.858	3.857	3.720	3.614	3.843	3.799	3.466	4.001	3.849
g. Fair exams	4.166	3.724	4.040	3.547	3.727	3.654	3.717	3.433	3.869	3.818
VIDEO TAPES:										
a. Can hear instructor clearly	4.240	4.040	3.868	4.018	4.234	3.977	3.944	3.728	4.170	4.015
b. Can hear students clearly	3.349	2.685	3.252	3.148	3.457	3.304	3.272	3.244	3.499	3.257
c. Can see instructor clearly	4.333	4.152	4.137	3.985	4.155	4.043	4.040	3.860	4.099	4.104
d. Read text and graphs easily	3.925	3.481	3.541	3.522	3.573	3.617	3.608	3.625	3.682	3.622
e. Lectures were well organized	4.275	3.675	3.877	3.817	3.890	3.972	3.850	3.610	3.890	3.898
f. Lectures were easy to follow	4.061	3.662	3.753	3.662	3.734	3.807	3.669	3.471	3.880	3.760
g. Lectures help me understand the material	4.148	3.673	3.877	3.792	3.830	3.859	3.726	3.703	3.855	3.840
ON-LOCATION LIVE TEACHING:										
a. Lectures were useful	4.621	4.537	4.577	4.190	4.355	4.403	4.204	4.138	4.310	4.384
b. Discussions with professor were helpful	4.518	4.464	4.447	3.869	4.279	4.352	4.220	4.064	4.287	4.284
c. Class activities with professor were valuable	4.492	4.486	4.430	3.938	4.280	4.320	4.252	4.023	4.157	4.281

(1=Strongly Disagree to 5=Strongly Agree)

By capturing the responses to comparable questions asked in the course evaluations completed by the "live" students, and categorizing these responses in a similar manner, it was possible to compare the evaluations by the TVI students to the evaluations of the "live" students in three of the five cohorts. (University policies regarding the public use of this information made such a comparison impossible for the two other cohorts). As shown in Table 3, course delivery, as evidenced by course evaluations, generally improved for the TVI students over time. Further, the average scores for questions grouped into the three categories were statistically higher for the CRC2 and CRC3 cohorts as compared to the average responses of the GD1 cohort.

Finally, comparing the average TVI student responses in each of these categories against the appropriate average student evaluation by "live" students during two academic terms, Fall 97 and Spring 98, showed that the TVI students, in general, found the quality of their "live" interactions superior to students whose entire MBA experience was conducted on a "live" basis. The analysis also showed that the content of the MBA courses offered on a TVI basis were judged as superior as well. However, the average of the three TVI cohort scores indicates that these students felt that the overall delivery of their instructors' lectures was statistically inferior to those delivered "live."

Table 3: Average of response means for comparable questions for on-site vs. off-site

	PROGRAM				
	CRC2	GD1	CRC3	USF Fall 97	USF Spring 98
COURSE CONTENT:					
a. Well defined course objectives	4.16	3.98	4.225	4.00	4.10
b. Appropriate difficulty level	3.83	3.66	3.935	3.50	3.50
c. Helpful assignments	3.99	3.64	4.024	3.50	3.40
d. Helpful to my professional activity	3.85	3.63	4.103	4.30	4.30
e. Helpful to my professional goals	4.11	3.81	4.158	4.00	4.00
f. Reading assignments helpful & easy	3.83	3.58	3.939	3.60	3.60
g. Fair exams	3.83	3.33	3.975	2.40	2.20
VIDEO TAPES:					
e. Lectures were well organized	3.86	3.66	3.990	4.00	4.10
f. Lectures were easy to follow	3.68	3.54	3.949	3.90	4.00
g. Lectures help me understand the material	3.80	3.58	3.985		
ON-LOCATION LIVE TEACHING:					
a. Lectures were useful	4.35	3.82	4.272	3.70	3.80
b. Discussions with professor were helpful	4.22	3.94	4.186	4.10	4.10
c. Class activities with professor were valuable	4.26	3.71	4.238		

(Off-site scale: 1=Strongly Disagree to 5=Strongly Agree; On-site scale: 1=Hardly Ever to 5=Almost Always)

Attitudinal Responses

For the purposes of making continuous improvements to the program, an attitudinal survey of the graduates of the CRC1, CRC2, GD1, and GD2 cohorts was conducted to get specific information about the delivery effectiveness of the TVI program and to see if it changed as problems were identified. Each student was asked to mark their degree of agreement with 17 attitudinal questions on a 7-point Likert scale. (A copy of that questionnaire is contained in the Appendix.)

As shown in Table 4, the average scores for each of the questions generally improved with successive cohorts. On an average, these four cohorts evaluated the impact of the program on the students' awareness of the international aspects of business (question 2) the highest, while the lowest evaluation was given for the attempt at equating the videotaped format with "live" instruction (question 11). As compared to the average evaluation for all 17 questions (5.399), questions 1, 2 (value for career progress), 7 (ROI on the company's investment), 9 (importance of discussant), and 17 (recommend program) were found to be statistically higher than the average response (p < .02). The responses to questions 11, 15 (investment in library resources), 16 (investment in telecommunications resources), 10 (adequacy of the video format), 13 (top leaders' support), and 12 (boss's support) were found to be statistically lower than average.

Table 4: Average of responses to attitudinal questions

Group	1	2	3	4	5	6	7	8	9	10	11	12	13	14	15	16	17
															QUESTION		
CRC1	5.92	6.00	5.46	5.38	5.23	5.00	5.62	5.15	5.31	4.77	3.38	5.08	5.69	5.46	5.08	5.08	5.85
CRC2	5.54	6.08	5.85	5.69	5.31	5.69	6.38	5.62	5.85	4.69	3.31	5.54	5.08	4.85	4.46	4.54	5.62
GD1	6.15	6.20	5.50	5.85	5.65	6.30	6.00	5.65	6.10	4.85	3.95	5.20	5.35	5.45	4.25	4.55	6.15
Grand Total	5.91	6.11	5.59	5.67	5.43	5.76	6.00	5.50	5.80	4.78	3.61	5.26	5.37	5.28	4.54	4.70	5.91

(Scale: 1=Strongly Disagree to 7=Strongly Agree; n=46)

From a direct comparison of attitudinal responses across the chronology of programs, we found that the CRC2 cohort (5.69) reported improvement in the delivery of technical skills (question 6) when compared to the earlier cohort, CRC1 (5.00). Similarly, the CRC2 cohort reported a much higher degree of satisfaction (6.38) with the decision by CRC to invest in this program (question 7) as compared to the earlier cohort, CRC1 (5.62). For the two GD cohorts, the only statistically significant improvement across programs occurred in the area of improved communications skills (question 4), while the GD2 cohort reported that they were less satisfied with the return on the company's investment in the program (question 7) when compared to the responses of GD1.

From a direct comparison of the second cohorts of both programs against one another it was noted that, in general, the GD TVI students were more satisfied with the program. Specifically, they rated career development (question 1), communication skill development (question 4), ethical considerations (question 5), technical skills (question 6), and the video format (question 10) more highly than did the students of CRC2. However, this GD cohort was less satisfied with their company's investment in library resources (question15) when compared to the CRC2 cohort.

Table 5: Statistically significant changes in average of responses to attitudinal questions

	GD1 vs. CRC1	GD1 vs. CRC2	CRC1 vs. CRC2	GD vs. CRC
Question 4	GD1 (5.65) vs. CRC1(5.38) p<0.05			
Question 6	GD1(6.30) vs. CRC1 (5.00) p<0.001	GD1(6.30) vs. CRC2 (5.69) p<0.02		GD (6.30) vs. CRC (5.35) p<0.01
Question 7			CRC1(5.62) vs. CRC2 (6.38) p<0.04	
Question 9	GD1(6.10) vs. CRC1 (5.31) p<0.02			GD (6.10) vs. CRC (5.58) p<0.05
Question 15	GD1(4.25) vs. CRC1 (5.08) p<0.03			
Question 17				GD (6.15) vs. CRC (5.73) p<0.04

(GD1 n=20; CRC1 n=13; CRC2 n=13)

CONCLUSIONS

Overall, the SOBAM faculty feel that their experiences with this distance teaching technology have been positive. The alumni of these programs are generally enthusiastic about their experiences. They believe their time and effort have paid off for them. They believe their companies have received good value for their investments in these programs.

The opportunity to teach in this program was also highly valued by SOBAM faculty because it gave them the opportunity to travel to China and be exposed to foreign culture. The logistical demands of the taping also meant that many of their lectures were better prepared, and in some cases this left them with better organized material for subsequent "live" classes on the same topics. In addition, the University became much more aware of the demands of doing this type of training and now has much greater capability to do it successfully.

Contrary to expectations, the average grade for the TVI students was lower than the average grade for the students that attended the "live" classes taped for this program. This is also contrary to the findings of the earlier research studies.

Table 6: Summary of student GPAs for all programs and all courses

	TEACHING AREA									
	ACC	COMM	DS	ECON	ENV/LAW	FIN	MGMT	MIS	MKT	**Grand Total**
Average of USF GPA	3.32	**3.56**	**3.39**	**3.22**	**3.70**	**3.41**	**3.51**	**3.30**	**3.59**	**3.43**
Average of China GPA	**3.41**	3.47	3.38	3.12	3.54	**3.41**	3.36	3.15	3.35	**3.36**

In retrospect, the faculty who taught in these programs have developed several hypotheses as to why program performances and student achievements differed from those expected. Few of the faculty used the tutor as intended. In the later cohorts in both programs, the role of the tutor was functionally downgraded to that of course assistant; e.g., starting the video, mailing the assignments, etc. Further, due to circumstances beyond the direct control of the SOBAM faculty, many of the students ended up watching videotapes individually (without the benefit of the group interaction and active questioning inherent in the TVI model). Specifically,

- The TVI was not used as designed because the client companies decided not to provide the required level of tutoring (for a majority of the courses that were offered) and would not enforce the group-oriented learning environment that is essential for effective TVI;
- Many of the SOBAM faculty were not fully aware of the underlying concepts of TVI, and the San Francisco-based program coordinators did not require that the TVI model be followed;
- Approximately one-third of the class contact hours "live"; and
- The TVI program did not take full advantage of the learning curve; i.e., the experiences of the faculty teaching in the program were not captured, analyzed, organized, and presented to faculty who were teaching in the program for the first time.

To summarize, the version of the TVI technology that was actually used in China by SOBAM faculty should be more properly labeled "VI" than TVI because the students actually received a "video instruction," devoid of any in-class discussion. Modifications in the TVI program actually reduced the effectiveness of the technology.

REFERENCES

Appleton, A., Dekkers, J. and Sharma, R. (1989). Improved teaching excellence by using tutored video instruction: An Australian case study. Presented at the *11th EAIR Forum*, Trier, Germany.

Arentz, H. C. (1995). A survey of TVI learners within cost engineering. *Cost Engineering*, 37(10), 26-35.

Chu, G. and Schramm, W. (1967). Learning from television: What the research says. Stanford University, ERIC Document Reproduction Service, *Report No. ED 014 900*.

Efendioglu, A. (1989). The problems and opportunities in developing international business programs. *Journal of Teaching in International Business*, 1(2), Haworth Press.

Gibbons, J. (1977). Tutored videotape instruction. *Presented at the Conference on Education Applications of Satellites*, Arlington, Virginia.

Gibbons, J., Kincheloe, W. and Down, K. (1977). Tutored videotape instruction: A new use of electronic media in education. *Science*, March, 1139-1146.

Moore, M. (1989). *Effects of Distance Learning: A Summary of the Literature*, Washington, DC, Office of Technical Assessment.

Murray, L. (1996). An analysis of the Chinese TVI programs. *Executive Council Report to the Faculty*, University of San Francisco.

Murray, L. and Efendioglu, A. (1999). Distance education: Delivery systems and student perceptions of business education in China. *Proceedings, Decision Sciences Institute Annual Meeting*, 281-283.

Schramm, W. (1967). What we know about learning from television. Stanford University, ERIC Document Reproduction Service, *Report No. ED 002 561*.

Sparkes, J. (1985). On the design of effective distance teaching courses. Presented at the *Annual Conference of the International Council on Distance Education*, Melbourne, Australia.

Stone, H. (1990). A multi-institutional evaluation of video-based distance engineering education. Presented at the *Frontiers in Education Conference*, Vienna, Austria.

Thach, E. and Murphy, K. (1995). Training via distance learning. *Training & Development*, 49(12), 44-47.

Wilkes, C. and Burnham. (1991). Adult learner motivations and electronic distance education. *The American Journal of Distance Learning*, 5(1), 43-50.

APPENDIX: QUESTIONS FOR THE CHINA EMBA PROGRAM GRADUATES

7	6	5	4	3	2	1
Strongly Agree	Agree	Slightly Agree	No Opinion	Slightly Disagree	Disagree	Strongly Disagree

Please enter the appropriate number in the box next to the question.

1. If I compare my career progress against the peers that I had before I entered the USF-EMBA, overall program was of great value to me.
   Please explain: _____

2. The EMBA program helped increase my awareness of international aspects of business.

3. The EMBA program helped increase my leadership skills.

4. The EMBA program helped increase my communications skills.

5. The EMBA program exposed me to consider ethical circumstances in my job and company.

6. The EMBA program helped increase my technical skills; e.g., use of the computer.

7. The investment of time and money made by my company in the EMBA program was a wise one as it developed skilled managers that the firm would not have had without the program.

8. The cohort system (taking the same classes with the same classmates throughout the entire EMBA program) improved my learning.

9. The use of a discussant, which attended classes with the students, improved my learning in the EMBA program.

10. The video delivery format used for the EMBA program was adequate.

11. I found that video delivery format used was not really much different from taking an entire course "live" with the instructor.

12. My boss during the time that I was taking classes in the EMBA program generally supported my educational efforts and gave me enough time off to complete the work required for the MBA classes.

13. In general, I feel that the top leaders of my company feel that the MBA program that I attended was a good investment.

14. In general, I feel that my company's investment in computer resources were sufficient to support the requirements for student activities in the EMBA program

15. In general, I feel that my company's investment in library resources were sufficient to support the requirements for student activities in the EMBA program.

16. In general, I feel that my company's investment in telecommunications resources (e.g., e-mail, fax) were sufficient to support the requirements for student activities in the EMBA program.

17. I would recommend the USF-EMBA program to friends and colleagues.

Chapter XV

Leveraging Distance Education Through the Internet: A Paradigm Shift in Higher Education

Zeynep Onay
Middle East Technical University, Turkey

In a global knowledge-based economy, with an ever-growing demand for learning, the Internet is seen as a vehicle for promoting effectiveness in teaching and reaching wider audiences. The number of online courses and programs offered by traditional higher education institutions, as well as new players in the education industry, has been increasing at an exponential rate. Yet the implementation of distance education through the Internet involves much more than a change of medium from face-to-face classroom interaction to an environment free of time and place constraints. Institutions are faced with the challenge of redefining their strategies to incorporate the e-learning paradigm. This chapter provides an overview of the different models that have emerged, and addresses the key issues that need to be resolved for integrating Internet-based learning in traditional universities. The breadth of strategic, administrative, academic and technological concerns encountered through the evolution of an Internet-based education system, from its inception to implementation, are discussed and illustrated by the e-learning initiative of Middle East Technical University in Turkey.

INTRODUCTION

The history of distance education can be traced back to the mid-Nineteenth century, when correspondence courses for teaching foreign languages by mail emerged in Europe. A hundred years later, televised courses heralded a new era. Distance courses were now enriched through sound and motion, and students were able to view classroom settings in their own homes. Commercial television stations started broadcasting university courses; a number of universities such as the University of North Carolina at Chapel Hill setup their own television stations. Televised instruction paved the way to the success of Open Universities. The advent of videocassette recorders, and later, CD-ROMs further removed the time constraint imposed by television program schedules. But it is the pervasiveness of the Internet in all facets of society that set the stage for the biggest revolution in distance learning and higher education.

The Internet has redefined the boundaries and promise of distance education by enabling the concurrent obliteration of time and place restrictions. Distance education through the Internet presents unprecedented opportunities for learners as well as providers of education. Learners can follow courses at anytime and from anywhere, at their own pace. Providers can reach a much wider and diverse population of learners than ever before, increasing their outreach and productivity. The use of new technologies also offers providers the potential to strengthen the quality and effectiveness of instruction.

However, distance education over the Internet entails much more than just a change of medium for the delivery of instruction. There are many stakeholders involved, each with a different perspective and set of priorities. The change is one that deeply affects the university as an institution, and the instructor and the student as individuals. For the university, the transition to an Internet-based learning environment requires a restatement of institutional missions and priorities, a revision of conventional structures. For the instructor and student, online courses represent a shift in educational philosophy and instructional design as the emphasis moves from "teaching" to "learning," leading to a student-centered rather than instructor-based system. The challenge for higher education is to find the best way to adjust to this paradigm.

Over the last few years, there has been an exponential growth in the number of courses, certificate and degree programs available through the Internet. In the United States (U.S.), the percentage of post-secondary institutions using the Internet as the predominant mode of delivery for distance education almost tripled from 1995 to 1998 (National Education Association, 2000). These trends are expected to continue due to several reasons:

- In a global knowledge economy, higher education establishments are faced with a growing demand for learning from people of all ages. The U.S. Department of Education's National Center for Education Statistics (NCES) estimated that in the 1997-98 academic year over 1.6 million students were enrolled in distance education courses offered by post-secondary institutions. This represents a twofold increase from 1995. A similar growth pattern was observed on the provider side: the number of credit-granting distance education courses offered by higher education institutions doubled between 1995 and 1998 (National Education Association, 2000). The National Household Education Survey (NHES) also shows that nearly half of the adult population in the United States is engaged in continuing education, of which more than half are studying for professional development (Kellogg Commission, 1999). Corporate sector spending for employee training and development rose to $2.9 billion dollars in 1999 (Ubell, 2000).

- The convergence of information and communication technologies is increasing the power and spread of global communication. Information accessibility and availability is accelerating, while the associated costs are decreasing. In the U.S., Internet access in households has risen by 123% since 1997. Over 40% of households now have access to the Internet (U.S. Department of Commerce, 2000). The Gartner Group predicts that by 2005, 75% of U.S. households will be connected to the Internet (Gartner Group, 2000).

- There is rising competition among providers of distance education. Just as the Internet brings increased educational opportunities for learners, it also means that the target student population for providers is no longer limited by geographic proximity. With over a hundred million students enrolled in higher education worldwide (U.S. Department of Education, The Web-based Education Commission, 2000), competition for this global market is not only among higher education establishments, but also between traditional universities and new players in the education industry. A large number of for profit and nonprofit organizations have emerged as providers and brokers of education; e-learning portals, service providers and virtual universities are a reality today.

Thus, the very structure of higher and continuing education is changing. In a knowledge-based society, the demand for learning will expand. Enrollments in higher education are expected to continue to increase over the next decade (U.S. Department of Education, National Center for Education Statistics, 2000). The International Data Corporation (IDC) projects that the distance education market will grow at a compounded annual rate of 33% over the next few years (Weinstein, 2000). On the other hand, Internet usage will spread even further. It is expected that one billion people around the world will be connected to the Internet by 2005 (Stone, 2000). As the number and type of organizations engaged in Internet-based instruction rises, competition among e-learning providers is likely to increase. Traditional universities are therefore no longer indifferent to the push of new technologies and confront the challenge of redefining their strategies in the 21st century.

The main question for institutions involved in higher and distance education is how to respond to this challenge. The answer requires the resolution of a number of academic, administrative and technical issues. This chapter explores these issues through the various phases involved in the development of an Internet-based distance education system, from its inception and planning to its implementation and maintenance. There are several options at each phase, and various institutions have opted for different courses of action. The next section covers some of the models adopted by traditional universities and nontraditional providers of education.

MODELS FOR DISTANCE EDUCATION THROUGH THE INTERNET

A number of established higher education institutions have responded to the challenge of new technologies by establishing their "virtual" campuses as extensions to their traditional settings. Washington State's Web University, Penn State's World Campus, the University of California-Berkeley Extension Online are only some examples of this approach. A majority of these universities have a long past in distance education through more conventional media. Appendix A presents a sample list of traditional universities with virtual campus extensions.

Among these traditional universities, two different strategies can be distinguished for producing and delivering online instruction. While some universities develop their own software tools and class management platforms, others turn to application service providers for establishing their virtual campuses. The first strategy involves high investment costs. However, it allows flexibility and customization to the institution's specific requirements. Indiana University developed its own course management system called OnCourse. Similarly, the University of British Columbia developed WebCT, for preparing and delivering its online courses. WebCT is now a commercial product used by a large number of institutions. The University of Illinois has built several authoring and teaching systems like Mallard, CyberProf and NetLearning Place.

The second strategy essentially consists of outsourcing all or part of the establishment and operation of the university's online learning platform to third-party companies. There is a vast array of services offered by such organizations, ranging from technical support to instructional design, expertise for content development and/or provision, all the way to entirely hosting and operating the instructional management system. Thus, the fixed costs of the university turn into variable costs, but as in all outsourcing ventures, the institution becomes dependent on the service provider. Many universities follow this strategy, as the time to market online courses and programs is significantly reduced. For example, Columbia University has an agreement with Cognitive Arts, a designer and provider of e-learning technology, to develop courses for Columbia Continuing Education Online. The courses are provided by Columbia University, the technology is supplied by Cognitive Arts. A sample list of e-learning platforms and service providers is presented in Appendix B.

In addition, many universities have relationships with external entities for purposes like funding, marketing, or just exposure through information portals. For instance, the University of California-Berkeley, like many other universities, has received substantial grants from the Alfred P. Sloan Foundation to start online programs (Asynchronous Learning Networks, 2001). The University of California-Berkeley Extension Online also has partnerships with marketing portals. These for-profit companies act as intermediaries between learners and providers and allow universities to gain access to a wide audience, without incurring up-front marketing costs. Education providers are represented on their portals, often in exchange for a commission per enrollment. Universities can also use pure information portals like Peterson's Distance Learning Channel and the World Lecture Hall, for passive marketing and exposure to learners. A sample list of marketing/information portals can be found in Appendix C.

Another model is for traditional universities to establish their own for-profit subsidiaries. This is illustrated by Cornell University's for-profit corporation, eCornell. eCornell produces, markets and delivers non-degree programs developed by faculty from the university's schools and colleges. Temple University and New York University have also launched their for-profit subsidiaries to market courses on the Internet. In contrast, on April 4, 2001, the Massachusetts Institute of Technology (MIT) announced its OpenCourseWare (MITOCW) project to make almost all of its courses accessible free of charge on the World Wide Web. More than 500 MIT courses will be available on the Web within two years (Massachusetts Institute of Technology, 2001).

On the other side of the spectrum, for-profit universities also establish their virtual extensions. The University of Phoenix, owned by Apollo Computers, is one of the largest for-profit universities in the U.S. The University of Phoenix Online was established as an extension to resident instruction, and has been experiencing a steady yearly growth rate of 50% in its online course enrollments. Park University's Distance Education extension has been experiencing a similar growth in online enrollments. Its degree completion programs have been accredited by the North Central Association of Colleges and Schools Commission on Institutions of Higher Education.

On the nontraditional side, there are nonprofit "virtual" universities like Western Governors University (WGU) and the Kentucky Commonwealth Virtual University (KCVU), that act as brokers for distance education programs available through traditional colleges and universities. WGU essentially facilitates student enrollment to courses delivered by around 40 post-secondary institutions. The model is based on guiding students about what is required to gain specific competencies and where to obtain them. Once students complete these requirements, they are assessed by WGU and obtain their competency-based certification degrees from WGU. Thus, through advising services and final assessment, WGU grants its own degrees.

Unlike Western Governors University, the Kentucky Commonwealth Virtual University does not award its own degrees or certificates. The model is based on outsourcing all programs and faculty from other colleges and universities. KCVU is managed by the Kentucky Council on Post-secondary Education, and is founded on a network of partnerships with traditional education providers, technology infrastructure and instructional management system providers.

In a similar way, The European Network University (TNU), a network of European and non-European universities, nonacademic institutions and nongovernmental organizations, does not grant academic credit itself, but offers courses that lead to a degree from participating universities. TNU is rooted at the University of Amsterdam, The Netherlands.

Still another approach is illustrated by one of the largest suppliers of online continuing education in the U.S., OnlineLearning.net. OnlineLearning.net offers its own courses and certification programs, but also has partnerships with universities, marketing their accredited courses and programs. The company provides online faculty development programs and aids course development. It holds the exclusive worldwide electronic rights to online courses from the University of California-Los Angeles Extension, and offers courses from the University of San Diego, among others. All such courses earn academic credit.

On the other hand, a number of companies have established their own virtual universities. Kaplan, Inc., an educational subsidiary of the Washington Post Company, founded the Concord University School of Law in 1998. Concord has its own full-time faculty and a number of visiting and supplementary lecturers. UNext founded Cardean University. Courses at Cardean are prepared by faculty from leading universities like Carnegie Mellon, Columbia, Stanford and the London School of Economics and Political Science, and are delivered by UNext adjunct professors. Corporate universities like Dell Learning, by Dell Computer Corp., and SunU, run by Sun Microsystems Inc., also cooperate with academic institutions to deliver online courses.

Jones International University (JIU) is an example for a not-for profit virtual university founded by a for-profit company. Established in 1993, JIU is the first fully accredited online institution of higher education. The model used at JIU involves "content experts" and "teaching faculty." Courses are designed and developed by "content experts" and delivered by "teaching faculty." Content experts are faculty from leading universities, including the University of California-Berkeley, Rutgers, Columbia, Purdue, Stanford and the University of Texas at Austin. Faculty facilitate the online instruction of these courses. A sample list of virtual universities is provided in Appendix D.

Other approaches include alliances between universities, and partnerships between universities and companies in telecommunications and publishing to exploit the power of new systems and technologies. In 1999, some of the largest research universities in the U.S. and Canada joined forces to market distance education courses through a central repository on the Web. The website, R1.edu, is maintained by the University of Washington. Hong Kong Polytechnic University has partnered with Pacific Century Cyberworks, a telecommunications products and services company, to create Hong Kong Cyber University. Pearson, the world's largest education publisher is rapidly expanding its share of the online education market. The company has alliances with universities and partnerships with solution providers like Blackboard and WebCT to supply a variety of online learning services (Blumenstyk, 2000). Similarly, Houghton Mifflin Company, a publisher of textbooks and other educational materials and technologies, has a strategic partnership with OnlineLearning.net.

Many institutions across the world are leveraging distance and continuing education through the Internet. NKI, one of the largest nongovernmental education institutions in Scandinavia, was the first European online college and has been providing online education for the past 15 years (Paulsen & Rekkedal, 2001). Last year, the British government announced its University for Industry (UFI) project. UFI is intended to be a vocational school that will offer most of its programs online (Walker, 2000). UNESCO's recent initiative to create an e-learning portal illustrates the thrust to facilitate access to education resources on a global scale. Open universities like the Open University U.K. and Athabasca University in Canada are also adopting the online mode of delivery to increase their outreach.

Traditional universities in different parts of the world are integrating Internet-based learning into their conventional structures. The University of South Australia and Deakin University (Australia) have undertaken major projects to convert courses and programs to the online mode. Similarly, Middle East Technical University (METU) in Turkey has developed an institutional e-learning system for both on-campus and off-campus students. The next section summarizes the METU experience.

THE METU E-LEARNING INITIATIVE

Middle East Technical University was the first, among 71 universities in Turkey, to implement an Internet-based learning environment: METU-Online. One of the leading universities in Turkey, METU has over 20,000 students enrolled in graduate and undergraduate programs offered by 39 departments in five facilities.

The university has taken a centralized institutional approach for the initiation of Internet-based learning. This allowed the consolidation of scarce resources and facilitated the coordination of activities. The task of establishing METU-Online was given to the university's Informatics Institute. The Institute is an interdisciplinary graduate school, offering degrees in areas where the theory and practice of a number of disciplines merge. Currently, the Institute has three programs: Cognitive Science, Information Systems, and Modeling and Simulation. The Cognitive Science program focuses on the cognitive aspects of computational approaches to speech and language analysis, teaching, and creative uses of computers in an information society. It amalgamates the fields of artificial intelligence, computer science, linguistics, psychology, cognitive neuroscience and philosophy. The Information Systems program integrates business administration, computer engineering, electrical and electronics engineering, and industrial engineering. The Modeling and Simulation program concentrates on the theoretical and practical aspects of modeling, virtual environments and computer simulation.

Since its foundation in 1996, the Institute has conducted several research projects on asynchronous learning. Thus, the responsibility for all planning, development and implementation activities concerning distance education through the Internet at METU was assigned to the Informatics Institute.

At the Institute, a team composed of faculty from the departments of business administration, computer engineering, education, and electrical and electronics engineering launched the METU-Online project in May 1998. The software platform for preparing and delivering online courses has been developed at the Institute and is being maintained by the Institute's Distance Education Laboratory. The first implementation took place in fall 1998 and within one year a total of 15 courses were offered to around 2,000 on-campus and off-campus students. All online courses come from the undergraduate and graduate curricula of various departments within the university, ranging from history to astronomy. The courses are developed and delivered by resident faculty. The mode of delivery varies among courses, from fully online course conduct, to the use of online material in addition to full class contact hours.

METU-Online also enables the efficient use of scarce faculty resources to teach large audiences. At METU, all first-year students (approximately 3,000 freshmen) are required to take an introductory computer literacy course. To meet this requirement, the Introduction to Information Technologies and Applications course (IS 100) has been designed by the Informatics Institute and is being delivered through METU-Online to 1,500 students each semester.

In February 1999, the Institute launched its online Informatics Certificate Program to train instructors from other Turkish universities to design and deliver introductory computer literacy courses such as IS 100 in their own universities. Instructors from various universities followed the program asynchronously from their respective institutions. The university's first online graduate program, leading to the degree of Master of Science in Informatics is the latest addition to its expanding portfolio of Internet-based learning applications.

The METU experience has recently prompted the Higher Education Council of Turkey, the governing body of all public and private universities in the country, to establish a national initiative for the development and exchange of Internet-based courses and programs between Turkish universities. The Higher Education Council provides funding, coordinates and regulates all aspects of interuniversity collaboration for e-learning.

The remainder of the chapter presents the evolution of an Internet-based education system, from its inception to its implementation, focusing on the issues that are of critical importance at each phase. It reflects the decision hierarchy and sequence of activities recommended for successfully integrating online courses, certificate and degree programs in universities. The recommendations are drawn from the lessons learned at METU during the development of its institutional e-learning system.

THE INITIATION AND PLANNING OF INTERNET-BASED LEARNING

Introducing the E-Learning Paradigm

Integrating a new educational paradigm into an existing system is often more complicated than establishing a totally new system. Entrenched organizational culture, academic norms, administrative bureaucracies, and technological constraints impose a greater challenge. Current experience shows that a fundamental rethinking of the missions, goals and operations is necessary in traditional institutions (Calvert, 2001; Harris & DiPaolo, 1999). Radical change is seldom possible; incremental change is often the preferred approach.

A prerequisite for success is the university's strong commitment to this paradigm (Bourne, 1998; King, McCausland & Nunan, 2001). Its strategies must reflect how the institution wants to position itself in the spectrum of e-learning applications. This will depend on the goals that are targeted. These might include:

- Enhancing the quality and effectiveness of education;
- Increasing outreach to serve different learner populations;
- Being more responsive to learner and faculty needs; and
- Improving efficiency in the utilization of scarce educational resources.

Accordingly, different institutions are likely to leverage the Internet in different ways. Some will use new technologies to reduce the cost of delivering courses and increase outreach to off-campus students; others to enhance the learning experience of on-campus students; others still, to facilitate large class management on campus. Needless to say, a combination of several objectives is the norm rather than the exception.

Based on the objectives set by the institution, the first step in initiating an Internet-based learning environment is to establish the scope and feasibility of such an undertaking. This in turn will be instrumental in determining the organizational arrangement for the development and implementation of e-learning. In addition, existing institutional policies have to be reviewed, and if necessary, revised at this stage.

Scope and Feasibility

In order to determine the scope of an institution's e-learning initiative a number of questions have to be answered: Should online instruction be available to off-campus students only? Should the emphasis be on individual courses or degree and certificate programs? Should priority be given to existing courses/programs or new ones tailored for specific markets? Should all online offerings be developed and delivered by regular faculty?

Alternative directions are possible. Online education can be targeted to resident students, either as a supplement to face-to-face instruction or as a substitute. It could be offered to off-campus students only, or serve both student constituencies. At METU, the decision was to make no differentiation between resident and off-campus students, since the university is seeking to enrich the learning experience on-campus, as well as provide opportunities for learners who are place bound. In terms of courses to be offered online, METU took an evolutionary approach, starting with individual courses already listed in the university's curricula, leading to the development of new online certificate and degree programs. With scalability in mind, the rationale for this approach was that encouraging the conversion of existing individual courses to the online mode would help to spread awareness to all academic units, and obtain the commitment of faculty and students. At METU, online course development and delivery is carried out by regular faculty in order to capitalize on the existing academic strength and reputation of the university.

The determination of the viability of online instruction for a particular institution requires the assessment of operational, technical and economic feasibility. At METU, the effects of organizational culture and the degree of resistance to change among administrators, faculty and students, as well as the constraints imposed by administrative procedures have been investigated to derive operational feasibility. The university's technical infrastructure and related skills portfolio were examined to establish technical feasibility. Possible sources of funding have been identified, and a preliminary three-year budget was derived to test economic feasibility.

Organization of the E-Learning Initiative

The next decision relates to the organization of the e-learning initiative. One possibility is to adopt a decentralized approach and delegate the development of online instruction to those academic units having or planning online offerings. Another option is to take a centralized institutional approach and assign the responsibility for the entire initiative to a single unit. The choice is of primary importance for long-term sustainability. At METU, the outcome of the feasibility study resulted in the derivation of a project plan and the formation of an interdisciplinary project team under a single independent unit, namely the Informatics Institute. The main factors leading to this final choice can be cited as follows:

- The need for coordination to uphold an institutional network;
- The concern for the efficient use of university resources, avoiding duplication;
- The fair allocation of resources to all units involved;

- The flexibility to extend the scope of services to different target groups;
- The necessity to maintain the ownership, management and balance of online offerings.

At this point, the institution's existing policies and procedures have to be reviewed to determine their suitability for incorporating a different mode of learning.

Institutional Policies

The integration of e-learning often requires the revision of institutional policies and development of new ones. Issues that are important in this respect include: the quality of online courses and programs, the administrative procedures for online learning, the ownership of intellectual property, faculty compensation, and the management of technology and support services for e-learning.

Quality of Online Instruction

A key concern for all institutions engaged in Internet-based education is the maintenance of academic standards for online courses and programs. Credit equivalencies with their traditional counterparts, and procedures for assessing their quality have to be established. Many stakeholders still question the effectiveness of online learning when compared to face-to-face instruction. Accreditation is seen as a way to "legitimize" the quality of online offerings. Therefore, some form of accreditation, whether national, regional or institutional, has to be instituted. On the other hand, existing accreditation standards mostly pertain to traditional education, therefore, their applicability to e-learning is a contentious issue. There is a need to develop specific standards for online education and improve coordination between different accreditation agencies (Stallings, 2000; U.S. Department of Education, Web-based Education Commission, 2000). Recently, the Institute for Higher Education Policy identified 24 benchmarks to ascertain quality in Internet-based distance education (The Institute for Higher Education Policy, 2000). The benchmarks are grouped under seven headings: institutional support, course development, teaching/learning, course structure, student support, faculty support, and evaluation and assessment. Together they provide a useful template for all stakeholders to determine what constitutes quality in online distance education.

Unlike the U.S., there are no national or regional accreditation agencies in Turkey. METU has therefore, developed its own internal accreditation procedure to assure the quality of online courses and programs. The process of accreditation at METU is described later in the chapter.

Administrative Issues

On the administrative side, conformance of this new mode of delivery to the university's existing statutes, rules and procedures has to be determined. Matters that have been considered at METU include alignment with the criteria set out by the academic rules and regulations of the university. Accordingly, the requirements for admission to and graduation from online programs are as strict as the ones for traditional programs. New administrative procedures have also been introduced to integrate the application and registration of online students into the existing system, enabling remote application, registration and payment of tuition fees. The procedure for the approval of new courses and programs by the university's academic boards has been revised to include online courses and programs.

Another issue to be addressed by the institution is the provision of Internet services to students. This is especially a concern in countries where connection to Internet service providers is costly and bandwidth limitations restrict the speed of communication. For its certificate and degree programs, METU gives each participant an unlimited Internet account through TR-NET, an Internet service provider directly connected to the university's ATM network. This facilitates access and allows faster communication among users.

Copyright

The digital age challenges the hitherto established principles of intellectual property and copyright. The Internet makes possible the almost limitless distribution and usage of information. Current legislation is inadequate to define the impact of copyright laws on online education. Although the Digital Millennium Act, passed by the U.S. Congress in 1998, addresses certain aspects related to electronic piracy, the concept of "fair use" of copyrighted material in a digital environment needs further clarification. This affects universities engaged in online education in two ways. First, the ownership of individual course content has to be established. Second, intellectual property has to be protected. Consequently, universities have to review their copyright policy, not only for the material produced in the courses, but also for the material used to produce the courses. So far, very few institutions have established policies with respect to the ownership of online material developed by faculty (Council for Higher Education Accreditation, 2000). The American Association of University Professors (AAUP) recommends that, in principle, faculty members who have developed material for distance education should own the copyright, except in the case of works made-for-hire that are not part of their normal workload, or when the university provides resources and services for developing the material, in which case joint ownership by a faculty member and the university is acceptable (American Association of University Professors, 1999). Another exception put forward by the AAUP is the situation where a faculty member makes a contractual agreement with the university (or a third party) to transfer part or all of his/her rights to the university (or third party). However, by and large, most universities own the rights to material, which is viewed as being part of the creator's normal workload, using institutional resources.

At METU, the ownership of online course material can be transferred to the university if the creator wishes to do so. An agreement is signed between the faculty member and the university whereby the member of the faculty gives the full copyright to the university, in exchange of a one-off royalty payment. In a way, the university purchases the rights to the online course. The practice of royalty payment encourages faculty to take part in the university's online initiative.

Faculty Commitment

In order to promote faculty commitment, the university needs to devote resources to faculty development on the use of new technologies and instructional pedagogies. Furthermore, specific incentives have to be developed to encourage the production and delivery of online courses. These can be in the form of giving release time for preparing online courses, reducing faculty teaching load for traditional courses, establishing revenue-sharing schemes, or counting contributions to Internet-based distance education towards academic promotion. At METU, online teaching is considered to be part of faculty's normal workload, however, the effort is taken into account in the determination of the university's yearly academic excellence awards. In addition, measures have been established for the distribution of revenues among the various contributors to Internet-based courses and programs.

Management of Technology and Support Services

Using the Internet for distance education also brings forth issues related to the management of the underlying technology to ensure the continuous operation, reliability, and maintenance of the system. Moreover, support services have to be provided to faculty as well as students. Often, the university's computer center is a natural candidate for these tasks. However, in institutional endeavors, as in the case of METU, care must be taken to clearly define the allocation of responsibilities between the unit in charge of Internet-based learning and the computer center. Currently, staff at the

Informatics Institute are responsible for the management of the technology supporting Internet-based courses and programs, including system administration, software upgrades, user support, and security issues. The university's computer center cooperates with the Institute, advises when necessary, and ensures that the infrastructure on campus meets the requirements of online course and program delivery.

THE DESIGN AND DEVELOPMENT OF INTERNET-BASED LEARNING

During the design and development stage, three major issues need careful consideration. The first one is related to the software platform to be used for Internet-based learning. The choice of platform greatly affects the efficiency and perceived value of online learning. The second issue deals with the selection and approval of courses and programs to be delivered online. Criteria for assigning priorities among courses/programs and the procedure for approval by the university's academic boards need to be established. Finally, the issue of quality assurance for online instruction has to be addressed in order to maintain the institution's academic standards.

The Online Learning Platform

The choice for the e-learning platform to be used for the preparation and delivery of online courses and programs is between in-house development and outsourcing all or part of the institution's "virtual" operations. As mentioned previously, there are a large number of companies providing systems for online instruction, offering a wide spectrum of services. Considerations of flexibility, customization, ease of use, scalability, and cost are primary determinants for the final decision.

METU developed its own e-learning platform: NET-Class. The first version of NET-Class was ready in five months. It is a learning management system designed to incorporate features that add value to student learning and enable instructors to achieve instructional effectiveness. NET-Class provides a user-friendly and secure environment for creating, delivering and managing courses. The system has three user views: the instructor, student and system administrator views. Access is authorized by the system, and the related view is presented to the user. The tools incorporated for each view are presented in Figures 1, 2 and 3.

Figure 1: System tools for instructors

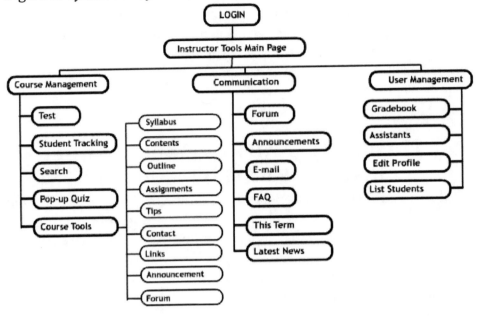

Figure 2: System tools for students

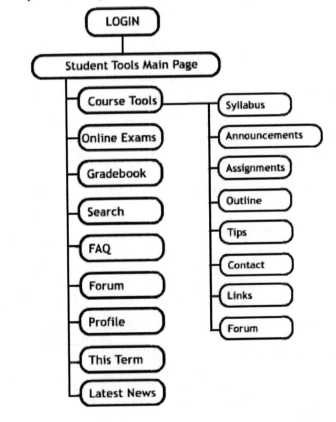

Figure 3: Tools for system administration

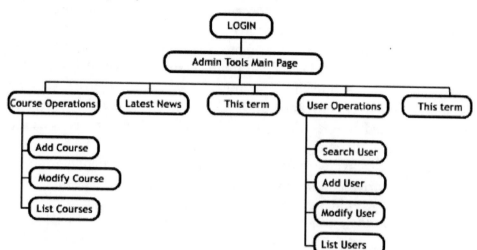

Instructors can organize course content, generate tests, activate the automatic grading utility, administer online discussion threads, and view student access rates graphically with the tools provided by the system. NET-Class includes templates to produce core parts of a course like the syllabus, announcements, and assignments. These templates ensure consistency in the format of presentation, which prevents user confusion, especially for faculty and students dealing with multiple courses. Students can take online tests and exams, see their results in the grade book, and perform searches in the course material. The system administrator is able to add/remove courses, register students, change their passwords, and monitor resource usage. New features and utilities are continuously added to NET-Class to promote active learning and facilitate course delivery.

Course Selection and Approval

The design and development stage also involves the determination of criteria for selecting the courses and programs to be offered online. These criteria are influenced by the scope of the institution's e-learning initiative and especially the nature of the target student population.

Given that METU adopted an evolutionary approach for integrating online instruction into its mainstream activities, the parameters used initially pertained to the selection of existing courses from the curricula of various departments. These include: the number of students enrolled in the course, whether the course is at the graduate or undergraduate level, the type of course (compulsory or elective), its frequency, faculty skills and willingness to develop the course online, and the suitability of the department's infrastructure (e.g., availability and adequacy of student computer laboratories) for delivery. These criteria have later been expanded to cover the determination of Internet-based certificate and degree programs.

Regarding the proposal and approval of courses and programs, the regulations for traditional instruction at METU stipulate that all new courses/ programs are first approved by the related Departmental Board, then the Faculty Board. New programs are further sanctioned by the University Senate, followed by the Higher Education Council. Online courses and programs follow the same procedure with a slight difference. If the course or program to be delivered online is an existing course/program from the university's curricula, a proposal is submitted directly to the Informatics Institute for support in preparation and delivery. Once the online version is ready, its delivery has to be approved by the related Departmental and Faculty Boards. On the other hand, new online courses and programs are first approved by Departmental and Faculty Boards, and then submitted to the Institute for support.

The preparation of all the university's online offerings is carried out through the Informatics Institute. Priorities for course and program preparation are assigned at the Institute, based on the selection criteria described above. The Institute provides faculty training, equipment if necessary, and support staff for instructional design, graphical design and programming. Once the course is ready, it goes through an accreditation procedure.

Quality Assurance and Accreditation

The accreditation procedure is an internal quality audit, instituted at METU, specifically for Internet-based courses and programs. An Accreditation Committee, established by the University Senate, evaluates all online courses and programs. Accreditation is in two stages. The first stage takes place at the end of course/program preparation, before online delivery. Each course is reviewed to establish its conformance to the university's Guidelines and Standards for the Design of Online Courses. These guidelines, developed at the Informatics Institute and endorsed by the University Senate, set out details pertaining to best practices for instructional design, format, layout, and navigation features of the course Web pages.

The second stage of accreditation takes place at the end of the semester in which the courses have been delivered. The Accreditation Committee assesses each course in terms of learning outcomes and effectiveness in using the various instructional tools incorporated in the e-learning platform (e.g., use of the forum by the instructor to communicate with students and encourage collaboration among students; the timeliness of feedback to questions). At this stage, the Committee also appoints an external reviewer for appraising course content. Only fully accredited courses qualify for transfer of copyright and royalty payment.

IMPLEMENTATION AND MAINTENANCE OF INTERNET-BASED LEARNING

Three issues stand out at this stage: the changing role of instructors and students, the choice between the different modes of online delivery, and the establishment of a regular post-implementation review to continually improve and maintain the system.

The Role of Instructors and Students

Internet-based education defies the traditional relationship and role of instructors and students (Bourne, Mayadas & Campbell, 2000; Kochtanek & Hein, 2000; McNeil, Robin & Miller, 2000). For the instructor, the challenge is to become a "moderator" in the students' learning experience, as the focus shifts from "teaching" to "learning," where interactivity and collaboration are key determinants of success (Andriole, 1997; Sherron & Boettcher, 1997). In this virtual environment, the instructor must be able to instigate discussions to keep interest alive, and maintain communication with students and interaction among students. Instructors must understand and cater to the individual learning styles of students, and has to be able to develop meaningful learning activities over the Internet. The instructor must anticipate problems and be available online to answer or route questions.

The instructor also often has to learn new skills for preparing/updating course content and conducting the course on the Internet. Institutions must be ready to support faculty on a continuous basis. Moreover, the e-learning platform must incorporate features that facilitate class management and the task of the instructor. In cases where the preparation of courses involves a team (e.g., instructional designer, graphics expert, technical specialists) to assist the instructor, coordination among team members is an added responsibility for the instructor.

On the other hand, the challenge for students is to change from being passive listeners to becoming active participants. Student-instructor and student-to-student interaction, through synchronous and asynchronous discussion groups, are essential components of Internet-based courses. Students must take part in discussions and learn to collaborate with other students virtually. In this paradigm, students are empowered to enhance their learning process and must have the ability to do so. This requires some degree of computer literacy and familiarity with the Web on the part of the student, but more importantly, students must possess self-discipline and motivation. They need to learn how to learn.

Students need to know how to access information for learning purposes and overcome hardware and software problems. Exposing students to using information technology as a natural part of the course is a good starting point for training in most cases, but more formal training support in the form of courses or tutorials provided by the university may be necessary. Thus, the effectiveness of online courses does not only depend on organizational support and instructor abilities; students also have to adapt to this new environment.

Modes of Delivery

Four modes of delivery are possible for the implementation of Internet-based courses. In the first mode, the course is conducted fully on the Internet, with no face-to-face contact. In the second mode, online material is used to supplement classroom instruction. In the third mode, regular class meetings are held each week but with reduced contact hours; the remaining credits being taken online. Lastly, the course is offered online to only a limited group of students, while the rest of the class follows traditional classroom instruction. The mode of delivery is primarily dependent on the characteristics of the course/program and the target student population.

At METU, for individual courses, the instructor and related department decide the delivery mode, but all certificate and degree programs are fully online, as the aim is to reach place-bound students. Residency is only required for two days at the beginning of each term for orientation purposes, and two days at the end of the term for proctored final exams.

Post-Implementation Review

Understanding the impact of Internet-based learning and the extent to which initial goals have been achieved is a very important aspect of the maintenance phase. Needless to say, overall impact is affected by the diverse issues discussed in this chapter. Piotrowski and Vodanovich (2000) present a review of recent research in the area, and note that empirical studies report a range of positive as well as negative results. Inevitably, what is theoretically possible does not always coincide with actual practice (Thomas, 2000). Therefore, learning outcomes and the effectiveness of the delivery platform have to be appraised on a regular basis. These two facets must be assessed by students as well as instructors. The results of these evaluations will enable the continuous improvement of the e-learning environment.

At METU, the learning outcomes and delivery platform are evaluated through an online questionnaire to students and interviews with instructors. Individual student reactions range from enthusiasm to constructive criticism, indifference (just printing lecture notes from the Web) and resistance (why this additional burden!). Nevertheless, overall results indicate that e-learning has a positive impact on student satisfaction. Similar findings have also been reported elsewhere (Motiwalla & Tello, 2000; Ward & Newlands, 1998). The effectiveness of Internet-based instruction is especially evident in courses incorporating "virtual laboratories" like astronomy, physics or image processing, where students are able to visualize phenomena through animations and interactive experiments. In courses where some degree of classroom contact is maintained, instructors also observed higher attendance to class meetings by students, compared to previous years, when the same course was delivered in the traditional way. In terms of grades, the class averages are at least equal and often better than the average grades for the same course delivered in the classroom environment.

Instructors admit that Internet-based education is a lot of work. Experience has shown that creating an online course often takes much longer than a traditional course. Indeed, preparing an online course can take up to 500% longer (U.S. Department of Education, The Web-based Education Commission, 2000). Moreover, being available online to administer threaded discussions and respond to questions takes a lot of time. Nevertheless, many faculty at METU find it a satisfying experience, positively influencing their other teaching activities. They also say that when compulsory courses are taught online, there is more demand for follow-up electives.

Results obtained from the assessment of the e-learning platform by students and instructors indicate that the attributes of the delivery platform largely influence learning outcomes, and consequently, the instructors' and students' perceptions on the effectiveness of e-learning. The usefulness of the utilities incorporated in the platform and their user-friendliness are of prime importance. The delivery platform is continuously upgraded at METU, based on the outcome of these assessments.

The results of evaluations carried out at METU so far suggest that in addition to the issues discussed in the previous sections, the effectiveness of online courses/programs is also influenced by the following factors:

- Degree of "prepackaging" in the course: It can be said that the less structured a course is, the more it can be customized to the pace and learning needs of students.
- Size of the class: The METU experience indicates that online courses increase effectiveness in large classes (over 100 students), mainly

because individual interaction with the instructor and communication among students can be established to an extent that is rarely possible in a traditional classroom.

- Mode of delivery: When full contact hours are maintained and the material on the Web is used as a supplement, effectiveness diminishes in proportion to the lecturing content during class. Class contact should be used for discussion of assignments, case studies and seminars by invited speakers, rather than teaching the material already available online.

- Degree of "homogeneity" among students: In the case of online courses, students who have been sharing the same environment for some time (e.g., 4th year undergraduates of the same department) tend to participate and collaborate more than students who come from different backgrounds (as in a typical MBA class). However, in the case of online programs, heterogeneity in the student population enriches the learning experience. This is especially valid for programs intended for working professionals, like the Informatics graduate program at METU, where interaction with fellow participants from different areas of expertise, exposes students to a rich and varied breadth of ideas and approaches.

No single factor is dominant. Rather, a combination of these factors is likely to affect outcome. Further research in this area could point to the determination of patterns that are most effective for Internet-based learning.

CONCLUSION

Technological developments are transforming the boundaries of work and education. Just as telecommuting and virtual offices challenge the workplace, virtual learning defies the traditional "lecture hour" and "classroom" confines of higher education. The growing demand for learning in a global economy, the availability of powerful technologies, combined with emerging competitors in the education market are driving universities to redefine their learning environment. The challenge for traditional universities is to adapt to this paradigm shift and strike a balance between the virtual and traditional components of their education services.

There is no single blueprint solution. Institutions have to develop their own models for integrating the virtual element into their mainstream activities. Nonetheless, the strategic, administrative, academic and technological issues to be addressed are common to all. Only the solutions will vary according to the particular goals and constraints of each institution. The METU case illustrates the phases in the evolution of an Internet-based learning environment, and highlights the breadth of issues to be resolved for an organized transition to a new mode of instruction.

The Internet holds enormous potential for leveraging distance education in universities. Yet adapting to a technology-enabled paradigm is not easy for traditional institutions with entrenched organizational hierarchies and practices. Initial costs are high, but equally high benefits are expected in terms of quality and outreach of education. The situation can perhaps best be described in the words of Pelton (1997): "Cyberlearning vs. the University: An irresistible force meets an immovable object." Although distance education through the Internet is not likely to supersede conventional instruction, the Internet is a perfect vehicle to be more responsive to learner needs and increase the quality and outreach of higher education. Universities are at a unique juncture to take part in one of the biggest revolutions in distance education and realize the opportunities that lie ahead.

APPENDIX A

Sample List of Traditional Universities with Virtual Campus Extensions

California State University CSU Institute (http://www.gateway.calstate.edu/
extension/Online/default.html)
Columbia University (http://www.ce.columbia.edu/online/)
Cornell University (http://www.ecornell.com)
Deakin University (http://www.deakin.edu.au)
Drexel University (http://online.drexel.edu/topclass/index.html)
Georgia Institute of Technology (http://www.conted.gatech.edu)
Indiana University (http://www.indiana.edu/~iude/)
Michigan State University (http://www.vu.msu.edu)
Middle East Technical University (http://www.ii.metu.edu.tr)
New Jersey Institute of Technology (http://www.njit.edu/DL)
New York University the Virtual College (http://www.scps.nyu.edu/dyncon/virt)
Pace University (http://online.pace.edu)
Park University (http://www.park.edu/DIST/DIST)
Pennsylvania State University World Campus (http://www.worldcampus.psu.edu)
Stanford University (http://scpd.stanford.edu)
State University of New York Learning Network (http://sln.suny.edu/domino/
slnhome.nsf)
Stevens Institute of Technology (http://www.webcampus.stevens.edu)

Temple University (http://www.temple.edu)

The University of Texas System TeleCampus (http://www.telecampus.utsystem.edu/)

The University of South Australia (http://www.unisanet.unisa.edu.au)

University of British Columbia (http://det.cstudies.ubc.ca/)

University of California-Berkeley Extension Online (http://learn.berkeley.edu)

University of Illinois Online (http://www.online.uillinois.edu)

University of Maryland University College (http://www.umsa.umd.edu/OnLine/)

University of Phoenix Online (http://online.phoenix.edu/)

University of Southern California (http://den.usc.edu)

University of Wisconsin Center for Learning Innovation (http://www.uwex.edu)

Washington State Web University (http://www.washington.edu/students/distance/)

APPENDIX B

Sample List of Online Learning Platforms and Service Providers

Blackboard (http://www.blackboard.com)

Cognitive Arts (http://www.cognitivearts.com)

Convene (http://www.convene.com/)

DigitalThink (http://www.digitalthink.com/)

Eduprise (http://www.eduprise.com/)

eCollege (http://www.ecollege.com/)

e-education (http://www.jonesknowledge.com/)

First Class (http://www.firstclass.ca/v2/launch.htm)

JonesKnowledge.com (http://www.jonesknowledge.com/)

Lotus LearningSpace (http://www.lotus.com/home.nsf/welcome/learnspace)

Outlook (http://www.outlookinteractive.com/)

Prometheus (http://www.prometheus.com/)

Topclass (http://www.wbtsystems.com/)

V Campus (http://www.vcampus.com/)

WebCT (http://www.webCT.com)

APPENDIX C

Sample List of Marketing and Information Portals

America's Learning Exchange (http://www.alx.org)
CyberU (http://www.cyberu.com/)
DistanceLearn (http://www.lifelonglearning.com)
Dr. Dobb's (http://www.ddj.com/)
Edupoint (http://www.edupoint.com/)
Ed-X.com (http://ed-x.com)
Embark (http://www.embark.com/)
Fathom (http://www.Fathom.com)
Globewide Network Academy (http://www.gnacademy.org)
Hungry Minds (http://www.hungryminds.com)
Learnon (http://www.learnon.org)
MindEdge (http://www.mindedge.com)
Peterson's Distance Learning Channel (http://www.petersons.com)
R1.edu (http://www.R1edu.org)
The Sloan-C Catalog of Online Educational Programs (http://www.sloan-c.org/catalog/)
THINQ (http://www.thinq.com)
UNESCO e-learning portal (http://www.unesco.org/education/e-learning/index.html)
World Lecture Hall (http://www.utexas.edu/world/lecture)

APPENDIX D

Sample List of Virtual Universities

American Coastline University (http://www.amercoastuniv.edu/)
Athena University (http://www.athena.edu/)
California Coast University (http://www.calcoastuniv.edu/)
California Virtual University (http://www.california.edu)
Capella University (http://www.capella-university.edu)
Cardean University (http://www.unext.com/)
Commonwealth Open University (http://off-campus.org/)
Concord University School of Law (http://www.concordlawschool.com/)
Cyber State University (http://www.cyberstateu.com/)

Greenleaf University (http://www.greenleaf.edu/)
Jones International University (http://www.jonesinternational.edu/)
Hong Kong Cyber University (http://www.hkcyberu.com)
Internet University (http://www.internet-university.com)
Kennedy Western University (http://www.kw.edu)
Kentucky Commonwealth Virtual University (http://www.kcvu.org/)
NKI Internet College (http://www.nettskolen.com)
OnlineLearning.net (http://www.onlinelearning.net/)
Open University U.K. (http://www.openuniversity.edu/)
South Dakota Electronic University Consortium (http://www.hpcnet.org/euc)
Southern California University of Professional Studies (http://www.scups.edu/)
Southern Regional Electronic Campus (http://www.srec.sreb.org)
The European Network University (http://www.netuni.nl)
University for Industry (http://www.learndirect.co.uk)
Virtual Online University (http://www.vousi.com/)
Western Governors University (http://www.wgu.edu/wgu/index.html)

REFERENCES

American Association of University Professors. (1999). Statement on copyright. June. Available on the World Wide Web at: http://www.aaup.org/spccopyr.htm. Accessed March 30, 2001.

Andriole, S. J. (1997). Requirements-driven ALN course design, development, delivery and evaluation. *Journal of Asynchronous Learning Networks*, 1(2), 57-67. Available on the World Wide Web at: http://www.aln.org/alnweb/journal/jaln_Vol1issue2.htm. Accessed March 30, 2001.

Asynchronous Learning Networks. (2001). *The Web of Asynchronous Learning Networks*. Available on the World Wide Web at: http://www.aln.org/sloan_aln. Accessed March 30, 2001.

Blumenstyk, G. (2000). How a publishing empire is changing higher education. *Chronicle of Higher Education*, September 8, 47 (2).

Bourne, J. R. (1998). Net-learning: Strategies for on-campus and off-campus network-enabled learning. *Journal of Asynchronous Learning Networks*, 2(2), 70-88. Available on the World Wide Web at: http://www.aln.org/alnweb/journal/jaln_Vol2issue2.htm. Accessed March 30, 2001.

Bourne, J. R., Mayadas, A. F. and Campbell, J. O. (2000). Asynchronous learning networks: An information technology-based infrastructure for engineering education. *Proceedings of the IEEE*, 88(1), 63-71.

Calvert, J. (2001). Deakin University: Going online at a dual-mode university. *International Review of Research in Open and Distance Learning*, 1(2). Available on the World Wide Web at: http://www.icaap.org/iuicode?149.1.2.8. Accessed March 30, 2001.

Council for Higher Education Accreditation. (2000). *Distance Learning in Higher Education: Update Number 3*. June. Available on the World Wide Web at: http://www.chea.org/Commentary/distance-learning-3.cfm. Accessed March 30, 2001.

Gartner Group Inc. (2000) Gartner's digital divide report: 50 percent of U.S. households now have Internet access: Gartner CEO advises congress on digital divide solutions. *Press Release*, October 2. Available on the World Wide Web at: http://www.gartner.com/5_about/press_room/pr20001002a.html. Accessed March 30, 2001.

Harris D. A. and DiPaolo, A. (1999). Institutional policy for ALN. *Journal of Asynchronous Learning Networks*, 3(1), 1-6. Available on the World Wide Web at: http://www.aln.org/alnweb/journal/jaln-vol3issue1.htm. Accessed March 30, 2001.

Institute for Higher Education Policy. (2000). *Quality on the Line: Benchmarks for Success in Internet-Based Distance Education*. April. Available on the World Wide Web at: http://www.ihep.com/quality.pdf. Accessed March 30, 2001.

Kellogg Commission on the Future of State and Land-Grant Universities. (1999). *Returning to Our Roots: A Learning Society. (Fourth Report)*, September, 20-22. Available on the World Wide Web at: http://www.nasulgc.org/publications/Kellogg/Learn.pdf. Accessed March 30, 2001.

King, B., McCausland, H. and Nunan, T. (2001). Converting to online course and program delivery: The University of South Australia case study. *International Review of Research in Open and Distance Learning*, 1(2). Available on the World Wide Web at: http://www.icaap.org/iuicode?149.1.2.7. Accessed March 30, 2001.

Kochtanek T. R. and Hein, K. K. (2000). Creating and nurturing distributed asynchronous learning environments. *Online Information Review*, 24(4), 280-294.

McNeil, S. G., Robin, B. R. and Miller, R. M. (2000). Facilitating interaction, communication and collaboration in online courses. *Computers and Geosciences*, 26(6), 699-708.

Massachusetts Institute of Technology. (2001). MIT to make nearly all course materials available free on the World Wide Web: unprecedented step challenges 'privatization of knowledge'. *MIT News*, April 4. Available on the World Wide Web at: http://web.mit.edu/newsoffice/nr/2001/ocw.html. Accessed March 30, 2001.

Motiwalla, L. and Tello, S. (2000). Distance learning on the Internet: An exploratory study. *The Internet and Higher Education*, 2(4), 253-264.

National Education Association, Higher Education Research Center. (2000). *Distance Education at Post-secondary Education Institutions: 1997-98.* Update, 6(2). Available on the World Wide Web at: http://www.nea.org/he/heupdate/vol6no2.pdf. Accessed March 30, 2001.

Paulsen, M. and Rekkedal, T. (2001). The NKI Internet college: a review of 15 years of delivery of 10,000 online courses. *International Review of Research in Open and Distance Learning*, 1(2). Available on the World Wide Web at: http://www.icaap.org/iuicode?149.1.2.4. Accessed March 30, 2001.

Pelton, N. (1997). Cyberlearning vs. the university: an irresistible force meets an immovable object. *IEEE Engineering Management Review*, Fall, 110-113.

Piotrowski, C. and Vodanovich, S. J. (2000). Are the reported barriers to Internet-based instruction warranted? A synthesis of research. *Education*, 121(1), 48-53.

Sherron, G. T. and Boettcher, J. V. (1997). Distance learning: The shift to interactivity. *CAUSE Professional Paper Series*, 17, 11-21. Available on the World Wide Web at: http://www.educause.edu/ir/library/pdf/PUB3017.pdf. Accessed March 30, 2001.

Stallings, D. (2000). The virtual university: legitimized at century's end: future uncertain for the new millennium. *The Journal of Academic Librarianship*, 26(1), 3-14.

Stone, M. (2000). Study shows 300 mil worldwide Web users. *Newsbytes*. March 22. Available on the World Wide Web at: http://www.newsbytes.com/pubNews. Accessed March 30, 2001.

Thomas, R. (2000). Evaluating the effectiveness of the Internet for the delivery of an MBA program. *Innovations in Training and Education International*, 37 (2), 97-102.

U.S. Department of Commerce, Economic and Statistics Administration and National Telecommunications and Information Administration. (2000). *Falling Through the Net: Toward Digital Inclusion.* October. Available on the World Wide Web at: http://www.esa.doc.gov/fttn00.htm. Accessed March 30, 2001.

U.S. Department of Education, National Center for Education Statistics.

(2000). The Condition of Education 2000. NCES 2000-602, Washington, DC: US Government Printing Office.

U.S. Department of Education, The Web-based Education Commission. (2000). *The Power of the Internet for Learning: Moving From Promise to Practice*. December. Available on the World Wide Web at: http://interact.hpcnet.org/webcommission/index.htm. Accessed March 30, 2001.

Ubell, R. (2000). Engineers turn to e-learning. *IEEE Spectrum*, October, 59-63.

Walker, D. (2000). British government plans online vocational university. *Chronicle of Higher Education*, July 14, 46(45).

Ward, M. and Newlands, D. (1998). Use of the Web in undergraduate teaching. *Computers & Education*, 31(2), 171-184.

Weinstein, B. (2000). Forecasting future of distance learning. *The Boston Globe*, October 29.

Chapter XVI

Teaching Enterprise Systems in a Distance Education Mode

Michael Rosemann
Queensland University of Technology, Australia

This chapter discusses the needs and opportunities for teaching comprehensive business applications, Enterprise Systems, in the form of academic distance education courses. Specific factors of the educational market in Enterprise Systems such as high demand, limited resources or the increased importance of Application Hosting Centers will be described. An appropriate learning model will be selected that stresses the role of the lecturer as a moderator. The subject, Process Engineering at Queensland University of Technology, is taken as an example in order to discuss different forms of distance and also collaborative education in Enterprise Systems. The summary includes recommendations and sketches possible future directions.

THE NEED TO TEACH ENTERPRISE SYSTEMS IN A DISTANCE EDUCATION MODE

Characteristics of Enterprise Systems

A new class of packaged application software has emerged over the past decade. Variously called Enterprise Resource Planning Systems, Enterprise-wide Systems, Enterprise Business Systems or just Enterprise Systems, these comprehensive software solutions seek to integrate the complete range of a business's processes and functions in order to present a holistic view of the business from a single information and IT architecture. An Enterprise System can be defined as customizable standard software that supports the main business processes of a company (Rosemann, 1999).

As off-the-shelf solutions, they consist of integrated applications for the main functions, such as procurement, production management, warehousing, sales and distribution, financial and managerial accounting, human resource management and quality management. In the most cases, industry-specific solutions are available, which include applications demanded by industries such as aerospace, automotive, banking, chemicals, consumer products, engineering, healthcare, higher education, insurance, mining, oil and gas, pharmaceuticals, retail, telecommunications or utilities. Enterprise Systems are based on one integrated logical database. Consequently, vendor master data entered in the materials management module are, for example, also available in the accounts payable module. Enterprise Systems have one common user interface across all modules that can be individualized for users or user groups.

Currently, the main Enterprise Systems vendors are SAP, J.D. Edwards, Oracle and PeopleSoft. Among these, SAP solutions are the dominant application, claiming more than 50 % of the Enterprise Systems market. The Gartner Group forecasts that the Enterprise Systems market will be greater than $20 billion by 2002 (with a probability of 80%) (Gartner Group, 1999). According to their prediction, more than 50% of this will be Enterprise Systems service revenue, while the total Enterprise Systems license revenue will amount to about $9 billion. The Gartner Group also estimates that more than 90% of Fortune 500 enterprises have purchased a module or a set of modules from an Enterprise Systems vendor. The market for small- and medium-sized enterprises is identified as the main customer group, as more than 50% of these enterprises have not yet selected a next-generation Enterprise Systems. For 2001 (2002), the Gartner Group predicts market growth of 25% (28%). These figures show that Enterprise Systems initiatives are among the biggest investments to which enterprises are currently committing. This trend is likely to continue as a second wave of Enterprise Systems (ERP II) is emerging, which extends these systems towards interbusiness processes such as Customer Relationship Management and Supply Chain Management (Gartner Group, 2000).

A range of influences has encouraged the increasing uptake of Enterprise Systems, which already account for a substantial portion of the world-installed base of application software. Global competitive pressures promoting the adoption of "best practices," the paradigm of continuous business engineering postulated by the large management consulting firms, and an international trend towards privatization of government services, have all contributed to a climate of change that has facilitated the growing acceptance and adoption of Enterprise Systems. The global rush to deploy information technology in support of re-engineering and rightsizing the firm demands both substantial and relatively rapid change to the information systems portfolio, a pace of change not possible with custom software development. The backlog in IS departments, problems integrating systems, the inability of legacy systems to cope with the "Year 2000" problem, and the introduction of the Euro currency have further increased demand for application software packages. Enterprise Systems are used because they allow a cost-effective, company-wide integration of data and processes.

Brief Overview about Enterprise Systems Education at Universities

While a significant and growing proportion of Information Systems graduates are integrally involved with the selection, implementation, operation, maintenance, support, management, development and use of software packages, Enterprise Systems as a distinct phenomenon of interest remain largely under-researched and absent in Information Management and Information Systems curricula (Gable, 1998; Klaus et al., 2000). Paradoxically, a serious dearth of Enterprise Systems expertise exists in practice. This shortage in supply contributes to heated competition for staff with related experience, project budget-overruns, and over-reliance on external consultants and contractors.

Universities started quite late with the integration of Enterprise Systems-related subjects into their curriculum. A main facilitator for the integration of Enterprise Systems is the range of university programs of the major Enterprise Systems vendors. This university to Enterprise Systems vendor link has spawned new curricula at the post-graduate level, either under the banner of a new breed of MBA program (Winter, 1999), or within the Information Systems area as a Master of Science program (Holmes and Hayen, 1999b). Individual experiences of universities implementing SAP R/3 into their IS curriculum can be found in Lederer-Antonucci (1999), Watson and Schneider (1999). Foote (1999) describes a SAP-accounting class and other SAP-related courses in the U.S. Shoemaker (1999) sketches a six-hour introduction to Enterprise Systems for sales and marketing professionals. Rosemann et al. (2000) and Hawking and McCarthy (2000) discuss Enterprise Systems courses with industrial work experiences.

The impact of reorganizing Enterprise Systems subject matter into existing curricula and the special challenges posed to faculty has been reported by Stewart et al. (1999). The benefits and pitfalls of teaching conceptual knowledge with Enterprise Systems as a learning vehicle have been critically evaluated in terms of learning outcomes and effort by Noguera and Watson (1999) and Scott (1999).

An example of a syllabus for the remote delivery of an introductory subject via the Internet is given by Holmes and Hayen (1999a). They describe the design of a course consisting of ten lessons that introduces the concepts, fundamentals and framework of Enterprise Systems (see also http://sap.mis.cmich.edu/sap-esoft00.htm). The main teaching tools were HTML-based websites generated from PowerPoint slides, Lotus Screen Cams and a web-based discussion forum. Stewart and Rosemann (2001) propose an increased international collaboration at universities in order to educate in the area of Enterprise Systems more cost-effectively.

In comparison with its dominance in industry, SAP is also the most popular Enterprise System in use at universities. A worldwide survey about teaching and research related to SAP R/3 showed that most universities (outside Germany) started in or after 1997 with their initiatives in Enterprise Systems (Gable & Rosemann, 1999). Since then, it has become an area of fast-growing interest in academia demonstrated by the continuously increasing number of subjects dealing with Enterprise Systems. The international survey, for example, consolidated data about more than 180 SAP-related subjects at universities. In the U.S., until 1997 almost no university was teaching SAP R/3, while in 2001 more than 200 institutes of higher learning are using SAP solutions. Most of these universities report a significant increase in enrolments due to their SAP offerings. SAP's Enterprise System R/3, as an example, is used worldwide by more than 400 universities in more than 35 countries and more than 50,000 students access this solution.

Moreover, research in Enterprise Systems is rapidly developing. In 2000, all major conferences on Information Systems (ICIS, AMCIS, ACIS, PACIS, ECIS) had a special track on Enterprise Systems. The Americas Conference on Information Systems (AMCIS) has, since 1999, a special track on Enterprise Systems that regularly includes papers on teaching Enterprise Systems (e.g., Holmes & Hayen, 1999a; 1999b; Noguera & Watson, 1999; Stewart et al., 1999; Rosemann et al., 2000).

Furthermore, many academic IS journals had special editions on Enterprise Systems in 2000 (e.g., Journal of Information Technology, Information Systems Frontiers, Communications of the ACM, Journal of Decision Systems, Journal of Management Information Systems, Business Process Management Journal, Australian Accounting Review).

Demand for Distance Education in Enterprise Systems

An analysis of the current course offerings shows that Distance Education in Enterprise Systems is still the exception, although various factors recommend an increase in the off-campus offerings of Enterprise Systems-related subjects. Overall, the market for Enterprise Systems education can be characterized as a situation of global demand and worldwide limited resources. These are the typical characteristics of a market for distance education.

On the one hand, the demand for graduates with Enterprise Systems experiences is significant. Experience at the Queensland University of Technology (QUT), Brisbane, indicates that many IT students (in this case especially from Southeast Asia) are selecting the QUT because it is offering subjects related to Enterprise Systems.

On the other hand, the number of lecturers with sufficient qualifications and Enterprise Systems hands-on expertise is still rather limited. This is also the case for appropriate, non-product-specific Enterprise Systems textbooks and teaching material. Furthermore, the management of Enterprise Systems at universities is a very challenging endeavour. These applications require immense hardware. Their implementation and continuous administration demand product-specific knowledge that cannot be found within the classical technical services of universities. This situation is further challenged by the continuous release of comprehensive upgrades of the Enterprise System. Thus, it is even more difficult to satisfy the students' demand.

Distance education is usually seen as a way to extend the market (providers' perspective) or as an approach to offer customers an increased course selection. In the area of Enterprise Systems, however, distance education can simply help to overcome the still under-represented offerings of Enterprise Systems subjects. It also allows sharing investments in Enterprise Systems made by one institution. Consequently, Enterprise Systems seem to be an important topic for distance education.

The Role of University Application Hosting Centers

As Enterprise Systems are very complex and comprehensive systems, an effective model has been developed in which selected universities host Enterprise Systems solutions for other universities. Instead of dealing directly with hundreds of universities (in the case of SAP), the Enterprise Systems provider donates the software only to selected Application Hosting Centers. Universities that want to use the Enterprise System have to have a contract with the Enterprise Systems vendor and an Application Hosting Center. In this model, universities can completely outsource their system administration and save significant costs. Instead of acquiring hardware and qualifying and paying a system administrator, they pay an annual fee for the system use. Lecturers and students can access the system via a web browser or through product-specific interfaces (e.g., SAP-Graphical User Interface). This also includes the very comprehensive online documentation, which is available in HTML format.

University Application Hosting Centers do not only provide system access. A main purpose of the establishment of these Application Hosting Centers is to build up a user community that shares experiences and actual course content. This model allows building up markets for course offerings and is an ideal platform for distance education purposes (Stewart & Rosemann, 2001).

Current University Application Hosting Centers for the market dominating SAP solution are at locations including Passau and Magdeburg (Germany), Taiwan, Seoul (Korea), Brisbane (Australia) and Chico (USA) (Gronwald, 1999).

LEARNING MODEL

Characteristics of Courses Related to Enterprise Systems

Teaching Enterprise Systems requires a model that takes the special characteristics of these applications into account. As part of the worldwide survey participants were asked to rate the importance of alternative SAP R/3 training opportunities for staff (1=unimportant, 5=highly important) (Gable and Rosemann, 1999). The results in Figure 1 clearly indicate the importance of hands-on experience.

This importance of hands-on experience (only one respondent rated this less than 3 out of 5) emphasizes the criticality of staff access to an operational SAP R/3 system. The breadth and depth of Enterprise Systems is difficult to comprehend and more difficult to demonstrate without hands-on access. University Application Hosting Centers conveniently offer at least the opportunity for hands-on exercises without the need for investments in hardware or software. Thus, the model of using University Application Hosting Centers could also be interpreted as distance education in the sense of using distant resources.

The necessity of hands-on expertise forms a major challenge for lecturers in Enterprise Systems, as they have to keep up with the speed of system upgrades as well as having to maintain a certain comprehensiveness of

Figure 1: Alternative training opportunities

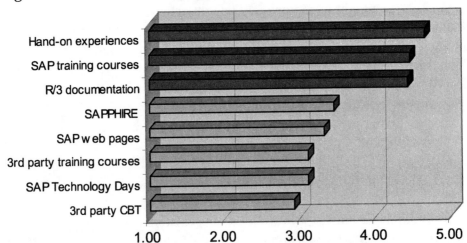

Enterprise Systems knowledge. This is virtually impossible given that many Enterprise Systems have more than 100,000 different screens and major updates annually. Thus, an academic instructor in Enterprise Systems is typically not familiar with the comprehensive and detailed system functionality.

An adequate learning model has to consider that Enterprise Systems are a fast developing area with high complexity. During one course, students will sometimes gain more product-specific knowledge in a certain area than the lecturer. Consequently, it is necessary to have a learning model in which the lecturer is more in the role of a moderator than an instructor. This demands a shift from a lecturer-centric paradigm to a more student-centric perspective.

Selection of an Appropriate Learning Model

The sheer size and degree of integration in Enterprise Systems packages often results in a steep learning curve, leading to problems in both classroom and corporate training environments. Critics argue that an Enterprise Systems learning model should avoid information overload and provide a strong bridge between concepts and hands-on experience (Scott, 1999). Scott (1999) has proposed five potential learning models that can be used to manage and enhance Enterprise Systems-related education. These models are based on the work of Leidner and Jarvenpaa (1995). Table 1 summarizes the key features of these models.

Due to the overwhelming importance of hands-on experiences and the extreme comprehensiveness and complexity of Enterprise Systems, the learning model has to consider that any academic instructor would struggle to provide detailed feedback on the entire system functionality. Thus, an

Table 1: Features of learning models

Learning model	Features
Objective Model	The goal is to transfer knowledge from the instructor to the students. It assumes that the instructor has all the necessary knowledge, provides the stimulus and is in control of the material and pace.
Constructive Model	The students decide the focus and control of the learning material. The instructor provides support more than direction. Engagement and motivation of the students are usually high.
Collaborative Model	Prior knowledge and experience of the participants are shared to enhance interpretation and learning. The engagement is typically high.
Cognitive Information Process Model	Assumes the importance of individual's learning styles and suggests the need for individualised instructions.
Socio-cultural Model	Heterogeneity of the learners in terms of prior knowledge and social and cultural backgrounds is carefully analysed to adjust the teaching process to the students' background.

objective model will often not be practical for Enterprise Systems education. If possible, students should rather be allocated to teams, in which experiences and interpretations can be shared (collaborative model).

The following two cases will describe examples of how the collaborative model can be used for Enterprise Systems distance education.

CASE 1: OFF-CAMPUS DELIVERY OF PROCESS ENGINEERING

Design and Techniques of this Distance Education Course

This paragraph discusses how one particular subject in Enterprise Systems, Process Engineering, has been offered over a period of two years in different forms of distance education. The subject is embedded in a comprehensive Enterprise Systems-related curriculum at the Queensland University of Technology (QUT), Brisbane, Australia. Built on an introductory course, Issues in IT Management, which explains the basics of Enterprise Systems and SAP R/3 as an example, two main streams are offered. In a more technical stream, students have the opportunity to gain knowledge in the areas of administering Enterprise Systems and in SAP's programming language ABAP. In a more business-oriented stream, process management represents, along with knowledge management, the main focus. The subject Process Engineering introduces the students to different approaches of process management like Business Process Reengineering or Process Innovation. Explanations are given as to how business processes can be modelled. Selected SAP processes are discussed and it is demonstrated how they can be configured and executed. This subject is a prerequisite for subjects covering extended Enterprise Systems concepts such as Customer Relationship Management and Workflow Management. In "Projects in Process Engineering" students are given the opportunity to apply their knowledge in a real-life context. Organized in groups, they analyze (with the support of SAP Australia and PricewaterhouseCoopers) selected business processes at a Queensland Government Agency (Rosemann et al., 2000). Figure 2 gives an overview of these process-related subjects within the Enterprise Systems curriculum at the Queensland University of Technology.

The course rationale of Process Engineering is described in the study guide as follows:

"This unit presents strategic and tactical, business and IT management issues involved with a process-oriented perspective on enterprises and their IT-applications. Based on a discussion of different Process Engineering approaches like Business Process Reengineering or Process Innovation, a procedure model for Process Engineering will be introduced. This procedure model includes the identification of relevant processes, as-is and to-be process modelling, process implementation, process execution and process change management. This unit focuses on process modelling issues. The participants will understand and use the ARIS-Toolset 5.0, the market leading business process modelling tool (Scheer, 2000). Regarding the IT applications, this unit emphasizes the Enterprise Systems marketplace. It gives students exposure to SAP R/3 4.6, the leading Enterprise System, and helps to prepare students for a range of Enterprise Systems roles in industry. The SAP-modules MM, SD, FI and CO will be discussed from a process-oriented

Figure 2: Subjects related to Process Engineering in the Enterprise Systems curriculum at the Queensland University of Technology

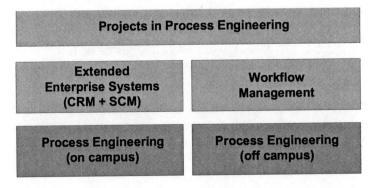

perspective using the SAP reference models and predefined processes. A main focus is the clear presentation of the interrelations between modelling, implementing, configuring and executing Enterprise Systems processes. Among others, the SAP implementation methodology, Accelerated SAP, and mySAP.com will be introduced.

This subject has the following theoretical objectives:

- Provide students with an awareness of the issues concerning the management of business processes.
- Develop in students the capability to identify, model, reorganize, introduce, and manage continuously processes in a business organization.
- Describe the characteristics of Enterprise Systems.
- Explain how the reference data and process models of Enterprise Systems are structured.
- Explain the relationships between the modelling, the customization, the execution, and the redesign of Enterprise Systems-based business processes.
- Develop in students the capability to understand and customize the processes of Enterprise Systems according to given requirements in a business organization.

Students have to work on three assignments. In these assignments they explore the Enterprise System SAP R/3. Students don't get step-by-step instructions on how to use the system, but only a general introduction into the system navigation. They have to explore the system on their own and follow predefined processes. In their assignments, they discuss how to model, execute and configure these processes. This learning style puts the students into an active role and helps to build general skills in understanding the system design. This approach is based on the selected learning model. It is of importance for any off-campus offering as it reduces the necessary conversation between lecturer and students.

Every student gets the required software, the user interface, in order to access the SAP software from home.

Coordinated On-Campus and Off-Campus Offer

Process Engineering is offered as a traditional on-campus unit as well as an off-campus unit. The content and the assignments of these two are nearly identical. The only difference is that off-campus students have a choice between a final exam and another assignment, whereas on-campus students must take the exam. This assignment usually applies the theoretical knowledge about process modelling and process improvement to a workplace. During semesters in which Process Engineering is offered on-campus and off-campus, local off-campus students have the opportunity to select one form of delivery. Most of these students prefer, if possible, attending the lectures.

All slides of the lectures are password-protected, published on the courses' website and available for download. They include further notes and audio data captured with the tool, RealPresenter (www.real.com). Further explanations and experiences regarding this software can be found at Lightfood (1999).

At the beginning of the off-campus offering of Process Engineering, students could interact with the lecturer in weekly Internet chats. These chats tried to simulate a classroom atmosphere. The slides for the week were the guideline for the chat session. Students could ask questions and the lecturer gave further information. Furthermore, he asked students questions so that they were actively integrated in the lecture. After this virtual lecture, the chat was saved, revised and uploaded to the homepage of the subject. Thus, it was available for all students.

Table 2 shows an extract from such a chat session. In fact, this chat was made in a semester in which the lecturer was located in Germany and the students were located all over Australia and New Zealand. A local tutor (Chris Nagel) supported this lecture. Microsoft's NetMeeting was used as a communication tool. The tutor hosted the session and controlled the participation to this chat session.

It turned out, that the students enjoyed these chat sessions very much. In fact, they tried to participate in these lectures even on their business trips. Extreme examples were the cases in which students were in airport lounges or even on an overseas holiday (Bahamas, 3:00 a.m.). It took approximately two weeks before all participants felt comfortable with this form of distance education. Furthermore, it took time before a "classroom atmosphere" with a moderating lecturer and attentive students was developed. Trials with participating students from other universities and more than one lecturer failed because of inexperienced participants. On average, 60-80 % of all off-campus students participated in these online chats. Their participation had no influence on their marks.

Occasionally, external experts were involved in these chat forums. In one case, for example, the SAP implementation methodology Accelerated SAP (ASAP) was discussed in the lecture. After one hour, a SAP employee from the German SAP headquarters, who was involved in the product development joined this chat session and students had the opportunity to ask questions. Later, a SAP consultant who was using ASAP for the implementation of

Table 2: Extract from an Internet-based chat with students

	....
Michael Rosemann	...and that is where ARIS can assist you can import processes from SAP into ARIS, modify them in ARIS and make additions, and export them again to SAP R/3.
Joseph Lam	You mean modify them in SAP?
Michael Rosemann	No, you modify process models in ARIS.
Frank Hilpert	Why export again to R/3? It doesn't change the module.
Michael Rosemann	It does not change the functionality - that is right, but you can individualise the exported models in ARIS.
Frank Hilpert	So you do process reengineering and then can not implement using SAP R/3?
Michael Rosemann	That is why you have to do customizing in SAP R/3.
Michael Rosemann	...to change the system in line with your business requirements.
Frank Hilpert	But customizing only goes so far.
Michael Rosemann	That is right - the implementation of R/3 will also affect established business processes, information flows and responsibilities within the company.
Paula and Adam	This way you can start with the reference models in R/3, export then and change then in ARIS. You don't need to start with blank models.
Chris Nagel	(*Privat*) I have to leave the PC for about 10 – 15 min.

Human Resource Management solutions in London, UK, participated in the chat. In that way, the students learned the concepts and could talk to the product developer and user.

In following semesters, off-campus students also received weekly video-tapes of the lecture, which they very much appreciated. Since then, the interest in weekly chats via the Internet was significantly reduced.

In the next semesters it is planned to use a more sophisticated environment for distance education that also allows bidirectional many-many audio communication (Virtual Classroom).

The comparable course content allowed an analysis of the differences in the performance of on-campus and off-campus students. In correspondence with similar studies (e.g., Dobrin, 1999; Smeaton & Keogh, 1999), it turned out that focusing just on the grades in the identical assignments, no significant differences could be observed. Table 3 shows the average results for the most recent semester (Second Semester, 2000).

Table 3: Comparison of students' performance (November 2000)

	number of students	assignment 1	assignment 2	assignment 3
on campus	31	8.19	8.26	8.39
off campus	10	8.10	8.40	8.20

CASE 2: COLLABORATIVE EDUCATION IN ENTERPRISE SYSTEMS

Collaboration in Education in Enterprise Systems

The participants of the international survey regarding teaching SAP R/3 (Gable & Rosemann, 1999) were also asked if they were collaborating with other universities in their SAP R/3 initiative. Interest in collaboration was also gauged. A surprising number—50% of all respondent institutes—stated that they are collaborating in various ways with other universities; 35 % of all collaborations are on an international basis. There are no obvious patterns of differences across countries. Only two universities indicated that they are not interested in collaboration. Table 4 shows the areas of interest in cross-university collaboration. Respondents often mentioned multiple areas.

Table 4: Areas of interest for cross-university collaboration

Area of Interest	Answers	Area of Interest	Answers
Research	19	Staff/Student Exchange	10
Teaching Material	15	Curriculum Design	8
Exchange of Knowledge/Experiences	15	Interactive Teaching	6
		Case Studies	3

Research is obviously the most popular reason for collaboration between universities (see also, Hazemi et al., 1998). It is expected that Enterprise Systems-related research will be the "second wave" of Enterprise Systems-related activities at universities once systems are established in curriculum. Sharing of teaching material like lecture notes and the general exchange of knowledge and experiences are further main reasons for collaboration. In many cases, universities that have just commenced their SAP initiative are interested in input from experienced universities.

Collaborative academic education in Enterprise Systems adds interaction between different faculties or universities to the distance education mode. An example for collaboration within one university is the Virtual Enterprise Project at the University of Missouri (University of Missouri, 2001). Participants from four campuses collaborate in this project in the design of a virtual enterprise. Each of the four participating institutes contributes knowledge from different areas such as logistics, accounting, human resource management, or data warehousing (see Figure 3). They all use the same SAP installation, which requires detailed coordination of activities.

Figure 3: The virtual enterprise project

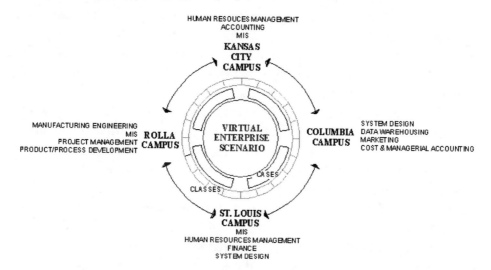

Collaborative Assignments

A simple starting point for *collaboration between universities* is the definition and use of the same assignment (content and specification, such as deadlines) for students at different universities.

This approach conforms with the proposed learning model. Rather than following the objective model and, for example, providing lectures from one university to other institutes, students interact and learn from each other under the moderation of more than one instructor. This format is open-ended and places responsibility on the participant. Instead of passive consumption, the participants have an active role and face a continuous pressure to contribute.

The following description of such an initiative in collaborative and distance Enterprise Systems education is based on a project between Queensland University of Technology (QUT) in Brisbane, The University of Texas at Austin (UT), and the Louisiana State University (LSU) (Rosemann et al., 2000). This pilot was the first step towards a more comprehensive participation and understanding of global collaboration in the area of teaching SAP R/3. It took place in September and October 1999.

The main objective of this project was to facilitate further exchange of knowledge and experiences among the lecturers as well as among the students. Furthermore, through interactive teaching between the universities, students gain valuable Enterprise Systems industry knowledge while they simultaneously learn how to communicate effectively using the latest Internet technologies and services (Hanna, 1998; Kimball, 1998).

The participating students had to work on one common assignment. Every student had to pick one of the following five topics. The numbers in brackets indicate how many students (first number) from how many universities (second number) were in each team: Customer Relationship Management (5/3), Supply Chain Management (4/2), Internet-based Processes (7/2), Workflow Management (4/2), and Activity-based Costing (5/2). Each team had to write one consolidated report within seven weeks (max. 25 pages) and to design a PowerPoint presentation. Both had to describe their chosen concept in general (50 %) and the current support offered by SAP-products in particular. The students had to present the results in their classes.

In addition to the three lecturers, every team received further support from associated "experts." These experts were academicians or experienced practitioners committed to

- provide the students with reading recommendations,
- recommend further material and information (e.g., web links),
- participate in a discussion group, and
- review the final assignment.

The following experts took part in this project:

- The head of the area Telecommunication at the German consulting company, Mummert & Partner. She was an expert in the area of Customer Relationship Management, in which she worked on various projects.
- A guest lecturer at the University of Tartu, Estonia, and head of the task force, 'Resource Modeling' within the Workflow Management Coalition.
- Two lecturers from the Cicade University in Rio de Janeiro, Brazil. They were experts in the area of Supply Chain Management and familiar with the SAP approach. Another supply chain management expert came from the Technological Educational Institution (TEI) of Thessaloniki, Greece.
- A lecturer, who has taught SAP R/3 for many years at the University of Harz, Germany, and at the Florida Gulf Coast University, USA. As an expert for Internet-based Enterprise Systems processes, he developed a workflow-integrated Internet scenario to have students from different countries collaboratively participate on an international sales process.

- Two lecturers from the Department of Information Systems at the University of Münster, Germany. They are both working within their Ph.D. thesis on topics related to Activity-based Costing.

The following three paragraphs describe the subjects and the participating students at the three institutions.

Queensland University of Technology, Brisbane

The 16 students from Brisbane were enrolled in the postgraduate subject Process Engineering, which was offered on-campus (in total 51 students) and off-campus (7 students) in the second semester 1999. Most of the off-campus students were not located in Brisbane. The students had the choice of working in a local team or participating in this international project. For these students this assignment was the last one of a total of five assignments. They had been working on group assignments before, although all previous group work was done with local students.

The University of Texas at Austin

Forty-three students were enrolled in an elective graduate course called "Cross-functional Systems Integration." The course is an overview of various aspects of Enterprise Systems and systems integration. Students were full-time, most studying for MBA, MPA and PPA degrees. A few students were from Engineering and Computer Science. The class had eight teams, each of which had four to six members. All teams had a group assignment due in the last week of the semester. They were given the option to participate in the global virtual team project. One group, with six members, chose to participate in the virtual team project. The other seven teams collaborated locally. The six students in the virtual team participated in the CRM, ABC and Internet projects, although their classmates did projects on just one topic.

Louisiana State University-Baton Rouge

Thirty-two students were enrolled in an elective graduate course called "Enterprise Systems." Similar to UT Austin's course, this course is an overview of Enterprise Systems and the processes that they support. These students were full-time graduate students from various programs: MBA and MS in Information Systems, Computer Science, and Engineering. Early in the semester, three students volunteered to participate in the global collaboration exercise as an extra credit project. These students turned out to be among the best in the class in terms of attitude towards learning. They each joined a global team: Customer Relationship Management, Supply Chain Management, and Workflow Management. Later in the semester, the class was split into five teams: Customer Relationship Management, Data Warehouse, Supply Chain Management, B2B, and Enterprise Application Integration. The original global team members became the natural leaders (and local experts) for their teams. These particular project teams produced a report that was clearly superior compared to the report from the teams that lacked the head start.

The Infrastructure

The entire communication between the three participating locations was done by Internet services. At the beginning, the list of all participants, lecturers, students and experts was distributed, including all email addresses. Chat sessions were recommended for the coordination between the group members. Moreover, a newsgroup was offered to all participants. An exchange of audio or video data did not take place.

Students' Feedback

After the assignment was completed, but before it was graded, the participating students were asked some questions related to their evaluation of this form of assignment. Nine of the twenty-five students answered (36 %). The main feedback was:

- 88 % of these students said they enjoyed this exercise.
- All students answered they would take part again.
- 77 % of these students thought the outcome was higher than in pure local teamwork.

  The students saw the following reasons for the improved outcome:
- shared knowledge,
- different ideas contributed to a higher level of work, and
- higher motivation, in part due to their attempt to impress their colleagues at the other universities.

However, the students believed their virtual teamwork required more effort than the corresponding local group work. Moreover, they saw problems in the existence of different deadlines per universities, which led to different motivation and pressure. Further suggestions from the students included the availability of pictures of all students on the web and the availability of more interactive chat sessions to improve the involvement of all members.

In a face-to-face interview with the Austin team at the end of the semester, the students expressed satisfaction with the project. However, they explained that there were communication problems at times and confusion on what to post and what to email. Apparently, other students told them "Don't post till the end because other teams could see the information." For the ABC project, it worked well. The student leader (QUT) organized and emailed the report and slides before posting. The students recommended an interim deadline for posting, "...we thought UT was late—but we were first to post." Although everybody was invited to use MS-NetMeeting, this Internet-based chat could not be conducted, because of the time differences within this project.

They thought it would be good, at the beginning of the project, if the members announce themselves. This could have been a worthwhile team-building exercise.

The students in Austin thought that the participants from QUT had an advantage as leaders of the project. They coordinated among themselves and probably got feedback instantaneously from the head of this project.

The students did not consider that trust was a problem, although the literature stresses the importance of trust in virtual teams (Knoll & Jarvenpaa, 1995; Lipnack & Stamps, 1997; Jarvenpaa et al., 1998). Students from Louisiana commented that trust was an issue only in the capability of all members to prepare the presentation; "For this, we all trusted each other."

Some further feedback received via email from the LSU students included the following:

- "Though this project provided an opportunity for collaboration, there was a lack of coordination for a very long time. Probably it would have been better if there were one person *assigned* to lead and coordinate in each team from the start."
- "Basically what happened is that I ended up doing my part of the presentation and the paper and emailing it to everyone. I couldn't get anyone to work. I tried emailing them assignments after I became 'Team Leader'. Most of the time that I wrote to them I didn't receive a reply – until another team member realized that his deadline was approaching quickly."
- "It is difficult to say if this was a successful collaboration. We were on time and we covered the scope of the project."
- "This project provided a good opportunity to learn virtual team management and coordination on a global scale. There was excellent support from the experts. This provided a unique learning experience."

Basically, the students perceived the fact that they were all being evaluated at different times as a major problem. Because of this, their time-based goals and priorities were misaligned. And although most students did not perceive trust as an issue, their behavior and comments indicate isolated incidences of unreliability, a symptom of lack of trust. The consolidated recommendations from the students for the design of these kinds of exercises were:

- "A leader defined from the outset with clear roles and responsibilities,
- teams of roughly equal size responsible for equal bodies of work,
- evaluation milestones that occur simultaneously across teams, and
- a better communication method than email - maybe chat room."

Although some of these comments are due to management and coordination issues, there was clearly an issue with the effectiveness of the communication mechanism for teams distributed across the globe. However, from various further statements, a quote from the Austin students' team summarizes the impression: "Overall, this has been a great and fun learning process for all of us." Other students' perspectives on Enterprise Systems distance education can be found in Figueroa and Foerster (2000). In this case, two students reflect on the learning outcomes of a German-American initiative (see also Scheruhn et al., 2000).

Collaborative System Configuration

The experience gained in this collaborative project was a useful learning experience not only for the students, but also for the involved lecturers. In the most current project, the common assignment is not only a theoretical exercise, but does also include hands-on experiences. This project was restricted to only two universities (Queensland University of Technology and Louisiana State University) and one group of students from both places.

The task was to define the system organizational units in SAP R/3 4.6b for a model company that was described regarding its organizational structure, product program and core business processes. System organizational units depict the structure of an organization in an Enterprise System. Examples of system organizational units are plant or distribution channel. The Australian students were responsible for the modules financial accounting and controlling, while the students from Louisiana were in charge of the logistics modules. Though this task could be done in parts independently, it definitely required interaction in order to design an integrated solution. Examples of interrelations are the structure of the profit centers (controlling) and its linkage with reporting units in sales or the links between factories (logistics) and legal entities (financial accounting). The students were provided again with an Internet discussion forum that allowed the upload of information. All students had access to the SAP system in Brisbane. The final report had to be delivered on the same deadline. All participating students got the same mark.

RECOMMENDATIONS AND FUTURE CHALLENGES

Enterprise Systems form the core business operating system in most medium-sized and big companies. Thus, most IT graduates will be exposed to problems related to Enterprise Systems. This leads to an urgent need to establish topics related to Enterprise Systems more comprehensively in the academic IT and business curricula. Universities, however, do not have technical support like the one that can be found in companies that typically use Enterprise Systems, as they lack the financial and personnel resources to implement Enterprise Systems. Rather, they depend on the services of University Application Hosting Centers. These Application Hosting Centers help at least to overcome the technical problem of running and maintaining the system. They allow distance education in the form of using distant resources.

Further resources such as staff members with Enterprise Systems-related knowledge including hands-on experiences are also often limited. Consequently, Enterprise Systems is an area that demands distance education with the opportunity that lecturers can be located at other institutes. A learning model for Enterprise Systems education has to consider the complexity of these applications. A collaborative model seems appropriate as it defines the lecturer more as a moderator than a traditional instructor. Forms of teaching an Enterprise Systems-related subject, not only in a distance education mode, but also collaboratively, have been presented.

Based on the above experiences, the following selected *recommendations* can be made to universities with interest in distance education in Enterprise Systems:

- *Use a University Application Hosting Center.*

A University Application Hosting Center facilitates concentration on the content delivery rather than the complex system administration. Students can easily access the system and in cases of technical problems interact directly with the Hosting Center.

- *Accept the necessity of a collaborative model, as the system complexity does not allow the classical objective model.*

Teaching Enterprise Systems requires accepting that at some stage students might have more insights into a particular sub-module than the lecturer. The likelihood that such a situation can occur has to be communicated frankly to the participants. The lecturer has to focus on the overall architecture and structure of the system. It is up to the students to experience the details of the system. Such an approach prepares the students for a real-life situation, in which they most likely will use modules of an Enterprise Systems they never saw before. Thus, they have to understand how to efficiently gain an understanding of the relevant functionality and interrelations.

- *Use the same assignments for on-campus and off-campus students.*

The utilization of identical on-campus and off-campus assignments reduces the efforts for the development of assignments. Some students appreciate the opportunity to select between the on-campus and off-campus offering during the semester. Furthermore, it allows a continuous comparison of the students' performance and the quality of content delivery.

- *Explore the quality and acceptance of videotaping on-campus lectures for distance education students.*

Videotaping is a reasonable low-cost approach that captures the entire content of a lecture. On-campus students value the opportunity to study certain parts of selected lectures at a later stage. Off-campus students can follow the entire discussion during a lecture.

- *Try to build up a good collaboration with the Enterprise Systems vendor and its implementation partners in order to have access to current knowledge.*

Enterprise Systems are very fast developing applications. Consequently, it is difficult for an individual to keep up with the speed of this development. Guest speakers and current product documentations can easily be integrated in distance education courses and guarantee the distribution of current knowledge.

- *Focus on the educational principles of distance education rather than the technologies.*

Various more or less sophisticated solutions for distance education are available. However, as most lecturers are experts in a certain domain rather than a distance education technology, there is a significant danger that the attempts to use a tool can distract from the actual content delivery. Thus, it is recommended to start, for example, with simple videotapes of a lecture combined with remote system access.

- *Try to collaborate with other universities in order to learn from their experiences.*

Instead of having many independent projects aiming to develop Enterprise Systems courses, it seems to be far more efficient for each participating individual and for the entire community to establish a network for the continuous knowledge exchange. The following two current projects will give an idea of how the establishment of such collaborations can be supported in the future.

The idea of 24x7 Enterprise Systems education describes *a worldwide collaborative model*, in which universities from different continents interact in coordinated Enterprise Systems lectures. Similar to the Virtual Enterprise project at the University of Missouri, each participating university has a certain role in the scenario of a worldwide business process. Such roles can be supplier, manufacturer, retailer, bank, logistical service provider or end consumer. This model allows the participating universities to take part quite independently from the others so that the differences in the semester periods between Australian, American and European universities can be handled. In phases of overlap between the semesters, intensive coordination and knowledge transfer between the participants has to take place. This model facilitates ongoing collaborative Enterprise Systems distance education and simulates collaborative worldwide business processes.

The project, "SMARTS," aims exactly for such a global collaborative approach. The following universities participate in this project:

- University of South Dakota, Vermillion
- University of Missouri, Columbia
- California State University, Chico
- Queensland University of Technology, Brisbane
- University of Sao Paulo

This project integrates SAP applications for business-to-business and business-to-consumer transactions. The final outcome will be robust global business processes, in which the participating universities trade virtual goods and services. Other universities can enter this scenario and take one of the available roles. This model will also be used for training purposes for SAP customers and implementation partners.

Further support for the worldwide communication between institutes of higher learning teaching Enterprise Systems can be expected from the *Marketplace for Higher Education*. This marketplace will increase the transparency about all activities at universities related to Enterprise Systems. Thus, it will include detailed information about universities, courses, lecturers, etc. Especially, it will also be used to trade Enterprise Systems-related lectures. Universities or individuals can offer their courses, which will be reviewed. After successful review, they will be available for purchase. This model aims to significantly reduce the costs related to the development of these courses. At the same time, it will be possible to extend the local Enterprise Systems-related offerings.

Both projects, the collaborative business scenario and the Marketplace for Higher Education, will contribute to the establishment of a worldwide community that shares experiences in Enterprise Systems education.

REFERENCES

Dobrin, J. (1999). Who's teaching online. *ITPE News*, 2(12), June 12.

Elam, J., Becerra-Fernandez, I., Nurphy, K. and Simon, S. (1999). ERP as an enabler of curriculum integration. In Sinnott, T., Gable, G. G. and Hawking, P. (Eds.), *Proceedings of the 3rd SAP Asia Pacific Institute of Higher Learning Forum-SAPPHIRE 1999*, Singapore, 1-2 November.

Figueroa, R. F. and Foerster, M. (2000). Learning ERP (SAP R/3) via the Internet: A student perspective. In Hawking, P., Rosemann, M., Byrne, T. and Stewart, G. (Eds.), *Proceedings of the 4th SAP Asia Pacific Institute of Higher Learning Forum-SAPPHIRE 2000*, Brisbane, 23-26 July, 28-40.

Foote, P. S. (1999). SAP R/3 curriculum development for undergraduate and graduate accounting information systems track. Presentation at the *1st Accounting Information Systems Educator Conference*. Denver, Colorado, 3 August.

Gable, G. G. (1998). Large packaged software a neglected technology? *Journal of Global Information Management*, Summer, 6(3), 3-4.

Gable, G. G. and Rosemann, M. (1999). An analysis of international university activities in teaching and research related to SAP R/3. In Sinnott, T., Gable, G. G. and Hawking, P. (Eds.), *Proceedings of the 3rd SAP Asia Pacific Institute of Higher Learning Forum-SAPPHIRE 1999*, Singapore, 1-2 November.

Gartner Group. (2000). Enterprise resource planning: The next five years. In *Proceedings of the Gartner Group Symposium/Itxpo2000. Brisbane*, Australia, 22-24 October.

Gartner Group. (1999). Enterprise resource planning vendors: The going gets tough. In *Proceedings of the Gartner Group Symposium/Itxpo99*. Brisbane, Australia, 19-22 October.

Gronwald, K. D. (1999). EMRPS education in the Internet environment. Presentation at the *First International Workshop Enterprise Management and Resource Planning: Methods, Tools and Architectures-EMRPS '99*. Venice, 25-27 November.

Hanna, D. E. (1998). Higher education in an era of digital competition: Emerging organizational models. *Journal of Asynchronous Learning Networks*, 2(1), 1998. Available on the World Wide Web at: http://www.aln.org/alnweb/journal/vol2_issue1/hanna.htm.

Hawking, P. and McCarthy, B. (2000). Transporting ERP education from the classroom to industry. In Hawking, P., Rosemann, M., Byrne, T. and Stewart, G. (Eds.), *Proceedings of the 4th SAP Asia Pacific Institute of Higher Learning Forum-SAPPHIRE 2000*, Brisbane, 23-25 July.

Hazemi, R., Hailes, S. and Wilbur, S. (1998). Supporting asynchronous collaboration in Academia. In Hazemi, R., Hailes, S. and Wilbur, S. (Eds.), *The Digital University*, Berlin: Springer-Verlag, 209-218.

Holmes, M. C. and Hayen, R. L. (1999a). An introduction to enterprise software using SAP R/3: A Web-based course. In Haseman, W. D. and Nazarath, D. L. (Eds.), *Proceedings of the 5th Americas Conference on Information Systems* (AMCIS), Milwaukee, WI, 13-15 August.

Holmes, M. C. and Hayen, R. L. (1999b). The master of science in information systems in a regional midwestern university. In Haseman, W. D. and Nazarath, D. L. (Eds.), *Proceedings of the 5th Americas Conference on Information Systems* (AMCIS) ,Milwaukee, WI, 13-15 August.

Jarvenpaa, S. L., Knoll, K. and Leidner, D. E. (1998). Is anybody out there?: Antecedents of trust in global virtual teams. *Journal of Management Information Systems*, Spring, 14(4), 29-64.

Kimball, L. (1998). Managing distance learning–New challenges for faculty. In Hazemi, R., Hailes, S. and Wilbur, S. (Eds.), *The Digital University*, Berlin: Springer-Verlag, 25-38.

Klaus, H., Rosemann, M. and Gable, G. G (2000). What is ERP? *Information Systems Frontiers*. 2(2), November, 141-162.

Knoll, K. and Jarvenpaa, S. L. (1995). Learning virtual team collaboration. In Shriver, B. D. and Sprague, R. (Eds.), *Proceedings of the 28th Hawaii International Conference on Systems Sciences-HICS '95*, 92-101.

Lederer-Antonucci, Y. (1999). Enabling the business school curriculum with ERP software: Experiences of the SAP university alliance. In *Proceedings of the IBSCA '99*, Atlanta, GA.

Leidner, D. E. and Jarvenpaa, S. L. (1995). The use of information technology to enhance management school education: A theoretical view. *MIS Quarterly*, September, 265-291.

Lightfood, J. M. (1999). Using the Internet to deliver audio-visual course content: A retrospective. In *Proceedings of the 10th Annual Conference of the International Information Management Association*, New Rochelle, NY, 13-15 October.

Lightfood, J. M. (1998). A blueprint for using the World Wide Web as an interactive teaching tool. *Journal of Educational Technology Systems*, 27(4), 325-335.

Lipnack, J. and Stamps, J. (1997). *Virtual Teams: Reaching across Space, Time, and Organizations with Technology*. New York: John Wiley.

Noguera, J. H. and Watson, E. F. (1999). Effectiveness of using enterprise systems to teach process-centered concepts in business education. In Haseman, W. D. and Nazarath, D. L. (Eds.), *Proceedings of the 5th*

Americas Conference on Information Systems, Milwaukee, WI, 13-15 August.

Rosemann, M. (1999). ERP-Software-Characteristics and consequences. In Pries-Jeje, J. et al. (Ed.), *Proceedings of the 7ᵗʰ European Conference on Information Systems-ECIS '99, Vol. III*, Copenhagen, Denmark, 23-25 June, 1038-1043.

Rosemann, M. and Chan, R. (2000). Structuring and modeling knowledge in the context of ERP. In Thong, J, Chau, P and Tam, K. Y. (Eds.), *Proceedings of the 4ᵗʰ Pacific Asia Conference on Information Systems-PACIS 2000*, Hong Kong, 1-3 June.

Rosemann, M., Scott, J. and Watson, E. (2000). Collaborative ERP education: Experiences from a first pilot. In Chung, H. M. (Ed.), *Proceedings of the 6ᵗʰ Americas Conference on Information Systems-AMCIS 2000*, Long Beach, 10-13 August.

Rosemann, M., Sedera, D. and Sedera, W. (2000). Industry-related education in enterprise systems. In Gable, G. G. and Vitale, M. (Eds.), *Proceedings of the 11ᵗʰ Australasian Conference on Information Systems–ACIS 2000*, Brisbane, 6-8 December.

Scheer, A. W. (2000). *ARIS-Business Process Framework, 3ʳᵈ ed.*, Berlin: Springer-Verlag.

Scheruhn, H., Johnson, D. and Rodriguez (2000). Collaborative teaching of enterprise resource planning on the Internet. In Hawking, P., Rosemann, M., Byrne, T. and Stewart, G. (Eds.), *Proceedings of the 4ᵗʰ SAP Asia Pacific Institute of Higher Learning Forum-SAPPHIRE 2000*, Brisbane, Australia, 23-26 July, 91-100.

Scott, J. (1999). ERP effectiveness in classrooms. In Haseman, W. D. and Nazarath, D. L. (Eds.), *Proceedings of the 5ᵗʰ Americas Conference on Information Systems* (AMCIS), Milwaukee, WI, 13-15 August.

Shoemaker, M. E. (1999). Introducing ERP systems to sales and marketing management graduate students: Discussion and exercises using SAP R/3. In *Proceedings of the 10ᵗʰ Annual International Information Management Association*, New Rochelle, NY.

Smeaton, A. and Keogh, G. (1999). An analysis of the use of virtual delivery of undergraduate lectures, *Computers and Education*, 32.

Stewart, G., Gable, G. G., Andrews, R., Rosemann, M. and Chan, T. (1999). Lessons from the field: a reflection on teaching SAP R/3 and ERP implementation issues. In Haseman, W. D. and Nazarath, D. L. (Eds.), *Proceedings of the 5ᵗʰ Americas Conference on Information Systems* (AMCIS), Milwaukee, WI, 13-15 August.

Stewart, G. and Rosemann, M. (2001). Integrating industrial knowledge into information systems curriculum. *Business Process Management Journal*–Special Issue on Enabling Process-Orientation through Enterprise Resource Planning (ERP) Systems, 7(3).

University of Missouri. (2001). *The Virtual Enterprise Project.* Available on the World Wide Web at: http://openssl.missouri.edu/paccess/umvep.html.

Victor, F., Mayr, R. and Otto, K. (1999). Doing the right thing right; Experiences of an interdisciplinary SAP R/3 education project. In Sinnott, T., Gable, G. G. and Hawking, P. (Eds.), *Proceedings of the 3rd SAP Asia Pacific Institute of Higher Learning Forum-SAPPHIRE 1999*, Singapore, 1-2 November.

Watson, E. F. and Noguera, J. H. (1999). Effectiveness of using an enterprise system to teach process-centred concepts in business education. In Haseman, W. D. and Nazarath, D. L. (Eds.), *Proceedings of the 5th Americas Conference on Information Systems*, Milwaukee, WI, 13-15 August.

Watson, E. and Schneider, H. C. (1999). Using ERP systems in education. *Communications of the Association for Information Systems*, 1(1), February.

Winter, R. (1999). HSG master of business engineering program: Qualifying high potentials for IS-enabled change. In Pries-Heje, J., Ciborra, C. and Kautz, K. (Eds.), *Proceedings of the 7th European Conference on Information Systems, Vol. II*, Copenhagen, Denmark, 23-25 June, 819-826.

About the Authors

Richard Discenza is a professor of Production Management and Information Systems in the College of Business and Administration at the University of Colorado in Colorado Springs. He received his BSF in Forestry from Northern Arizona University, an MBA from Syracuse University, and a PhD in Management from the University of Oklahoma. Dr. Discenza was formerly dean of the college where he helped establish and oversaw the development of a distance MBA program. His current research focuses on business process reengineering, distance education, project management and supply chain management. He has published numerous articles in professional and academic journals and is a member of APICS, the Academy of Management, and PMI.

Caroline Howard is on the faculty of the Goizueta Business School of Emory University where she teaches in the Decision Information area. She has an MBA from the Wharton School of the University of Pennsylvania, and a PhD from University of California, Irvine. She researches, consults and publishes in the areas of distance education, electronic commerce and telecommuting.

Karen D. Schenk holds a PhD in Information Technology and an MBA in Finance from the University of California, Irvine. She has been a professor of Information Systems at the University of Redlands, California, and North Carolina State University, teaching courses in Information Technology and Systems Design. Her research has focused on distance education, lifelong learning, decision support systems and human-computer interfaces. She is currently Senior Partner of K. D. Schenk and Associates Consulting, working with companies on decision support systems development and IT internal customer relationships.

***

Christine Bagwell heads up the University of California, San Diego's Instructional WWW Development Center, a division of Academic Computing Services. Her duties focus on assisting and training faculty in the development of WWW-based courseware, as well as a for-hire Web development service for the UCSD campus. Christine is also involved in research regarding the psychology and pedagogy of online and distance learning.

Angela Benson is a PhD candidate in Instructional Technology at the University of Georgia. Her research interests are distance learning, technology integration, instructional design, and educational change. Ms. Benson has designed and taught courses using a variety of online technologies, including a bulletin board-based online writing course that she taught for three years. In addition, she has given numerous conference presentations and published several academic articles related to distance and online learning. She holds undergraduate degrees in Math and Industrial Engineering, and masters degrees in Operations Research and Human Resource Development. In August 2001, Ms. Benson will join the Department of Human Resource Education at the University of Illinois at Champaign-Urbana as an Assistant Professor of Educational Technology.

Elizabeth A. Buchanan is Assistant Professor and Co-Director of the Center for Information Policy Research at the School of Information Studies, University of Wisconsin-Milwaukee. Prior to her faculty appointment, she was the school's Distance Education Coordinator. Her research interests include distance education and institutional strategies and planning, pedagogical issues in online teaching and learning ethics and information technologies, and research methods in virtual space.

Cathy Cavanaugh, PhD (University of South Florida) is Assistant Professor in Curriculum and Instruction at the University of North Florida. She has been an educator since 1982. She taught science to children in the Caribbean and Florida, and directed an education staff development center for math, science and technology. As assistant director of the Florida Center for Instructional Technology at the University of South Florida, she developed online resources for teachers and studied distance education effectiveness. Her distance education experience includes producing distance learning programs for children, teaching distance workshops and courses to teachers, and publishing reports about distance education.

Linda Cooper is a Professor in the Division of Business Administration at Macon State College and has been teaching Business Computer Applications for nine years. She began offering her class online during summer term 1998 and was the first instructor to offer an online class at Macon State College.

Since that time, she has published numerous articles and made several presentations to instructors on the topic of designing and implementing online courses. She earned her doctorate degree at the University of Tennessee in Adult and Technological Education.

Geoffrey N. Dick is a Senior Lecturer at the School of Information Systems, Technology and Management at the University of New South Wales in Sydney, Australia. During part of 2001, he was a Visiting Professor at Georgia Southern University. The focus of his PhD was telecommuting and he has been involved in both conducting distance education and research into it for several years. He regularly teaches distance classes in the Master of Business Technology programme at UNSW and he pioneered the use of technology as a distance education aid in that programme. Dr. Dick is on the UNSW Pro Vice-Chancellor's Committee on Information Technology in Distance Education, and in 2001 was the President of the International Academy for Information Management.

Kim E. Dooley is Assistant Professor of Agricultural Education at Texas A&M University. Her area of specialization is distance education. She has developed faculty training programs for distance delivery for more than five years. Her graduate course, *Advanced Methods in Distance Education* uses interactive video and the web as delivery tools. Dr. Dooley's research focuses on change facilitation (diffusion of innovation) of distance education in K-12, Higher Education, and Corporate Settings. One particular research project investigated the effects of computer animation on the asynchronous learning of scientific phenomena. She has served as distance education consultant for the Inter-American Institute for Cooperation in Agriculture (Costa Rica) and the International Potato Center (Peru).

Alev M. Efendioglu is a Professor of Management and Information Systems at the School of Business and Management (SOBAM), University of San Francisco (USF). Having joined USF in 1977, he has served at various times as chair of SOBAM's many faculty committees (including Peer Review and Academic Standards Committees), Coordinator of the Management Teaching Area, and the Coordinator of USF-EMBA Program (1998-2000) for Guangdong Enterprises in China (Hong Kong, Shenzhen, and Guangzhou). He has extensive consulting experience and is the author of two books and numerous professional publications. He is a member of and holds administrative positions in a number of domestic and international professional organizations. You can find more detailed information on Dr. Efendioglu at his Internet home page (http://www.usfca.edu/alev/alev.htm), developed and maintained by him on an ongoing basis.

Shirley Gregor holds the Chair of Information Systems at the Australian National University, Canberra. Prior to taking up this position in May 2001, she was Associate Professor and Head of the School of Computing and Information Systems at Central Queensland University, Rockhampton, Australia, where she also headed the Electronic Commerce Research Group. Professor Gregor's current research interests include electronic commerce and the theory of interorganizational systems, intelligent systems, and information systems development. She has led several large projects in this area funded by the Meat Research Corporation, the Department of Communications, Information Technology and the Arts, and the Australian Research Council. Professor Gregor spent a number of years in the computing industry in Australia and the United Kingdom before beginning an academic career. She obtained her PhD in Information Systems from the University of Queensland. Professor Gregor has published widely, with articles in journals such as *Management Information Systems Quarterly, Information Technology & People,* and the *International Journal of Human-Computer Studies.*

Jane Magill is a Professor of Genetics at Texas A&M University. Her research has been in the area of gene expression and she teaches undergraduate biochemistry and genetics. In 1980, Dr. Magill received the Texas A&M University award for Excellence in Teaching. She began teaching at a distance in 1993, by doing a course, Biotechnology, in 13 weeks on satellite TV. In 1994, she hosted an international satellite conference on Agricultural Biotechnology that allowed scientists at universities in Africa to interact with scientists at Texas A&M University. Dr. Magill is the Faculty Coordinator for distance education in the College of Agriculture and Life Sciences and teaches online courses in biochemistry and genetics.

Stewart Marshall is the founding Dean of the Faculty of Informatics and Communication at Central Queensland University in Australia. Although originally an electrical engineer with the Central Electricity Generating Board in the UK, he has worked in higher education for 27 years in England, Papua New Guinea, Australia and Southern Africa. He was the foundation Professor of Communication at the Papua New Guinea University of Technology, foundation Professor of Communication in the Faculty of Arts at Monash University, and foundation Coordinator of Academic Studies and Professor of Distance Education at the Institute of Distance Education at the University of Swaziland in Southern Africa. Professor Marshall's research interest is in the role of communication and information technologies in distance education, especially in developing countries.

William Benjamin Martz, Jr. is an Associate Professor of Information Systems whose teaching interests include e-business, software development, groupware and team-based problem solving. Ben received his BBA in Marketing from the College of William and Mary, his MS in Management Information Systems (MIS) and his PhD in Business, with an emphasis in MIS, from the University of Arizona. He was one of the founding members, as well as President and COO, of Ventana Corporation–a technology, spin-off firm from the University of Arizona–incorporated to commercialize the groupware software product, GroupSystems. In 1994, GroupSystems won PC Magazine's Editor's Choice Award for Best Electronic Meeting System Software. Ben has published his groupware research in *MIS Quarterly*, *Decision Support Systems*, and the *Journal of Management Information Systems*, and his student learning environment research in *Journal of Cooperative Education* and the *Journal of Computer Information Systems*.

Diane A. Matthews is Program Director and Professor of Accounting and Finance, in the Division of Business and Information Management at Carlow College, Pittsburgh, Pennsylvania. Diane is a Certified Public Accountant, holds a BS from Indiana University of Pennsylvania, and an MS from Robert Morris College. Diane is currently a PhD student at the University of Pittsburgh where she has done extensive research in distance education. Diane directs Carlow's distance education offerings in accounting, and has taught a multitude of online accounting courses. Prior to joining Carlow College, Diane held various corporate positions. She was employed by Arthur Young & Co., a CPA firm, by Equibank, N.A. as vice-president of the Telecommunications Division, and by Fisher Scientific Company as manager of the Customer Systems and International Telecommunications Division. Diane enjoys sports and traveling. She and her husband, Bill, have twin sons, Brad and Nicholas.

L. William Murray is a Professor of Finance at the School of Business Administration and Management (SOBAM), University of San Francisco (USF). Having joined USF in 1978, he has served at various times as chair of SOBAM's many faculty committees, Coordinator of International Programs, and Associate Dean for Academic Affairs. He is the author of more than 75 professional publications and holds membership in a number of international professional organizations. Professor Murray has held visiting faculty positions at the University of California at Berkeley; Clark University; Beijing's University of International Business and Economics, the Estonian Business School; the Catholic University of Uruguay; the International Graduate School of Freiburg, Germany; Southern Cross University in Lismore, Australia; and the Fachhochschule Ludwigshafen in Germany. He has conducted programs for executive training in locations throughout the world.

Zeynep Onay is an Associate Professor of Operations Management and Information Systems at the Department of Business Administration, Middle East Technical University (METU), Turkey. She is a founding member of the Informatics Institute at METU, served as Associate Director at the Institute, and is a member of the Institute's Executive Committee. She is also a member of the university's Accreditation Committee for online courses and programs. Sine 1997, Dr. Onay has been actively involved in the groundwork, development and implementation of the university's Internet-based education system, METU-Online. She took part in the design of the online Certificate Program in Informatics as well as the Informatics Online graduate program. She has prepared and delivered courses through METU-Online since 1998.

Valerie E. Polichar holds a PhD in Experimental Psychology and an undergraduate degree in Cognitive Science. She works as a technical manager for networking technology groups in Academic Computing Services at the University of California, San Diego. Her recent research and writing is on the applications of psychological principles to computer-based education; she has a particular interest in the use of MUD/MOOs in education. She frequently speaks on these subjects to government and educational groups.

Michael Rosemann is Associate Director of the Information Systems Management Resource Centre and Senior Lecturer at the School of Information Systems at the Queensland University of Technology (QUT), Brisbane, Australia. He received his MBA (1992) and PhD (1995) from the University of Münster, Germany. He is a regular guest lecturer at the Nanyang Technological University, Singapore, and the Northern Institute of Technology, Hamburg. In 1998, he was teaching a post-graduate IT course for the Queensland University of Technology from Germany. Since then, he has continuously offered distance education courses related to Enterprise Systems. Michael Rosemann is author of two books, editor of two books and author of more than 50 papers and articles in books and journals. He presented his work at conferences such as ICIS, PACIS, ECIS, AMCIS, ACIS, HICSS and

CAiSE. He has comprehensive consulting experiences in the areas of Enterprise Systems, process and workflow management through projects in Germany and Australasia.

Richard Ryan is an Associate Professor at the University of Oklahoma in the Construction Science Division of the College of Architecture. He has been actively involved in teaching and using information technology for construction applications since 1992. He has done web development and technology consulting for construction companies. In Spring 1998, he offered to Associated Schools of Construction programs the first complete, semester-length online construction class, cns4913online, Construction Equipment and Methods. His experiences have fostered many observations pertaining to creation, organization, promotion and administration of web-based distance learning. Currently, he is developing online automated teaching applications for an infrastructure construction portal and working with interactive information delivery and assessment techniques.

Gary Saunders, DBA, CPA earned his doctorate at the University of Kentucky. He is currently Professor of Accountancy at Marshall University, Huntington, West Virginia. Dr. Saunders has published extensively and has authored two accounting simulation textbooks, a cost accounting textbook and a spreadsheet textbook. He operates Integrated Business Systems, a publishing company, and BrightFutures, a nonprofit corporation to promote educational opportunities in developing countries.

Lynne Schrum is an Associate Professor in the Department of Instructional Technology at the University of Georgia. She received a PhD in Curriculum and Instruction from the University of Oregon in 1991. She has taught courses on distance learning, telecommunications, research methods, and introduction to instructional technology. Dr. Schrum's research focuses on online and distance learning, implementation of technological innovations in education, and appropriate uses of information technology in K-12 education. She is the immediate past-president of the International Society for Technology in Education (ISTE). She has written two books, numerous articles, and several monographs on these subjects, and consults and speaks to educators, administrators, and policymakers throughout the US and around the world.

Vicky A. Seehusen is Associate Vice-President for Distance Education for the Community Colleges of Colorado. She manages the consortial program called CCCOnline and has been with the program since its inception in 1997.

Previously, she worked for Red Rocks Community College, Colorado, as the full-time director of computer services and a part-time faculty member. Prior to this, she was a manager and trainer in private industry. Vicky has written numerous articles and books chapters about governing consortial distance education programs and administering instructional and student services in cooperation with colleges that are geographically separated.

Morgan Shepherd spent ten years in industry, most of that time with IBM. His last position with IBM was as a technical network designer. He earned his PhD from the University of Arizona in 1995, and has been teaching for the I/S Department at the University of Colorado in Colorado Springs since then. His primary teaching emphasis is in telecommunications at the graduate and undergraduate level. He has also taught numerous courses on computer literacy, web design and systems analysis and design. In addition, he has been teaching courses via distance education for several years. His primary research emphasis is on making distributed groups productive and applying this research to business as well as education. His research has appeared in the *Journal of Management Information Systems*, *Informatica*, and *Journal of Computer Information Systems*.

Index

A

academic integrity 185
accreditation 7, 172, 245
adaptive structuration theory 113
advantages and disadvantages of distance
    education 5
American Association of Collegiate
    Schools of Business 223
application hosting centers 263
assessing 94
assessments 184
asynchronous 99
asynchronous communication 132
attitudinal responses 228
Australian 221

B

behavioral 93
Beijing 224
benchmarks 176
best practices 142, 174
Blackboard's CourseInfo 99
bulletin board 2, 93
business services issues 213

C

cameras 224
career development 229
challenges 141
chat room 93
chat sessions 131
China Resources Holding Company 222
Chinese 219
chunks 104
cognitive 93

cohort 222
college teams 209
communication 177
communication skill development 229
communications skills 229
comprehension 94
consortia/collaboratives 13
consortial 206
consortial model 208
continuing education 236
copyright 246
correspondence courses 54
costs of entry 6
course design 194
course management system (CMS) 125
course-in-a-box 96
courseware 3, 94
cramming 104
CRC MBA 222
cross-university collaboration 275

D

DISCUS 99
distance education 4, 36, 75, 108, 192
distance learning 54, 93, 108, 126, 191
distant students 142
drives and constraints 37

E

e-learning 2, 234
educational 25
educational effectiveness 219
educational psychology 95
effectiveness 9, 174
elaborative encoding 93
electronic networks 192
engineering 220

Enterprise Resource Planning 263
Enterprise Systems 263
ethical considerations 229
extensions 237

F

faculty training 75
fade back 111
"falling fruit" 101
field theory 111
financial aid 12
fraud 8

G

global issues 12
globalization 22
goals 222
grades 220
Graduate Management Aptitude Test 223
group support systems (GSSs) 113
groupware 3
Guangdong Enterprises 224

H

Hewlett-Packard 220
high schools 173
higher education 21, 173
Hong Kong 221

I

incentives 75, 103
Informatics Institute 241
institutional services 141
instructional services issues 212
intellectual property 12
interaction 178
international aspects 228
Internet 54, 234
Internet courses 54
Internet degrees 57
interrelating 103
investment in library resources 229
investors 15
isolation effect 104

L

leadership 208
learning centered education 109
learning model 263
learning network 33
learning/teaching network 26
library services 142
long–term memory 95

M

management 206
management team 207
managers 219
Marketplace for Higher Education 284
MBA 221
media 2
Media Richness Theory 114
memory 95
METU-Online 241
microphones 224
Microsoft PowerPoint 105
Middle East Technical University (METU)
    241
models 234
MS Office 125
MUD/MOO 93

N

need for affiliation 108
needs theory 111
NET-Class 248
NetMeeting 273
Norway 220

O

online 21
online business computer applications
    course 125
online classes 125, 156
online course evaluations 134
online courses 125
online education 141
online instruction 126
online interactive discussion 99
online learning 7
online learning process 126

online testing 133
operant conditioning 102

P

participation 94
partnerships 238
pedagogical approaches 94
perception 93
personal attributes 38
platforms 237
players in distance education 12
policies 207
portal 236
portfolio 184
practices 172, 212
procedures 207
process engineering 263
professional development 173
punisher 101

Q

qualitative perceptions 158
quality assessment 158
quality assurance 7, 156, 172
quality expectations 158
quests 97
quizzes 96

R

real presenter 105
real streaming server 105
real-time sessions 131
reinforcement 93
reinforcers 100
remote learner 4
resources 173
results 173
retention 94
return on the company's investment in the
      program 229

S

San Francisco 221
SAP 264
satisfaction 227
School of Business and Management

(SOBAM) 221
self–paced 96, 104
service providers 236
serving 141
shaping 102
short–term memory 104
Singh effect 103
SOBAM 221
social exchange theory 111
Social Information Processing Theory 113
social interaction 110
Social Learning Theory 110
Social Presence Theory 114
spacing effect 93
standards 8, 174
strategic alliances 26
strategic plan 176
streamed audio and video 105
student course evaluation 226
student performance 219
student services issues 209
student-centered perspective 142
synchronous communication 132

T

tabula rasa 109
task suitability 42
teaching network 26
technical skills 229
technologies 16
technology lens 116
telecommuting 36
text–based virtual environments 97
theory of structuration 22
threaded discussion 3, 131
time-strapped adult learners 4
topics 103
Total Quality Management 182
tutor 220
Tutored-Video Instruction 220
TVI MBA 224

U

University of Central Florida 180
University of San Francisco 221

V

vertical disintegration 24
virtual 236
virtual classroom 4
virtual high school 186
virtual office hours 99
virtual university 7

W

Web CT 136
Web-assisted course 3
Web-based 141
Web-based course 3
WebBoard 99
WebCT 99
Western Association of Schools and
        Colleges 222